EDUCATION AND PSYCHOLOGY OF THE GIFTED SERIES

James H. Borland, Editor

*Planning and Implementing Programs
for the Gifted*
James H. Borland

*Patterns of Influence on Gifted Learners:
The Home, the Self, and the School*
Joyce L. VanTassel-Baska
Paula Olszewski-Kubilius
EDITORS

*Reaching the Gifted Underachiever:
Program Strategy and Design*
Patricia L. Supplee

The Academic Acceleration of Gifted Children
W. Thomas Southern
Eric D. Jones
EDITORS

*Understanding the Gifted Adolescent:
Educational, Developmental, and Multicultural Issues*
Marlene Bireley
Judy Genshaft
EDITORS

Understanding the Gifted Adolescent

Educational, Developmental, and Multicultural Issues

Edited by
Marlene Bireley
Judy Genshaft

Teachers College, Columbia University
New York and London

Published by Teachers College Press, 1234 Amsterdam Avenue, New York, NY 10027

Copyright © 1991 by Teachers College, Columbia University

Library of Congress Cataloging-in-Publication Data

Understanding the gifted adolescent : educational, developmental, and
    multicultural issues / edited by Marlene Bireley, Judy Genshaft.
    p.   cm. — (Education and psychology of the gifted series)
    Includes bibliographical references and index.
    ISBN 0-8077-3073-4 (alk. paper) — ISBN 0-8077-3072-6 (pbk. : alk. paper)
    1. Gifted teenagers.   I. Bireley, Marlene.   II. Genshaft, Judy.   III. Series.
BF724.3.G53U53   1991
155.5—dc20   90-23940
                                                                      CIP

ISBN 0-8077-3073-4
ISBN 0-8077-3072-6 (pbk.)

Printed on acid-free paper
Manufactured in the United States of America

98 97 96 95 94 93 92 91   8 7 6 5 4 3 2 1

To Laura and Chris
my best and most beloved teachers —M.K.B.

To Steve
for his infinite patience,
encouragement, and affection —J.L.G.

Contents

Foreword   ix
James Borland

Preface   xiii

1. Adolescence and Giftedness: A Look at the Issues   1
   Marlene Bireley and Judy Genshaft

2. Parenting the Gifted Adolescent—Special Problems,   18
   Special Joys
   Sylvia B. Rimm

PART I   PERSONAL ISSUES   **33**

3. Psychosocial Needs of the Gifted Adolescent   35
   Diane E. Frey

4. Eating Disorders in the Gifted Adolescent   50
   David M. Garner

5. Perfectionism and the Gifted Adolescent   65
   Miriam Adderholdt-Elliott

6. Stress Management with the Gifted Adolescent   76
   Judy Genshaft and Jim Broyles

PART II   EDUCATIONAL ISSUES   **89**

7. Encouraging Higher Level Thinking in   91
   the Gifted Adolescent
   Susan R. Amidon

8. Encouraging Creativity and Talent in Adolescents   104
   Jane Piirto

9. Leadership and Gifted Adolescents   122
   Frances A. Karnes and Suzanne Meriweather-Bean

10. Patterns of Underachievement Among Gifted Students   139
    E. Susanne Richert

11. The Paradoxical Needs of the Disabled Gifted   163
    Marlene Bireley

12. University and Community-Based Programs for the   176
    Gifted Adolescent
    Raymond H. Swassing and George R. Fichter

PART III   LIFESTYLE AND CAREER ISSUES   **187**

13. Learning Styles: One Way to Help Gifted Adolescents   189
    Understand and Choose Lifestyles
    Marlene Bireley

14. Career Choices for Gifted Adolescents: 201
    Overcoming Stereotypes
    Constance L. Hollinger

15. Moral and Spiritual Development of   215
    the Gifted Adolescent
    Karen B. Tye and Marlene Bireley

PART IV   MULTICULTURAL ISSUES   **229**

16. Gifted Black Adolescents: Beyond Racism to Pride   231
    Alexinia Young Baldwin

17. Gifted Hispanic Adolescents   240
    Vicente Z. Ortiz and Alexander Gonzalez

18. Gifted Adolescents in the Emerging Minorities: 248
    Asians and Pacific Islanders
    Robert Woliver and Gail Muranaka Woliver

THE GIFTED ADOLESCENT IN PERSPECTIVE   **259**
    Judy Genshaft

About the Editors and the Contributors   265

Index   273

Foreword

The publication of *Understanding the Gifted Adolescent* represents, to my knowledge, a first, and a long-overdue one at that. For despite the obvious importance of adolescence in the development of the individual, I am not aware of a book-length treatment of the problems and issues of adolescence as they affect the gifted. This is all the more puzzling since adolescence is a period during which much of the transition from potential to accomplishment, the realization of what Terman called "The Promise of Youth," takes place.

The reasons for this neglect are no doubt many. Two spring immediately to mind. First, most of our research and especially our attempts at special education for the gifted have been focused on children, not adolescents. Thus, we have directed our attention to where the action has been educationally, neglecting, to a certain extent, educational and psychological issues that affect gifted individuals after they leave programs for the gifted. Second, to state the obvious, adolescence is a difficult period, for adults as well as adolescents. Although we have all gone through it, we seem to understand it poorly. Why else do we fatuously persist in advising teenagers, when they give voice to the depression and frustration that often come with having to confront adult problems with a child's limited understanding and power, to stop worrying and enjoy "the happiest time of their lives"?

Yet, for all its difficulties, the study of adolescence is an endeavor that is rich in the potential for understanding a range of issues related to giftedness. As humans move from the relatively sheltered period of childhood and begin, tentatively, to try on the real world for size, they encounter, often without the protective mediation of adults, aspects of human existence of which they previously only heard hints. To what extent does intellectual giftedness affect one's ability to contend with these issues? Unfortunately, we do not have a good answer to this question. The value of the present volume is found, I think, in the fact that variations on this question are posed for our consideration.

I would like to highlight a few of the crucial but neglected topics raised by the contributors to this collection. The issue of sexuality, addressed by Diane Frey, is of obvious importance in the study (and experience) of adolescence, but it has been largely ignored in discussions of the needs of the gifted. Broaching this topic in relation to the lives of gifted adolescents suggests the need to explore a variety of complex issues in future writings. For example, how do gifted adolescents deal with the contradictory messages from the adult world that relentlessly encourage them to be preoccupied with sex (through advertising, for example), while moralistically insisting that they not carry this preoccupation to its logical conclusion? How do stereotypical notions of sexual attractiveness affect adolescents' regard for their talents and gifts, especially when demonstrations of those talents and gifts are not congruent with the stereotypes (the issue of female mathematical precocity springs to mind here)? And how do gay and lesbian gifted adolescents deal with the double marginality that the labels "gifted" and "homosexual" impose? These and other questions ought to be taken up by our field.

A related issue is raised by David Garner in his chapter on eating disorders. The prevalence of such disorders among achievement-oriented females has been largely ignored in discussions of the multitude of problems society creates for gifted girls. That an alarming number of young women react to familial and societal pressures by literally making themselves gradually disappear physically ought to tell us something about how we regard female giftedness in this culture.

Karen B. Tye and Marlene Bireley discuss moral and spiritual issues confronting gifted adolescents. Once again, as they point out, the dearth of writings on the topic belies its importance. Little is known in this area, and little research exists beyond the work inspired by Kohlberg's problematic stage theory. But again, opening the discussion prompts a number of questions for subsequent analysis. For example, if, as is likely, gifted individuals are precociously concerned with metaphysical and moral issues, where can they turn for guidance? To what extent are our attempts to encourage critical thinking in gifted adolescents constrained by or antagonistic to the strictures of organized systems of belief? Do the gifted, as Tannenbaum suggests, bear a heavier moral burden that results from their potential to produce, rather than merely to consume, ideas?

The last part of this volume deals with issues faced by gifted African Americans, Hispanics, and Asians and Pacific Islanders in a society in which they are outside the mainstream. The failure of our field to understand and meet the needs of gifted individuals from racial and ethnic minorities is a long-standing source of shame for us collectively. This should be a particular concern given the upsurge in overt racism that, I believe, has been encouraged, subtly and not-so-subtly, at the highest levels in our country. We talk about the problems of prejudice and discrimination quite a bit in this field, but pious lamentations do not take us very far toward doing the right thing. Understanding the specific conditions and needs of gifted children from various subcultures is a start. For example, it is useful to understand that the "positive" stereotype of the "model minority" has been pernicious for Asian Americans, just as negative stereotypes have been for African Americans and Hispanics, if perhaps not to the same degree. Both kinds of stereotypes have been the pretext for overt and covert policies of exclusion. We have talked about these issues in relatively polite language thus far. Perhaps it is time for the role that programs for the gifted play in increasing access to positions of privilege in society to be discussed in less polite terms by those who are systematically, if not always intentionally, excluded from those programs.

These and a host of other issues, problems, and questions are raised by the various chapters of this book. If the issues are not addressed definitively, if the problems are not solved once and for all, if the questions are not answered conclusively, it is hardly the fault of the authors whose thoughts are contained herein. We have neglected the needs and concerns of gifted adolescents for far too long. We owe a debt of thanks to Marlene Bireley and Judy Genshaft—and to the contributors to their volume—for making it more difficult for us to continue to do so in the future.

JAMES H. BORLAND, EDITOR
Education and Psychology
of the Gifted Series

Preface

This book is a testament to the life force that we call serendipity. Responding to an invitation from Teachers College Press to submit a book proposal, the co-editors agreed on the topic and direction of this book during a very long dinner in Chicago during the 1988 convention of the National Association of School Psychologists. After listing and critiquing possible topics in our combined areas of interest, we narrowed the choice to two great needs in the current literature—preschool or adolescent gifted. Our personal expertise and interest led us to choose the latter.

Once the topic was decided, the vision quickly took shape. Our contributors should be a balance of known experts in gifted education who were recognized as authorities on issues related to the gifted, and less-known authors who were either emerging in the field or were establishing good local or regional reputations. Once a serious literature search was started, we added a third category—those with expertise in a topic we had selected as pertinent to adolescent gifted but for which no "gifted educator" expert could be found. These contributors were asked to discuss their area of interest and, where a limited research base existed, extrapolate the meaning for gifted adolescents.

It was with great delight that we found that most of those invited to contribute, readily and enthusiastically agreed. The few who declined did so because of prior commitments but were equally supportive of the project and the topic.

The book we now share with you is a product of the continuation of that enthusiasm through the harsh reality of getting the manuscript to press. We believe that it is a real contribution to gifted education. As programs for elementary school children become well established, we turn our attention more directly to the needs of secondary school students. We have chosen a balanced focus—our major themes are the adolescent in the family, the developmental needs and potential crises of the adolescent, educational issues, and the unique needs of the culturally different. We see them all as crucial components in developing an understanding of adolescent gifted students.

We have tried to balance the theoretical and the practical. As academicians, we believe that it is important to understand the knowledge base of any discipline. A recurring theme in most of the chapters is the need for more research in the specific needs of the adolescent gifted as it relates to that topic. Many of our contributors have expressed an interest in devising such research. We hope these plans come to fruition.

As practitioners, we know that it is important to have concrete ideas and materials to wage the daily battle. We have tried to include some ideas and interventions that have immediate practical application. When space has limited extensive descriptions of interventions, we have tried to provide specific references to more detailed sources.

Finally, we wish to thank the many behind-the-scenes contributors who always exist in such a project. They include our families and friends who have patiently listened and supported us through our conceptual and gestational periods; Jim Broyles, graduate assistant, who has spent hours completing or checking references; and Autumn Harless Phelps, who retyped much of the manuscript. Finally, to you, the reader! That you have been moved to pick up this volume and, hopefully, to read it, provides us the ultimate support and gives us the greatest pleasure.

Understanding the Gifted Adolescent

*Educational, Developmental,
and Multicultural Issues*

CHAPTER 1

Adolescence and Giftedness: A Look at the Issues

Marlene Bireley
Judy Genshaft

"Struggling toward maturity" is an appropriate description of American adolescents as they move from childhood to their final integration as adults in our society. Being an "average" teen brings with it the drive for acceptance, the struggle to preserve self-esteem in a time of self-doubt, and the need to choose a career and lifestyle. If the choices made during this quest contradict those chosen by previous generations or the desires of one's family, multiple pressures can develop. Being "gifted" does not relieve one of making the same choices or feeling the same pressures. Indeed, special labels, even those with positive connotations, bring additional special problems.

The literature on the gifted has exploded in the last 15 years. Advice to, for, and from gifted children and their families and teachers has emerged from many sources. Yet, the literature seems to be most lacking in guidance for the gifted adolescent. The issues we have chosen to address are those faced by all teenagers. The contributors to this book have incorporated into their discussions the unique needs of the gifted adolescent who is facing these common concerns. To lay the groundwork for those discussions, in this chapter we will review the various definitions of giftedness and intelligence that have shaped our understanding of those two concepts, and we will review briefly those areas of adolescent development upon which the contributing authors will elaborate.

THE MANY FACES OF GIFTEDNESS

Expanding the Terman Stereotype

As any student of gifted education knows, the benchmarks of history in this field are the works of Lewis Terman (1925) and his collaborators (Burks, Jensen, & Terman, 1930; Cox, 1926; Terman & Oden, 1947, 1959) and those of Leta Hollingworth (1926, 1942). The children identified by Terman were a truly exceptional group. Throughout their lifetimes they have been brighter, more achievement oriented, more successful, healthier, and better adjusted than their contemporaries. They certainly have proven that basic ability can be the steppingstone to a productive, happy life. They consisted as well of a California population, with a mean IQ of 150, skewed toward middle class, white, and urban families. While the lessons we have learned from this group form the cornerstone of gifted education, the Terman group does not represent all of those children we are now serving. We must broaden both our understanding and our concerns if we are to address present reality. Hollingworth was a pioneer in recognizing the needs of two atypical populations, the highly gifted and gifted females (Silverman, 1989). Recently, concerns about meeting the needs of other atypical groups have been raised. Specifically, how do we identify and serve minorities, economically disadvantaged, and handicapped persons whose giftedness may be overlooked because of these other characteristics (Richert, Alvino, & McDonnel, 1982)?

Some Modern Perspectives on Giftedness

While most discussions of giftedness begin with the federal government's definition (Marland, 1972), many other frameworks can be used to define the gifted population. Gardner (1983), Sternberg (1985), and Dabrowski and Piechowski (1977) have focused on the variety of gifts and the levels of intelligence. Renzulli (1978) raised the question of task commitment (do we have to use our gifts productively to be considered gifted?), a seemingly restrictive view, but couched it in an inclusive identification model that considers giftedness more as a behavior to be taught than a condition to be identified (Renzulli, Reis, & Smith, 1981). Others (Betts & Neihart, 1988; Richert, 1986; Rimm, 1986) have identified a number of subtypes based on affective needs and achievement/underachievement dimensions. Since each of these constructs adds to our understanding of the multifaceted condition of giftedness, each will be discussed in some detail.

The Marland Report. An extensive study of gifted and talented persons was completed and published by the federal government during Sidney Marland's tenure as Commissioner of Education. From that report came a description of six types of giftedness, which have formed the basis for much of the programmatic and curricular concerns of the past 2 decades. Those types were general intellectual ability, specific academic ability, creative or productive thinking, leadership ability, talent in the visual or performing arts, and psychomotor ability.

While confusion over the meaning of the last category (do athletes, dancers, and those with mechanical or fine motor ability all qualify?) has dropped it from common usage, each of the other five categories continues to be widely used within the literature and the profession.

Gardner's Multiple Intelligences. Howard Gardner (1983) identified seven types of intelligence. These "multiple intelligences" include linguistic, logic and mathematical, musical, visual and spatial conceptualization, bodily kinesthetic, interpersonal and intrapersonal intelligences. It is his belief that each person has the capability to develop to a certain degree in each of these areas, but that cultural values and biological components combine to determine those areas in which a given person can excel. Since the first two types correspond most closely with the schooling demands of our society, students identified as gifted most often excel in one or both of those two areas. Gardner's emphasis on the possibility of considerable variance in ability across domains and his concept of creativity as the attainment of a high level of competence in any domain are major contributions to our understanding of the complexity of high ability.

Sternberg's Triarchic Theory of Intelligence. One of the most prolific and intriguing of the current theorists of intellectual development is Robert Sternberg. His work is important in that he has not only proposed a theoretical framework, but with his colleagues has developed specific approaches for developing the thinking potential of children (Baron & Sternberg, 1987; Sternberg, 1985, 1986).

Sternberg describes his triarchic theory as consisting of three subtheories, a componential subtheory, a contextual subtheory, and an experiential subtheory. Sternberg describes intelligent behavior under his componential subtheory as behavior that effectively uses *metacomponents*, *performance components*, and *knowledge-acquisition components*. Metacomponents are higher order control processes that are used in executive planning and decision making in problem solving; performance components are lower order processes used in executing a problem solving strategy; and knowledge-acquisition components are lower order processes used in acquiring, retaining, and transferring new information (Sternberg, 1986).

Under Sternberg's contextual subtheory, exceptional intelligence consists of "purposive adaptation to, shaping of, and selection of real world environments relevant to one's life" (Sternberg, 1986, p. 225). His experiential subtheory holds that one displays exceptional intelligence when one demonstrates "either or both of two skills: the ability to deal with novel kinds of tasks and situational demands, and the ability to automatize information processing" (p. 229).

Dabrowski's and Piechowski's Psychic Overexcitabilities. A theory that connects the concepts of intelligence and creativity to an overabundance of or heightened response to stimuli is that of the late Polish psychiatrist, Kazimierz Dabrowski. His theory identifies five types of psychic overexcitabilities: psychomotor (high energy, restlessness); sensual (sensitivity to the environment and to beauty, openness to experiences); imaginational (fantasizing, playfulness, creativity); intellectual (curiosity, insight, concentration); and emotional (high degree of empathy, depth of emotional intensity) (Dabrowski & Piechowski, 1977). His colleague, Michael Piechowski (1986), described the five areas as channels of information flow and modes of experiencing. When any or all of the channels are stronger than those of a child's peers, the child often feels "different, apart from others, guilty and embarrassed for being different" (p. 191). Piechowski argued that, to counterbalance this feeling of being different, persons concerned with the development of the gifted should assist children in developing their potential so that they may become self-actualized adults, which Dabrowski described as the two highest of five levels of personality development. Level IV is characterized by a "strong sense of universal values" and "extraordinary sense of responsibility" (p. 193), as exemplified by Eleanor Roosevelt; Level V "epitomizes universal compassion, self-sacrifice, and total dedication to the service of others" (p. 194). Dag Hammarskjold's dedication to the ideals of the United Nations is cited as an example of this level.

Renzulli's Three-Part Definition and Talent Pool Models. Joseph Renzulli (1978) identified three components that are necessary ingredients for gifted behavior. He labelled these: (1) above average intelligence, (2) creativity, and (3) task commitment. According to Renzulli, each must be present for the individual to be considered gifted. In recent elaborations on the three-ring concept (Renzulli, 1986; Renzulli, Reis, & Smith, 1981), Renzulli has stated that above average intelligence should include a talent pool of about 15%–20% of the population. From that group, those who have the most potential for developing "gifted behaviors" in certain circumstances will also display aptitude for creative production and persistence or commitment. The extent to which these latter characteristics will manifest themselves varies widely across setting, topic, and time, thus giving support to the concept of the revolving door identification and programming model, which allows enrichment opportunities for the entire talent pool rather than the top 3%–5% served in many other program models.

Subtypes of Giftedness. George Betts and Maureen Neihart (1988) suggested six categories or subtypes of giftedness, which address both the cognitive and affective dimensions of the superior person. The persons described include such types of adolescents as

1. The *successful* gifted, who are achieving, conforming, and perfectionistic. While they are admired and liked by adults and peers, they need to become more risk-taking, assertive, and intrinsically motivated.
2. The *challenging* gifted, who are creative, bored, frustrated, rebellious, and inclined toward power struggles. They need to become more self-aware and self-controlled, to develop a sense of group belonging and flexibility, and to be supported for their creativity.
3. The *underground* gifted, who are insecure, quiet/shy, and have a poor self-concept. They are unrecognized as gifted or are seen as compliant and poor risk takers. They need to develop self-awareness and self-acceptance, more interactions with other types of gifted, and freedom to make choices.
4. Gifted *dropouts*, who are angry, resentful, explosive, and burned out. Adults see them as loners who are rebellious and dangerous; peers may see them as "dopers" and "airheads."
5. The *double-labelled* gifted, who may be learning disabled or physically handicapped, or have emotional problems. They are frustrated, powerless, angry, and have low self-esteem. Adults and peers may see them as weird or of only average ability, or may see only the handicap. They need coping skills, emphasis on strengths, skill development, and a gifted support group that reinforces the concept of giftedness.
6. The *autonomous* gifted, who have a good sense of self, are enthusiastic, accepting of both strengths and weaknesses, intrinsically motivated, and psychologically healthy. Adults and peers admire them and view them as responsible. They need support, advocacy, facilitation, and opportunities.

While the Betts and Neihart schema provides the most extensive subtype discussion, two of our contributing authors, Susanne Richert and Sylvia Rimm, have developed similar models. In Chapter 10 Richert provides an elaborate description of the characteristics of subtypes she has labelled the conforming, nonconforming, and transcendant gifted. She suggests different approaches for parenting or working with each type.

In Chapter 2 Rimm focuses on the gifted child in the family. Else-where, she has described the role of dominant and dependent behavior in the development or absence of achievement (Rimm, 1986). While her discussion of underachievement is aimed at all levels of intelligence, she contends that major factors contributing to achievement below one's potential include "the overwelcome child, early health problems, par-ticular sibling combination, specific marital problems and giftedness" (Rimm, 1986, p. 23). Betts and Neihart (1988), Richert (1986), and Rimm (1986) have contributed greatly to our understanding of the need to find and assist those who are not reaching their gifted potential.

The Concept of Creative Production

The concept of creativity or creative production is embedded in most of the above theories of intelligence. The highest level of achieve-ment (Gardner, 1983), insight (Sternberg & Davidson, 1985), and devel-opment of potential (Piechowski, 1986) all address this dimension of human development. It is difficult to assess creativity without acknowl-edging the influence on gifted education of the study conducted by Getzels and Jackson (1962). These researchers compared the high school academic performance of what they called high-IQ/low-creativity stu-dents with that of low-IQ/high-creativity students. They reported that they found that these low-IQ/high-creativity students did as well in terms of scholastic achievement as did the high-IQ/low-creativity students. Their conclusion was that there was a large number of creative students whose actual scholastic performance shows them to be gifted and that these students are being ignored by schools as not being gifted because they did not perform well on an IQ test. Furthermore, they argued that since the low-IQ/high-creativity students were found through the use of creativity tests, then these tests are an important instrument for finding gifted students who are missed with IQ tests.

Fundamental to the validity of the conclusions of Getzels and Jack-son (1962) was the concept of the low-IQ/high-creativity student. If indeed their low-IQ subjects did demonstrate a low IQ, then perhaps their conclusions would be sound. However, the low-IQ group actually had a mean IQ of 127, placing the group at the 97th percentile nationally, well within the range where they would be classified as intellectually gifted by regular IQ standards. It should come as no surprise, then, that efforts to replicate the study generally have not confirmed the hypothesis of Getzels and Jackson (1962) except where the IQ of the entire popula-tion is unusually high (Tannenbaum, 1983). Unfortunately, the original conclusions of the study were not read critically by many practitioners in the field of the education of the gifted, leading to the controversial use (or misuse) of creativity tests as instruments for identification of children for gifted programs. For example, the work of Paul Torrance and his associates has relied heavily on the concept of identifying gifted students who achieve high scores on creativity tests although not necessarily on IQ tests. Their work with the Torrance Tests of Creative Thinking, future problem solving, and disadvantaged youth has alerted us to the importance of the various dimensions of creativity such as fluency (quantity of ideas), flexibility (variety of ideas), originality (uniqueness of ideas), and elaboration (complexity of ideas) (Torrance, 1963, 1966, 1969; Torrance, Blume, Maryanopolis, Murphey, & Rogers, 1980). Finally, the work of Barbara Clark (1986, 1988) should be acknowledged. Her synthesis of the work of those concerned with creativity, intuition, and brain/behavior research, which culminated in her concept of integrative education, provides a model of personal creativity and a curricular model for incorporating the thinking, feeling, sensing, and intuiting functions into the educational process (Clark, 1988).

The Concept of Talent

The above theorists have stressed the concepts of intelligence, achievement, and creativity, and the relationship of the cognitive/affective domains. The concept of talent is somewhat different in that it is less tied to the presence of general or global intelligence. Dancers, artists, musicians, actors, and professional athletes may or may not have distinguished themselves as students. Our increasing understanding of the neuroanatomical correlates of the skills required by the talented may help us to understand why many of our best known athletes and arts personalities were poor, even disabled, learners. If we accept the current notion that, for most, the right hemisphere of the brain is concerned with "getting the big picture" and "is more musically inclined, and more apt to take governance in gross-motor activities, particularly as to how the body arranges itself in space," while the left hemisphere controls our higher level speech and language and is "more directly associated with skilled, fine-motor movements" (Lewandowski, 1987, p. 20), then accepting the publicly acknowledged learning disability of such modern high achievers as Cher, Greg Louganis, Tom Cruise, and Bruce Jenner becomes less problematic. Indeed, the skills of Olympic class athletes, of actors, and of visual and performing artists correspond well with the psychomotor, sensual, imaginational, and emotional overexcitabilities of Dabrowski (Dabrowski & Piechowski, 1977) and with superiority in Gardner's (1983) domains of bodily kinesthetic, musical, interpersonal, intrapersonal, and spatial intelligences. It can be argued that, in the individuals cited above, their particular biological and cultural imperatives allowed them to develop their talents to a remarkable degree without achieving in traditional academically related skills (perhaps even to the detriment of acquiring the latter).

The Concept of Leadership

Whether the focus is on the identification of potential leaders or the development of curricular approaches that encourage leadership skills in all the gifted (we prefer the latter), this trait continues to be recognized as a separate area of concern. Again, using Gardner's scheme, those who exhibit leadership qualities may be more highly developed in interpersonal and intrapersonal intelligences. The ability to know oneself and others to a remarkable degree may allow one to exert one's influence in a leadership capacity. Contributions by Karnes, Meriweather, and D'Llio (1987); Feldhusen and Richardson (1986); and Sisk (1986, 1987) have established ways of identifying different leadership styles and specific content, which can be incorporated into curricular studies of this topic.

Who Are the Gifted?

We end this discussion with the same question with which it began. Yes, the gifted are those who are intelligent, achieve well, and display creative potential. Most agree that they are also those who may hide or never discover their potential because of cultural disregard, disdain, or neglect (based on gender, ethnic, or socioeconomic issues or physical impairment), or because of lack of self-esteem based on family or societal circumstances. In adolescence, each of these potential deterrents to "being gifted" can be reinforced by the powerful imperatives of the adolescent experience. In the process of breaking away from the family and achieving independence, the role of the peer culture as the primary group becomes paramount. Many who were content to accept the status "gifted" as elementary children may choose to reject it in adolescence. The natural and anticipated behavior of this life stage is discussed below to clarify its impact on the development of the gifted adult.

THE ADOLESCENT EXPERIENCE

Havighurst (1972) identified tasks for each stage of human development, including eight tasks for the adolescent period. Havighurst acknowledged the influence of Erikson (1963, 1968) on his work and considered his developmental tasks to be an elaboration of Erikson's psychosocial crises. (Erikson defined these crises as the achievement of trust, autonomy, initiative, and industry in early and middle childhood; the achievement of identity in adolescence; and the achievement of intimacy, generativity, and ego identity in adulthood.) The tasks of adolescence (based on the achievement of identity crisis) were described by Havighurst as

1. Acquiring more mature social skills
2. Achieving a masculine or feminine sex role
3. Accepting the changes in one's body, using the body effectively, and accepting one's physique
4. Achieving emotional independence from parents and other adults
5. Preparing for sex, marriage, and parenthood
6. Selecting and preparing for an occupation
7. Developing a personal ideology and ethical standards
8. Assuming membership in the larger community

How does being gifted complicate the above tasks? Roedell (1984) identified seven "vulnerabilities" that may plague the highly gifted child. They are perfectionism; pressures from adult expectations; intense sensitivity to the "messages" of others; self-definition (an early existential search for personal meaning); alienation from the peer group because of disparate abilities; frequent placement in inappropriate environments; and societal, age, or gender conflict because of disparate development.

When the tasks of Havighurst and the vulnerabilities described by Roedell are analyzed, they appear to fit into four broad categories of human concern, namely, social/emotional, educational, ethical/spiritual, and career/lifestyle. These are, in a very real sense, the major themes of this book. Although our organization does not follow that exact framework, these broad categories provide a way of looking at the literature on the gifted adolescent and the apparent differences that can be anticipated when one is both "gifted" and "adolescent."

Social and Emotional Issues

Burks, Jensen, and Terman (1930) reported in the third volume of the Terman longitudinal studies that their group maintained in adolescence the superiority that was evident in the childhood assessment of a number of social traits. This superiority was determined by instruments that ascertained "character," fair-mindedness, and social intelligence and by questionnaires that provided home and school information and personal interests. Specific areas in which the Terman group excelled or exhibited normal tendencies were "sought as companions," "interested in the opposite sex," and "not considered different or peculiar."

In response to Hollingworth's (1926) contention that the lack of congenial playmates tended to throw the child with an IQ over 180 into solitary, intellectual play, 35 of the Terman children with IQs over 170 were considered as a separate group in the follow-up reported by Burks, Jensen, and Terman (1930). The average age of the group was near 14, and all but two had been accelerated (from 1 to 6 years). On a 5-point scale of sociability and leadership (5 indicating serious maladjustment), the mean was 3.0. There was a trend toward more serious maladjustment in those who had been accelerated 3 or more years. About two-thirds of this group were described by teachers as "poor mixers," and none were "conspicuous" leaders, although 21 of 31 reported holding offices in classes or clubs. The authors concluded that "the members of the gifted group whose IQ's are in the neighborhood of 170, 180, or 190 tend to have considerably more difficulty in making social adjustments than do the more typical members of the gifted group" (p. 183). However, much later in their lives, Feldman (1984) followed up 26 of the Terman subjects with IQs above 180 and found no way to distinguish them from another group with a mean IQ of 150.

In a recent post-high school follow-up of persons who had been identified in the 1976 and 1978 talent searches of the Study of Mathematically Precocious Youth at Johns Hopkins University, Brody and Benbow (1987) found that students who had accelerated one or more grades or had taken in-school acceleration options, such as Advanced Placement (AP) tests, showed higher achievement than students with enrichment or no accelerative experiences. The AP group was involved in more school activities; the AP and enrichment groups were most involved in athletics and community organizations and were most likely to hold leadership positions; while the nonaccelerated group was most involved in the performing arts. The accelerated group had the highest educational aspirations, had the least interest in marriage and a happy family life, and indicated the most willingness to experiment. No significant differences were found among the groups on an Adjective Check List of social/emotional characteristics. Brody and Benbow interpreted their findings as supportive of acceleration, without the fear of social and emotional maladjustment.

While social ability or disability can be attributed to either males or females, there appear to be gender differences in this area. Kerr (1985) identified a sense of isolation as a common theme among the prominent women whom she studied. Reis and Callahan (1989), in their extensive review of the literature on gender differences, noted the continued existence of sexual stereotypes in parental expectations, classroom attention and communication, occupational values, and career aspirations as blocks to fulfillment of the gifted female. Alvino (1989), on the other hand, described "boy problems" as the need to conform to the "macho" image; to suppress their feelings and not cry, to the detriment of developing their creative and sensitive sides; to separate from their mother's caregiving instincts while finding emotional connectedness to their fathers; and a tendency toward perfectionism and/or underachievement. He urged that as much concern be shown for these gender-related issues as for the needs of gifted females.

One of the classic studies of attitudes toward academic excellence (Tannenbaum, 1962) pointed out nongender-related issues of social acceptance. In that study, 615 junior students in New York City were given the dichotomies of brilliant–average, studious–nonstudious, and athletic–nonathletic in the eight possible combinations of these three pairs. Brilliant and average nonstudious athletes were ranked highest, while average and brilliant studious nonathletes were given the seventh and eighth ranks. Tannenbaum concluded that "academic brilliance" per se was not a stigma, but could become one when linked with other attributes that the respondents considered undesirable.

Even though both positive and negative social indicators exist for the gifted person, Clark (1988) concluded that her summary of studies of the social-emotional characteristics of gifted children presented a very positive profile. However, she concluded, and we agree, that the gifted must be assisted in learning to value themselves as unique persons. The way to do this is through creating opportunities for them to learn with intellectual peers and through encouraging intrinsic, rather than adult-imposed, motivation.

Social and emotional issues often are considered together and are very difficult to separate. Certainly, any of the dilemmas discussed above, if left unresolved, can result in emotional distress. For our purposes, we shall define social issues as those involving the gifted person's interaction with others, while emotional issues are the internal concerns that one must resolve with oneself. Three of "the eight great gripes of gifted kids" have to do with internal feelings: "We feel overwhelmed by the number of things we can do in life"; "We feel too different, alienated"; and "We worry a lot about world problems and feel helpless to do anything about them" (Galbraith, 1983, p. 17).

The potential vulnerability of gifted persons is evident, as is their general superiority in addressing emotional stresses. When given proper support, superior problem-solving capabilities can be used to overcome or dilute the impact of affective problems in much the same way that cognitive challenges can be met and overcome.

Educational Issues

Concern for the gifted often centers around their educational needs. Programs serving the gifted have grown tremendously over the past 2 decades. Many models for serving the able child have been tried, and many problems remain. Maker (1988) and her contributors cite identification, gender-related problems, qualitatively different curriculum, enrichment vs. acceleration, and program policy, procedures, and evaluation as critical issues in the education of the gifted. Homogeneity vs. heterogeneity, elitism vs. fairness, intellectual vs. chronological/social placement, and thematic vs. subject matter orientation are but a few of the other dichotomies that come quickly to mind as educational dilemmas. While the body of knowledge about each is growing, few answers acceptable to all exist. Educational achievement is a topic of this book primarily as it relates to the growth of the gifted individual as a well-adjusted, fulfilled adult, but it is a topic of considerable importance and controversy.

Ethical and Spiritual Issues

We have alluded several times to the unusual sensitivity of the gifted individual. It follows that the search for answers and for moral and spiritual guidelines and their subsequent application to the quality of life should be of special concern to this group. Surprisingly, the research relating this topic to giftedness has been sparse, but three recent books on human development (Conger & Petersen, 1984; Craig, 1989; Nielsen, 1987) revealed considerable discussion of these issues in relation to adolescents in general.

In a particularly thorough discussion of moral development, Nielsen (1987) compared four theoretical perspectives: cognitive, psychoanalytic, social learning, and cognitive-social learning. Perhaps the best known of these is the cognitive approach of Lawrence Kohlberg (1983, 1984), who proposed a three-level, six-stage model of moral development. He believed that most adolescents and adults function in the conventional mode (living up to others' expectations and obeying societal and religious rules), while a few will reach the highest stage of postconventional reasoning in which moral conflicts and universal principles will take precedence over laws (as exemplified by Gandhi and Martin Luther King).

In the psychoanalytic framework, Freud described the change in the superego from child to adolescent as the replacement of the childhood reliance on parental values by a period of evaluation after which parental values may be accepted or rejected (Freud, 1925/1961, cited in Nielsen, 1987).

Nielsen (1987) described the social learning approach as one based on reward and punishment, rather than as a given stage of development. Since the reward process is based on community norms, different cultures reflect different values. The cognitive-social learning theorists (notably Hoffman, 1980, 1983, 1984) attribute moral development to parental values and parenting approaches. Hoffman compared *power-assertive* parents, whose children conform to escape detection and punishment, to *inductive-approach* parents, who stress the rationale for behavior and use logical consequences as a basis for encouraging conformity. A third group, those who practice *love withdrawal*, supplant punishment with emotional deprivation, a potentially more dangerous practice (Conger & Petersen, 1984).

Religious practices and the search for spirituality are neither synonymous with each other nor with moral development. Certainly, the adolescent questioning of adult values must include those pertaining to religion. Conger and Petersen (1984) described changes in adolescent religious belief as moving from the concrete to the abstract, as more tolerant and less dogmatic, and as a gradual lessening of church attendance in later adolescence. Whether the outcome for the individual is to remain within traditional religion, join unorthodox groups, or pursue a highly personal path, the search for spirituality appears to be a powerful human force and another way in which adolescents can assert their independence.

Career and Lifestyle Issues

Much of our adult identity is tied to the work we do. Determining our eventual lifestyle through choosing our career path, balancing work and family, and finding economic and personal fulfillment are issues that each adult must face. The gifted adolescent who is deciding on an initial career (life expectancy changes have produced many sequential career options) may be hampered by the heavy burden known as "you can be anything you want to be." There is a particular need for guidance in this area. While the capabilities of the gifted teenager may lead counselors and parents to stress higher status professions, happiness and fulfillment are not linked totally to economics and traditional societal values. The concept of learning styles has been helpful in providing clarification in this regard. Working with many people or preferring more solitary en-

deavors, preferring ideas or practical applications, concern with justice
or concern for human comfort, and the need for order or the preference
for changeability are only some of the dimensions that can be explored
through the use of learning style and vocational preference instruments
(Myers & McCaulley, 1985).

Gender stereotypes are as critical in this area as they are in many
others. The absence of female models in many professions (especially
those relating to math and science) and the necessity to make a "choice"
between career and family or to undertake the stressful role of "superwoman" continue to plague young women. Similarly, though they are less
arduously defended in the literature, young men who wish to choose
"women's work" need support and guidance (Alvino, 1989). Young men
are often pushed into math and science with the same fervor that young
women are discouraged from those fields. Although in this age of affir-
mative action and expectations of gender equality one might assume the
situation to be otherwise, the reality is that adolescents are often discouraged by teachers, counselors, parents, and societal reaction when they
attempt to make atypical choices. This discouragement demands consideration. Advocates for the gifted must provide strong support to adolescents who wish to reject the advice and preferences of family members
whom they respect and love.

A LOOK AHEAD

Completion of the developmental tasks of adolescence and attaining
fulfilling adult competency are overriding goals for adolescents. This
book tends to focus on the stumbling blocks that gifted teens may
encounter in their personal quests. We are not pessimistic. We believe that
the vast majority of those who now struggle with difficult decisions will
overcome the temptations, weather the developmental inconsistencies,
and make the hard choices that will propel them into adulthood. Eventually, most will join in the great advantages this society offers to those with
intelligence and the desire to use it productively. Some, however, will be
lost to themselves and to society if they do not receive assistance in
dealing with problems emanating from family needs, self-imposed pressures, or the weight of the burden that society unwittingly places on those
who seem to "have it all."

To complete the introduction to the subjects of this book, Chapter 2
provides a discussion of the critical role of the family in the life of the
gifted adolescent. Then in Part I, Chapters 3–6 consider those personal
issues that are most closely related to the stresses facing the gifted
adolescent. Variables in educational success or underachievement, and

critical issues related to career and lifestyle choices are delineated in Parts II and III, respectively. Finally, in Part IV the joys and frustrations of racial or ethnic difference are discussed.

It is our intent in this book to cover issues, present solutions, and pose questions for further exploration. We hope that among our suggestions are some that will provide guidance, comfort, and direction for gifted adolescents and their teachers, mentors, and parents.

REFERENCES

Alvino, J. (1989, Spring). Gifted boys have problems, too! TAG *Update, 12*, 1.

Baron, J., & Sternberg, R. (Eds.). (1987). *Teaching thinking skills: Theory and practice.* New York: Freeman.

Betts, G., & Neihart, M. (1988). Profiles of the gifted and talented. *Gifted Child Quarterly, 32*, 248–253.

Brody, L., & Benbow, C. (1987). Accelerative strategies: How effective are they for the gifted? *Gifted Child Quarterly, 31*, 105–110.

Burks, S., Jensen, D., & Terman, L. (1930). *Genetic studies of genius: Vol. 3. The promise of youth: Follow-up studies of a thousand gifted children.* Stanford: Stanford University Press.

Clark, B. (1986). *Optimizing learning: The integrative education model in the classroom.* Columbus, OH: Merrill.

Clark, B. (1988). *Growing up gifted* (3rd ed.). Columbus, OH: Merrill.

Conger, J., & Petersen, A. (1984). *Adolescence and youth: Psychological development in a changing world.* New York: Harper & Row.

Cox, C. (1926). *Genetic studies of genius: Vol. 2. The early mental traits of three hundred geniuses.* Stanford: Stanford University Press.

Craig, G. (1989). *Human development* (5th ed.). Englewood Cliffs, NJ: Prentice-Hall.

Dabrowski, K., & Piechowski, M. (1977). *Theory of levels of emotional development* (Vol. 1). Oceanside, NY: Dabor Science Publications.

Erikson, E. (1963). *Childhood and society* (2nd ed.). New York: Norton.

Erikson, E. (1968). *Identity: Youth and crisis.* New York: Norton.

Feldhusen, J., & Richardson, W. (1986). *Leadership education: Developing skills for youth.* West Lafayette, IN: Star Teaching Materials.

Feldman, D. (1984). A follow-up of subjects scoring above 180 IQ in Terman's "Genetic studies of genius." *Exceptional Children, 50*, 518–523.

Freud, S. (1961). Some psychical consequences of the anatomical distinction between the sexes. In J. Strachey (Ed.), *Standard edition of the complete psychological works of Sigmund Freud* (Vol. 19). London: Hogarth Press. (Original work published in 1925).

Galbraith, J. (1983). *The gifted kids survival guide.* Minneapolis: Weatherall.

Gardner, H. (1983). *Frames of mind: The theory of multiple intelligences.* New York: Basic Books.

Getzels, J., & Jackson, P. (1962). *Creativity and intelligence: Explorations with gifted children.* New York: Wiley.

Havighurst, R. (1972). *Developmental tasks and education.* New York: Longman.

Hoffman, M. (1980). Moral development in adolescence. In J. Adelson (Ed.), *Handbook of adolescent psychology* (pp. 295–344). New York: Wiley.

Hoffman, M. (1983). Affective and cognitive processes in moral internalization. In E. Higgins, D. Ruble, & W. Hartup (Eds.), *Social cognition and social development* (pp. 236–274). Cambridge: Cambridge University Press.

Hoffman, M. (1984). Empathy, its limitations and its role in comprehensive moral theory. In W. Kurtines & J. Gewirtz (Eds.), *Morality, moral behavior and moral development* (pp. 283–302). New York: Wiley Interscience.

Hollingworth, L. (1926). *Gifted children: Their nature and nurture.* New York: Macmillan.

Hollingworth, L. (1942). *Children above 180 IQ Stanford-Binet: Origin and development.* Yonkers, NY: World Book.

Karnes, F., Meriweather, S., & D'Llio, V. (1987). The effectiveness of the Leadership Studies Program. *Roeper Review, 9,* 238–241.

Kerr, B. (1985). *Smart girls, gifted women.* Columbus: Ohio Psychological Publishing.

Kohlberg, L. (1983). *Moral stages: A current formulation and a response to critics.* London: Karger.

Kohlberg, L. (1984). *The psychology of moral development: Essays on moral development.* San Francisco: Harper & Row.

Lewandowski, L. (1987). Brain–behavior relationships. In L. Hartlage, M. Asken, & J. L. Hornsby (Eds.), *Essentials of neuropsychological assessment* (pp. 12–29). New York: Springer.

Maker, J. (Ed.). (1988). *Critical issues in the education of the gifted.* Rockville, MD: Aspen.

Marland, S., Jr. (1972). *Education of the gifted and talented. Report to the Congress of the United States by the U.S. Commissioner of Education.* Washington, DC: U.S. Government Printing Office.

Myers, I., & McCaulley, M. (1985). *Manual: A guide to the development and use of the Myers-Briggs Type Indicator.* Palo Alto, CA: Consulting Psychologists Press.

Nielsen, L. (1987). *Adolescent psychology: A contemporary view.* New York: Holt, Rinehart & Winston.

Piechowski, M. (1986). The concept of developmental potential. *Roeper Review, 8,* 190–197.

Reis, S., & Callahan, C. (1989). Gifted females: They've come a long way—or have they? *Journal for the Education of the Gifted, 12,* 99–117.

Renzulli, J. (1978). What makes giftedness? Reexamining a definition. *Phi Delta Kappan, 60,* 180–184.

Renzulli, J. (1986). The three-ring conception of giftedness: A developmental model for creative production. In R. Sternberg & J. Davidson (Eds.), *Conceptions of giftedness* (pp. 53–92). Cambridge: Cambridge University Press.

Renzulli, J., Reis, S., & Smith, L. (1981). *The revolving door identification model.* Mansfield, CT: Creative Learning Press.

Richert, E. (1986, March). *Underachievement in the gifted.* Paper presented at the Ohio Association for Gifted Children, Columbus.

Richert, E., Alvino, J., & McDonnel, R. (1982). *National report on identification, assessment and recommendations for comprehensive identification of gifted and talented youth.* Sewell, NJ: Educational Information and Resource Center.

Rimm, S. (1986). *Underachievement syndrome: Causes and cures.* Watertown, WI: Apple.

Roedell, W. (1984). Vulnerabilities of highly gifted children. *Roeper Review, 6,* 127–130.

Silverman, L. (1989). It all began with Leta Hollingworth: The story of giftedness in women. *Journal for the Education of the Gifted, 12,* 86–98.

Sisk, D. (1986, May). Leadership: A special type of giftedness. *Gifted Children Monthly, 7,* 14–15, 20.

Sisk, D. (1987, May). Leaders are made, not born. *Gifted Children Monthly, 8,* 1–3.

Sternberg, R. (1985). *Beyond IQ: A triarchic theory of intelligence.* New York: Cambridge University Press.

Sternberg, R. (1986). A triarchic theory of intellectual giftedness. In R. Sternberg & J. Davidson (Eds.), *Conceptions of giftedness* (pp. 223–243). Cambridge: Cambridge University Press.

Sternberg, R., & Davidson, J. (1985). Cognitive development in the gifted and talented. In F. Horowitz & M. O'Brien (Eds.), *The gifted and talented: Developmental perspectives* (pp. 37–84). Washington, DC: American Psychological Association.

Tannenbaum, A. (1962). *Adolescent attitudes toward academic brilliance.* New York: Teachers College Press.

Tannenbaum, A. (1983). *Gifted children.* New York: Macmillan.

Terman, L. (1925). *Genetic studies of genius: Vol. 1. Mental and physical traits of a thousand gifted children.* Stanford: Stanford University Press.

Terman, L., & Oden, M. (1947). *Genetic studies of genius: Vol. 4. The gifted child grows up.* Stanford: Stanford University Press.

Terman, L., & Oden, M. (1959). *Genetic studies of genius: Vol. 5. The gifted group at midlife.* Stanford: Stanford University Press.

Torrance, E. P. (1963). *Education and the creative potential.* Minneapolis: University of Minnesota Press.

Torrance, E. P. (1966). *Torrance Tests of Creative Thinking: Norms—technical manual.* Princeton, NJ: Personnel Press.

Torrance, E. P. (1969). Creative positives of disadvantaged children and youth. *Gifted Child Quarterly, 13,* 71–81.

Torrance, E. P., Blume, B., Maryanopolis, J., Murphey, F., & Rogers, J. (1980). *Teaching scenario writing.* Lincoln: Future Problem Solving Program, Nebraska Department of Education.

CHAPTER 2

Parenting the Gifted Adolescent— Special Problems, Special Joys

Sylvia B. Rimm

Imagine driving a country road on a foggy morning. You turn on your car lights, then turn them off to see if it improves your visibility. You occasionally see familiar landmarks that give you the security that you are continuing on the right route. You emerge from the fog intermittently and see especially clear, blue sky and green fields only to again return to the fog and lose your sense of direction. You feel a tension while you drive, which seems delightfully relieved each time you emerge to patches of clarity. Finally the fog lifts permanently, and you see the clear day.

Emerging from the fog lifts your spirits. You have stayed firmly in the driver's seat and have successfully negotiated the miles of misty insecurity. The view seems more spectacular than ever and you appreciate it differently than you might have on a less challenging day.

Parenting an adolescent holds the same foggy insecurities and the same patches of joyful clarity. If you've driven carefully and stayed firmly at the wheel, it provides the same satisfying view as your adolescent emerges from the fog into young adulthood.

The foggy, rural route and the tense parenting drive in the passage between childhood and adulthood challenge parents of average children as well as of gifted children. However, there are some dramatic differences in terms of both the insecurity of the fog and the clarity of the magnificent open stretches, which may increase the challenge of steering gifted adolescents through to the clearing of adulthood. The heightened insecurity that the fog provides for the driver may come because gifted adolescents often sound so much like adults and expect so much adult power that parents may feel threatened or less certain in their parenting. They may indeed feel that their adolescents are in a better driving position than they are. In addition, the requirements of a lengthy education may cause an extended period of financial, and therefore psychological, dependence—almost like a protracted adolescence, so the foggy

18

drive may indeed be longer. The clarity of the open stretches may be more fulfilling as parents participate in some of the heightened experiences in which gifted adolescents become involved.

CASE STUDIES

Gifted adolescents can be as different from each other as they are from adolescents with average abilities. Thus their family interrelationships may also vary as much as do those of average adolescents. There are, however, some family characteristics which are more typical for achieving gifted children and some that are typical for underachieving gifted children. Here are two case examples of gifted adolescents to draw some prototypical pictures.

Jenny

Jenny is 13 years old. She almost always gets A's. She loves drama and has participated in some high-powered eastern drama camps. She almost always gets a part in the school play, but she never gets the lead. Jenny says that's because she is overweight. She may be right. She is assigned to be the mother or the grandmother, and observes that pretty, thinner peers get the lead roles despite, from her perspective, their lesser talent.

Jenny hasn't had a close friend since her best friend moved away in fourth grade. She's not sure why she is not accepted by the "popular crowd." "Is it my weight?" she wonders. Other kids say she's too bossy. She tries not to be, but "I have to tell them when they do dumb things." Her friends have started to "go with boys" in school. The boys don't seem to be interested in Jenny. "Is it the weight?" she wonders again.

When Jenny's social life goes awry, and that is fairly often these days, she heads for the refrigerator. "How come," she wonders, "my mom is thin, my brother is thin, my spoiled, little sister is thin, and I have to be fat, like my dad? It doesn't seem fair!" she exclaims, as she shoves her little sister, "accidentally."

Jenny gets along well with her parents and teachers. She enjoys good and open communication with them. She even copes pretty well with her own perfectionism and competition in schoolwork and on stage. Her peer relations and her weight problem, however, frustrate Jenny and her parents. She won't take any suggestions or criticism when it comes to either of those two areas even though both cause her a great deal of sadness.

Andrew and Bryan

Andrew and Bryan are brothers. Andrew is 16 years old and a good-looking, conservatively dressed junior. His grades are excellent and his eleventh-grade courses are all accelerated or honors level. He verbalizes extensively about how he doesn't really study much or take notes. He says he can memorize the material effortlessly and enjoys demonstrating his excellent memory. He confidently states that he could learn anything presented to him.

He has lots of friends. He's part of the "band group," and he's trumpet section leader and searches for a way to explain "humbly" that he is the best trumpet in the school.

He is responsible, works part-time, and participates in extracurricular activities. He has his sights on Harvard and has been determinedly mastering PSAT practice tests and measuring his score improvements.

Although he's basically a good kid, he takes curious delight in winning arguments with each of his parents. He almost always wins, because, he says, "he's right." His parents feel a bit frustrated with the arguing but feel helpless about avoiding it. Andrew takes charge of himself, and does so fairly effectively. He also takes charge of keeping his brother, Bryan, in his place, also fairly effectively. Andrew likes to describe himself as "perfect" to his brother.

Bryan, an eighth grader, comes to see the psychologist attired in a black T-shirt with a gold "heavy metal" design. He explains to the therapist that he is a "metal head." His friends are important to Bryan because for years he had almost no friends. He explains that his present success is due to his realization that he had to use two languages—one for adults and one for kids. He used the latter so that his friends wouldn't feel as if he was putting them down.

Bryan's IQ is in the high 130s, but he has repeated seventh grade. Bryan has diligently refused to do any homework since second grade; thus the retention in seventh grade. He has always asserted that school is boring and blames his problems on his teachers or on his brother; the teachers because they didn't like him, and his brother because Bryan felt so terrible about not doing anything as well as Andrew.

Bryan's mother was very supportive when he explained to her about his feelings of losing. She kept trying to find something Bryan could do better than Andrew. That only heightened the competition between the two brothers since it served as a further challenge to Andrew to again outdo Bryan, and it provided a subtle message to Bryan that he was expected to do something better than Andrew in order to feel successful.

Bryan's parents describe him as very imaginative. They also say that he has always "marched to the beat of his own drummer." Curiously enough Bryan plays the drum very well—although he does not play the drum as well as Andrew plays the trumpet.

Andrew was adopted; Bryan was his parents' birth child. Andrew is closer to his father, while Bryan clearly identifies with his mother. He communicates better with her, too. Andrew spends much of the weekends with his father. Bryan devotes his time to listening to heavy metal music, reading anything but his homework, and feeling sad. He rarely remembers doing anything with his father alone. His brother was always there too.

The boys' parents are delighted with Andrew's progress and feel desperately worried and helpless about Bryan. They wonder if he will ever begin to do his schoolwork.

The special joys that go with parenting the Jennys and the Andrews come from observing their competence, their special talents, and their many successes. Less capable children do not usually provide their parents with the same sense of pride in their accomplishments. The special problems come mainly from the heightened competitiveness that frequently accompanies giftedness. Perhaps because gifted children receive so much recognition for their talents, they internalize a pressure to achieve, to win, and to compete. That heightened competition often generalizes to all facets of their lives. Parents who may counteridentify with their gifted children also feel increased pressure for their children to excel. During adolescence these pressures heighten. Involvement in competitive school activities and applications to colleges increase the realities of competing with others beyond the high school environment. Parents waiver between treating their youngsters as children and expecting them to behave as adults.

Jenny's parents worry about her nonacceptance by peers. Will Jenny feel so badly about her nonacceptance that she will compromise her parent-taught values to be accepted? Will Jenny feel frustrated enough about her weight problem to become eating disordered or bulimic as do other teenage girls? Will she become depressed when she realizes that she may not be able to make drama her career? They notice some unusual sadness now. Will it get worse?

Andrew's and Bryan's parents don't feel too worried about Andrew, but feel very concerned about Bryan. Will he finally begin doing his work? Will he ever change his image as a "lazy, oppositional kid"? What about the "heavy metal" crowd he's friends with? Will they get into drugs, and will Bryan, who for the first time has friends, be pressured into experimenting? Or will he, with his need to "march to the beat of his own drummer," decide to be the first of his crowd to try drugs, perhaps as an effort to heighten the excitement of his drumming experience or to imagine that he's the best?

Although Andrew's parents don't yet feel worried about him, should they be worried? Where will his perfectionism and need for power lead him if Bryan begins achieving and outperforms him? How will Andrew cope with a possible rejection from Harvard? And after Andrew enters college and is no longer the best and the smartest, will he fall apart and feel like a failure as many perfectionists do when they enter extreme competition?

Parents of gifted adolescents do indeed have increased opportunities for enjoying the successes of their adolescents. The problems that their adolescents struggle with are not entirely different from those of average adolescents. Concerns with peer pressure, emphasis on appearance, increased demands for adult power; and alcohol, drugs, and promiscuous sexual activities are equally worrisome to parents of less gifted adolescents. However, the problems of heightened competition and pressure to excel in everything add a special intensity to those normal adolescent problems.

SUPPORTING THEIR TALENTS, INTERESTS, AND ACTIVITIES

If adolescents exhibit special talents, their parents have probably already been heavily involved in cultivating those talents. However, adolescence brings with it new calls to greater involvement.

Time and Financial Commitment

Adolescents who excel in music, art, drama, or dance undoubtedly have previously been involved in local lessons, school bands, orchestras, choruses, and community art activities. According to Bloom's (1985) study of talent development, adolescence brings with it the need for a different level of instruction. If these talents are to be nurtured, much greater commitments of time and finances will be required by both the adolescents and their families.

High level teachers who are able to guide these youngsters through the complexities of their more advanced training are typically found in urban areas and are far more costly to engage. That may involve long drives and great expenses. The usual neighborhood car pools no longer serve to relieve the time commitments. Extended time with the special-talent child may limit time with other members of the family and may invade scarce financial resources. High priced musical instruments or art supplies to support their talents are considered a "necessity" and cause havoc for normal family budgets. The pressures on families to support these youngsters' talents become extraordinary. Their parents struggle to weigh the value of investing $10,000 in a fine violin, as they are further plagued by doubts about whether their adolescent is sufficiently talented to be the success the music teacher only cautiously predicts. They wonder if they are stealing from their child a more socially balanced development. They are anxious about the new teacher's requirements for 3 hours of nightly practice. How will the adolescent have time for the normal experiences of youth?

Parents feel torn between the overwhelming commitments required and the joyful recognition of their adolescent's unusual talents. How can they deny opportunities when so few others have such extraordinary talents? As they observe their child's conflicts, the youngster's immersion in the art form seems almost as if the art is required nurturance, like food or sleep. They wonder how they can possibly deny the child these special opportunities despite their own personal sacrifices and doubts.

Research on eminence and achievement consistently documents family commitment and support (Albert, 1980; Bloom, 1985; Olszewski, Kulieke, & Buescher, 1987). Clark and Zimmerman (1988) emphasized again the importance of parental encouragement for artistically talented students. Parents invest energy and resources. They drive to lessons, concerts, performances, and contests. They provide practice rooms, instruments, and supplies—never knowing whether their adolescent will emerge from the competitive art arena to become a concert violinist, starring artist, high level ballerina, Olympic gymnast, or Broadway star. There is no other way, it seems. There appears to be no choice.

The time and financial commitment that parents are often required to provide for children talented in the arts is only slightly different from requirements for children's talents that fall into other areas of giftedness. Mathematicians, scientists, historians, and creative writers may not require the expensive supplies initially, although they surely will eventually. However, their requirements include support for special summer courses, contests, classes, and teachers. Although financial investments tend not to be as high, time involvement may equal that of the artist's parents. While much more of the student's involvement is related to curriculum and direct school experience, parents may be required to advocate to schools to be sure that opportunities for challenge are provided. Schools don't always make a commitment to gifted students unless parents organize to prove that there is support for gifted education.

How Much Is Too Much?

While it is true that extraordinarily gifted adolescents require parental support to discover whether their talent qualifies them for a lifetime career in an art field, parents' responsibility becomes equally heavy to prepare adolescents for the possibility of alternative careers. If special-talent areas demand flexibility from school assignments, parents should ensure that the youngster's talent does not provide "an easy way out" from other reasonable school responsibilities.

As parents advocate for gifted education, positive patience and perseverance are extremely important. While they are negotiating for special services, they should not allow students to use the lack of challenging curriculum as an excuse for not fulfilling homework and study responsibilities. Parents' battles with schools were apparent among the families of underachieving gifted children, but not typical in biographies of eminent and achieving adults (Rimm & Lowe, 1988).

While parents provide large amounts of time and financial resources for their extremely gifted adolescents, they must always ask themselves that most difficult question, how much is too much? The answers are ambiguous at best and result in further questions, as such: Are the adolescents matching adult investments with their own efforts? Are high level teachers and judges continuing to project successful careers? Are other siblings suffering as a result of lack of resources and paucity of attention? Are the parents managing to maintain an adult life that is not entirely child centered, or is the marriage suffering as a result of the gifted child? Is the gifted child learning to function in a competitive environment so that he or she will not become depressed because of failures? Are alternative careers being explored should the first choice prove to be a disappointment?

Families will want to weigh the answers to these questions in deciding "how much is too much" for their individual gifted child.

Teaching Competition

Families of gifted adolescents may wonder why this section is included under parent support. Of course parents always support their adolescents' winning. The problem is truly related to what parents model to their children about losing, mistakes, and failures.

If parents feel too sorry for their adolescents in defeat, then adolescents will learn to feel too sorry for themselves. They will become more anxious about competition, thus encouraging even more protection from their parents. Too much parent sympathy, anxiety, and disappointment convey the subtle unintended message to adolescents that they are always expected to win at something. This unrealistic competitive partnership pressures children into feeling that they are failures and that they are disappointing their parents. Parents are often unaware that they are increasing their children's pressures by increasing their empathy. A matter-of-fact approach to losing, accompanied by a good dose of humor, will encourage children's resilience about losing and will strengthen their character and resolve for engaging in further competition. Overanxiety and sympathy will only encourage them to avoid competition.

Gifted children tend to become more competitive as they experience more winning. Since they will not and cannot win forever and since there is almost always someone more talented than they, learning to cope with losing without quitting is a requirement for functioning in a competitive society.

Respite from competition can also be provided with activities that are noncompetitive and provide intrinsic rewards. Emerick (1989) used adolescents' involvement in personal interests as a means of helping gifted underachieving students to emerge from underachievement in school. Also, competition with oneself to improve a skill or activity is a good source of building self-confidence.

Sharing Interests

Biographies of eminence and achievement are replete with family histories of talented young people who shared intense common interests with at least one parent (Albert, 1980; Bloom, 1985; Goertzel & Goertzel, 1962). On the other hand, gifted underachievers (Rimm & Lowe, 1988) tended to outgrow their earlier shared interest with their parents. Instead, busy family members all seemed to move in so many different directions that the bond of common interests seemed to be almost eradicated.

A parent's modeling of a talent area in his or her vocation or avocation heightens adolescent interest in that area, provided that the other parent does not describe that interest or vocation in negative terms. If he or she does, it may worsen competition and opposition between the adolescent and the potential parental role model, thus discouraging the sharing of common interests (Rimm, 1986, 1990a; Rimm & Lowe, 1988).

Parent-School Relationships

A positive parent-school relationship models for adolescents a respectful attitude for education. That seems obvious, yet so many parents of gifted children find themselves enmeshed in conflicts with schools. The opposition usually involves differences in philosophy about educating gifted children and is intended to benefit children. However, the results may be seriously detrimental to their education, particularly during adolescence. Children who are allied with their parents against a school may simply refuse to continue to function in the school environment because they protest that the curriculum does not provide for their learning preference. While they might benefit from alternative lifestyles, the battling attitude prevents success for all involved. Parents and adolescents do not want to lose face, and principals and teachers may fear losing control (Rimm & Lowe, 1988). The result can easily be dramatic underachievement, which may close doors for a positive school education.

Gelcer and Dick (1986) observed that among gifted underachievers, when a philosophical difference occurred between a gifted child and a teacher, parents supported the child against the school authorities. Support was expressed as the assertion that the family's values were better than those of the school. This continuous conflict escalates cyclically and results in increased unhappiness and insecurity for the child.

Sensitive adult negotiations to benefit the adolescent are required. Compromises will undoubtedly be necessary. Much harm may be done for the adolescent in rigid battle stances taken by either school or parents. After all, there are multiple ways in which gifted children learn successfully. How can any way be all right or all wrong? A parent-school "united front" (Rimm, 1990a) is much more effective than school opposition for encouraging the adolescent to learn.

If high school experiences lack adequate challenge, adolescents and their parents may select from summer supplementary experiences and extracurricular activities to enrich the normal high school experience. Gifted students may also study abroad for a year or may graduate a year or more early and attend college, which may prove more suitable than continued high school attendance. While it would be better if schools could provide appropriate experiences for gifted adolescents—and parents should advocate for these—the supplementary experiences may serve the adolescent as substitutes. Continued opposition with the school will be likely to harm the student.

Parent volunteers in the school may also enrich opportunities for gifted students. Thus, providing mentorships, teaching in specific talent areas, or chaperoning enrichment field trips are all ways that parents can actively foster gifted programming for their own adolescents as well as for other young people. An active parent partnership with the schools provides a clear message of parent respect for education.

Extended Adolescence

Adolescents of average abilities frequently take on the responsibilities of adult roles after high school or after a 2-year technical school. Achieving adolescents with above average abilities are likely to extend the time of quasi-adolescence through at least a 4-year college program before they are able to be self-supporting. Gifted adolescents may embark on 6 to 12 years of training beyond high school, and although part of their graduate education may provide stipends, that amount is rarely enough for their complete support. They may continue to be financially dependent on a combination of family support and loans throughout their 20s. While they can hardly be described as truly adolescent, the independence that comes with financial self-sufficiency is postponed and leaves both them and their families in a strange kind of limbo. In many ways they are adults with adult insights and career responsibilities. In other ways they are adolescent, somewhat dependent on their parents and very much within the control of their teachers. The postponement of the privileges of adulthood is part of the deferred gratification in which they invest while becoming involved in a lengthy educational process.

Families of these gifted young adults are in the peculiar position of any ambiguous relationship. While they may want to encourage and do take pride in their youngster's accomplishments, they may feel uncertain about how to advise these young people. They continue to bear major financial responsibility for them. The conflict between independence and dependence may put a substantial strain on what earlier may have been a reasonably good parent-child relationship.

SIBLING RELATIONS

Sibling relationships among gifted adolescents may not be very different from those of average adolescents, or there may be some very dramatic differences. There are three areas where giftedness may contribute to some special sibling problems.

Families with Multiple Achieving Gifted Children

When several siblings have already established themselves as achievers, pressure is likely to be felt by younger siblings to maintain the family achieving tradition. Even when parents especially avoid making comparisons, younger children may feel that they must meet the performance standards of their older siblings. Although they may be capable of similar high performance, they may nevertheless feel frustrated at the preset standards established by older siblings.

Their responses to greetings from teachers welcoming them with high expectations, are not always predictable. They may fear that they cannot maintain the family standard, or they may appreciate the positive reputation set by their older siblings.

Families with Especially Gifted and Less Gifted Children

This difference probably causes the most frustation for parents and siblings alike. Parents are hesitant to give the especially gifted children their due for fear that it will hurt the less gifted children. They find themselves constantly searching for qualities in the less gifted children that they can point to as superior. That only causes greater problems. The children "see through" the technique and neither the more gifted nor less gifted feel good about this approach. They assume from their parents' response that everyone must be *best* at something to be acceptable. They also assume that if someone is best, someone else must be second best or not good at all. The impact on children appears to be an increase in competition between the siblings.

A more appropriate way to cope with this situation is to teach children to accept the differences, including invidious comparisons. Being honest with children about apparent limitations in abilities is probably more supportive in the long run. Explaining to them that they may not be as capable as their siblings is probably in their best long-term interest. After all, don't all people have to come to terms with their inadequacies? Even the most intellectually or artistically gifted adults eventually learn that they are not as talented as they wish they were.

Families with Achieving and Underachieving Gifted Children

Birth order appears to affect achievement patterns. The literature on achievement and eminence finds more first born, only, and youngest among the eminent (Albert, 1980). These same birth orders also appear to be high risk for underachievers (Rimm & Lowe, 1988). Sibling rivalry affects the various members of many families almost as if to provide them with individual labels, for example, the achiever, the athlete, the social one, the creative one, the behavior problem child, or the underachiever. Successful clinical work with an underachiever has predictable effects on all other children in the family. If the earlier scapegoat's problem is removed, and he or she is identified as successful, the adolescent who formerly held the "first" status feels threatened. Being the most gifted and achievement-oriented in a family is a precarious position. It is not at all surprising for the child in first position to subtly, or sometimes not so subtly, attempt to maintain his or her first place at the expense of siblings. The example of Andrew and Bryan fits this pattern. Andrew actively sabotaged Bryan's efforts. Even in my meeting with Andrew, he gave me some "secret" information to point out Bryan's inadequacies. It was clear his first-place position was precariously maintained.

PRECARIOUS POWER

The roadway through adolescence to adulthood feels exploratory to adolescents and their parents. Assertiveness and aggressiveness are precariously attempted by most gifted adolescents, and permitting appropriate power while setting limits is always difficult for parents.

Guiding Adolescents by Positive Trust

For gifted adolescents to feel trusted, parents must allow them a continuum of freedom and power that resembles the shape of a V (Rimm, 1986). If as small children they were given clear limits and power appropriate for a child, rather than an adult, it would be as if they were moving up the V of development, and their sense of responsibility would bring them to the broader top of the V, where they would continue to feel trusted but respect adult limits. When they are ready to move out of the V to young adulthood, they will have internalized some values that will assist them in establishing both identity and intimacy, the developmental tasks of adolescence and young adulthood. A study of 60 achieving gifted adolescents (Leroux, 1988) found that family relationships were described as positive by these high school seniors. They said they could "count on their parents." The rebelliousness that is more evident in underachieving gifted students was not typical of the achieving gifted adolescents. Studies of high achievement typically indicate the importance of a positive family environment (Albert, 1980; Bloom, 1985; Olszewski et al., 1987).

Sometimes gifted children whose vocabulary may sound very adult are treated to too much power and freedom too early (Gelcer & Dick, 1986), as in an inverted Λ. They may be unwilling to accept parents' limits in adolescence because they are accustomed to adult power. If their parents attempt to control them even with reasonable rules, they become angry and depressed and rebel. Once adolescents have been given too much power, only gentle negotiations and careful guiding are effective for maintaining relative peace in the household. Indeed the resulting behavior may become very difficult, and even gifted adolescents are at risk of dropping out of high school and college.

Parents and teachers have the right and responsibility to set limits. The degree with which that can be done comfortably is very much *relative* to the power and freedom given in early childhood. If a level of trust has been established, few punishments should be necessary during adolescence (Rimm, 1990b).

Coping with Debaters

Adolescents who argue incessantly often think of themselves as debaters. They are frequently told by parents that they will make good lawyers. The more parents call them "lawyers," the more determined they will be to win all arguments. They pride themselves on their reasoning skills and may extend their debating to teachers and friends (Rimm, 1990a).

Although parents may sometimes enjoy their adolescents' critical-thinking ability, they also find themselves feeling pushed, frustrated, manipulated, and very negative. When "debaters" approach, an automatic no appears on the parents' forehead. They say no before they even hear the request. Saying no feels almost instinctive and, at least, protective. However, arguers don't accept a "no" answer. They pursue parents with further convincing discussion until finally, either out of guilt, frustration, or desperation, or just to deliver themselves from pain, the parents respond with a negative "all right, yes." They've now, unintentionally, increased the debater's arguing skill by demonstrating that if the adolescent perseveres, the parents will surely change their decision. Parents feel trapped.

When parents ask a favor of a debating adolescent, oddly enough the youngster also responds with an automatic "no, why do I have to?" Parents then find themselves pursuing the adolescent, providing a nagging rationale for their request, until finally the youngster responds with a negative "all right, if I have to." Parents don't understand the negativism when they've been so good to the adolescent. The youngster has copied the parents' pattern!

Adolescents naturally become more skilled in arguing with continued experience. While it's important to encourage critical thinking and discussion, a regular arguing mode is more a power struggle than a discussion. Furthermore, these youngsters are accumulating experiences in always winning power struggles. This is a habit that will make it difficult for them to live and work with others in the future.

The goal is to encourage thinking and reasoning, but to discourage dominating power struggles. Adolescents need to be given the opportunity to respect the experience and intelligence of their parents and teachers, while retaining their own rights as adolescents to think, question, and discuss. This isn't an easy balance to maintain.

Avoiding Dysfunctional Power Alliance

Adolescence is a most critical time for parents to provide a "united front" for their youngsters (Rimm, 1986, 1990a). Since their children are almost adults it becomes easy for one parent to form a "friendship" relationship with a son or daughter and unintentionally sabotage the other adult's power. This sabotaging alliance will definitely cause heightened rebellion and competition with the sabotaged parent and steal from that parent the opportunity to be a role model for the adolescent. Fine (1977) notes that these competitive struggles between the gifted child and his or her parents is a crucial loss for the adolescent. Newman, Fox Dember, and Krug (1973) referred to this problem as a "diffusion of generational boundaries." This becomes even more precarious in a divorce situation. If gifted adolescents who are almost grown up are given more power and status than a parent, they are almost certain to become oppositional (that is, continually and irrationally opposing their parents' requests and expectations). If parents are positive and supportive of each other, extreme oppositionality rarely occurs.

In steering the adolescent on the road between childhood and adulthood, empowering gradually and sufficiently, but not too much, is probably the trickiest of tasks.

REFERENCES

Albert, R. S. (1980, Spring). Family positions and the attainment of eminence: A study of special family positions and special family experiences. *Gifted Child Quarterly, 24*(2), 87–95.

Bloom, B. S. (Ed.). (1985). *Developing talent in young people*. New York: Ballantine.

Clark, G. A., & Zimmerman, E. D. (1988, Fall II). Views of self, family background, and school: Interviews with artistically talented students. *Gifted Child Quarterly*, *32*(4), 340–346.

Emerick, L. J. (1989, November). *The gifted underachiever: Classroom strategies for reversing the pattern*. Paper presented at National Association for Gifted Children, 36th Annual Convention, Cincinnati, OH.

Fine, M. J. (1977). Facilitating parent–child relationships for creativity. *Gifted Child Quarterly*, *21*(4), 487–500.

Gelcer, E., & Dick, S. (1986). Families of gifted children: Achievers and underachievers. In K. K. Urban, H. Wagner, & W. Wieczerkowski (Eds.), *Giftedness: A continuing worldwide challenge* (pp. 447–459). New York: Trillium.

Goertzel, V., & Goertzel, M. G. (1962). *Cradles of eminence*. Boston: Little Brown.

Leroux, J. A. (1988). Voices from the classroom: Academic and social self-concepts of gifted adolescents. *Journal for the Education of the Gifted*, *11*(3), 3–18.

Newman, C. J., Fox Dember, D., & Krug, O. (1973). He can but he won't. In R. S. Eissler, A. Freud, M. A. Kris, & A. J. Solnit (Eds.), *The Psychoanalytic Study of the Child* (Vol. 28). New Haven, CT: Yale University Press.

Olszewski, P., Kulieke, M., & Buescher, T. (1987). The influence of the family environment on the development of talent: A literature review. *Journal for the Education of the Gifted*, *2*, pp. 6–28.

Rimm, S. B. (1986). *Underachievement syndrome: Causes and cures*. Watertown, WI: Apple.

Rimm, S. B. (1990a). *How to parent so children will learn*. Watertown, WI: Apple.

Rimm, S. B. (1990b). Parenting and teaching gifted children: A theory of relativity. *The Gifted Child Today*, *13*, 32–36.

Rimm, S. B., & Lowe, B. (1988, Fall). Family environments of underachieving gifted students. *Gifted Child Quarterly*, *32*(4), 353–359.

PART I

PERSONAL ISSUES

Gifted adolescents are not immune to the many psychological and sociological traumas that can beset any of us. We do know that the development of certain conditions or reactions to stress is more likely in the gifted population. These predictable conditions are associated with the external or self-imposition of unusually high expectations on those who wish to please themselves or others. These conditions are discussed in Chapters 3–6.

Many of the problems of the gifted child and adolescent stem from the condition known as developmental dysplasia, or uneven development. Those who can mentally compete with much older children may be expected to do so physically and socially as well. The gifted child and adolescent, like all other human beings, is a combination of abilities, disabilities, and mediocrities. When the right to be average, or even to fail, is denied the gifted person, stress will result. This will occur whether the stress is self-imposed or a reaction to the expectations of others.

Among the best documented reactions to stress in the gifted adolescent are eating disorders and perfectionism. In fact, the former is often but one manifestation of the latter. Because they are so often associated with high intelligence, especially in gifted young women, we have devoted entire chapters to each of these topics. Notably missing is a discussion of addiction in the gifted population. While it is a topic of primary interest in the adolescent population and one that we had hoped to include, no research exists linking addiction and giftedness. It is one of the many areas in which we found a need for basic research relative to the gifted adolescent population. We challenge our readers who have expertise in this subject to begin to build this much needed knowledge base.

Each of the four chapters in this part contains specific knowledge and suggests intervention strategies for the targeted conditions. Fulfillment of potential depends as much on emotional stability as on intellectual and educational opportunity. Identifying and intervening in the social/emotional problems of the troubled gifted adolescent constitutes a major challenge for each of us.

CHAPTER 3

Psychosocial Needs
of the Gifted Adolescent

Diane E. Frey

As Descartes stated, "The greatest minds are capable of the greatest vices as well as the greatest virtue." What seems to make the difference between the vices and the virtue lies in the affective domain. History is replete with examples of gifted individuals who had an extensive knowledge base, but who affected societies in negative ways, frequently due to a lack of self-understanding and of a satisfying life adjustment. While it is certainly true that the "future is in our minds" (American Association for Gifted Children, 1978, p. 5), the future is also in our hearts. Gifted adolescents who do not have their psychosocial needs met are likely to have difficulty using their abilities wisely.

While the past decade has evidenced an increase in the interest in gifted programs and educational research about the gifted, there are other indications that much more needs to be accomplished in the study of giftedness. Inquiry into the psychosocial needs of the gifted is long overdue.

Although helping professionals acknowledge the interrelation of emotional, social, and cognitive domains of development, programs for the gifted frequently neglect the emotional and social development areas (Betts, 1986; Betts & Neihart, 1985; Horowitz & O'Brien, 1986; Levine and Tucker, 1986). The complexity of gifted students' multipotentiality and the greater attention given to their intellectual adjustment may obscure their emotional and social adjustment needs (Barnette, 1989).

Various professionals have posited that gifted adolescents have a unique set of affective needs compared with their nongifted peers (Colangelo & Pfleger, 1979; Silverman, 1983). The vast emotional range and intensity of feelings that gifted adolescents experience may make them seem quite contradictory: mature and immature, arrogant and compassionate, aggressive and timid. Outer composure and self-assurance often mask deep feelings of insecurity in gifted adolescents.

A review of the literature of psychosocial adjustment of gifted adolescents indicated that the gifted suffer no more adjustment difficulties than do their nongifted peers (Holahan & Brounstein, 1986). Research has revealed that gifted adolescents in general are not clinically maladjusted; however, they do have unique concerns manifested by a lack of self-understanding and of coping skills in the social and emotional aspects of their lives. Lacking these abilities, gifted adolescents, in extreme cases, abandon their abilities and struggle through a seemingly endless adolescence (Buescher, 1985). Only when the social and emotional concerns of gifted adolescents are understood can concerned adults guide the adolescents to effective adjustment—an adjustment that does not necessitate tremendous, stressful, "trial and error," or "hit or miss" approaches for the gifted.

This chapter will explore the social and emotional needs of gifted adolescents and the interventions appropriate for the gifted. In addition, preventive approaches for gifted adolescents in the socioemotional area will be reviewed.

GENERAL PSYCHOSOCIAL NEEDS
DURING ADOLESCENCE

Studies indicate three major changes occurring within every adolescent: biological maturation, attainment of new ways of thinking and learning, and shifts in psychosocial needs. Buescher (1985) identified the latter as needs for independence, autonomy, adult role models, achievement of coping skills, individuality, recognition, acceptance, and self-knowledge. The gifted adolescent's response to these needs is frequently unique.

Independence and Autonomy. Independence is a common affective trait of the gifted. Since gifted adolescents often have developed this trait throughout childhood, it does not usually represent an area of difficult adjustment for them in adolescence. Gifted adolescents also score higher than their nongifted peers on scales designed to measure autonomy (LeResche, Strobino, Parks, Fischer, & Smeriglio, 1983). Since autonomy is also a characteristic of the gifted from childhood, the meeting of this need in adolescence usually does not present a problem.

Adult Role Models. An adolescent need that is more difficult for the gifted is finding gifted adult role models. Gifted adults could have a tremendous positive effect by mentoring the gifted in the psychosocial domain. While schools and organizations such as Mensa frequently provide mentors for the gifted in the cognitive domain (such as pairing a student interested in chemistry with a chemist in the community), seldom do the gifted have a chance to be mentored by a gifted adult who might possess, for example, the decision-making skills or self-esteem the adolescent is seeking to develop.

Coping Skills. The gifted adolescent often lacks information about specific coping skills that are effective in dealing with everyday problems of psychosocial adjustment. It has been suggested (Roedell, 1984) that adults frequently expect the social maturity of the gifted to match their intellectual development. When these two levels of development are uneven—a concept often referred to as dysplasia—adults may characterize the gifted individual as having a behavior problem. In actuality the gifted adolescent is responding as effectively as possible given the difference between intellectual maturity and socioemotional maturity that is frequently common in this population. Another reason gifted adolescents lack coping skills is that throughout childhood they are given positive feedback primarily for their intellectual prowess. Ultimately this leads to the development of the belief in adolescence that only by being smart can one be accepted (Powell & Haden, 1984). Thus social and coping skills are developed more slowly in the gifted. This leads to emotional distancing of the gifted from others, as well as an emotional detachment from their own emotional life (Powell & Haden, 1984).

Individuality. Individuality frequently represents a problem for gifted adolescents in that there may be a conflict between society's stereotypical expectations for age, sex, and racial groups and the gifted adolescent's need to fulfill individual expression. It is often the macho football star who is the hero of the school, not the mathematical wizard (Roedell, 1984). The desire to fulfill role expectations for adolescent males, for example, can deter a young gifted male from aesthetic appreciation or involvement in literature or mathematics. Gifted adolescent females, by the same token, are often less likely than their male peers to pursue high level mathematics or science courses (Fox, Brody, & Tobin, 1980). Gifted females frequently experience the conflict between traditional concepts of femininity and their inner desire to excel (Roedell, 1984). Consequently, discovering and expressing one's individuality can be difficult for gifted adolescents.

Recognition. Recognition needs of gifted adolescents are often obscured. Adults tend to become accustomed to gifted children performing well. As a result they often do not offer praise and encouragement but just assume the child will do well, as always. Gifted adolescents also lack recognition from peers inasmuch as friendship skills are often less well developed in the gifted. The characteristics of popular children (friendliness, peer dependency, conformity to peer rules and routines; Coleman, 1980) are not common among the gifted. Thus the gifted often have fewer friendships and fewer opportunities for recognition from peers.

Acceptance. The intense sensitivity and internal responsiveness characteristic of many gifted adolescents can lead to difficulty in feeling accepted by others. A highly sensitive gifted adolescent may perceive social rejection where there is none, thus enhancing a sense of alienation. This heightened sensitivity in gifted adolescents often takes the form of intense inner experiences, leading gifted teenagers to assume that something is wrong with them. Peers may ridicule a gifted adolescent for reacting strongly to a trivial incident, thereby increasing the gifted individual's sense of being odd and not accepted. In addition, the myths perpetuated about the gifted often lead to their being labelled as "gifted" and not feeling truly accepted for being themselves.

Self-Knowledge. The self-knowledge needs of most adolescents result in unique issues for the gifted. Self-knowledge needs arise earlier for the gifted, whose intense analytical approach to life results in earlier self-analysis (Roedell, 1984). The perfectionism of the gifted, coupled with inappropriate adult expectations, can make the process of identity very difficult for gifted adolescents, who report low social self-esteem but high academic self-esteem (Frey & Carlock, 1989). Being different from their peers seems to have a negative effect on the self-esteem of the gifted (Janos & Robinson, 1985).

In summary, the adolescent's need for independence and autonomy do not seem to present a developmental problem for gifted adolescents. The need for self-knowledge and self-esteem is partly met in the academic area but not the social area. The remaining needs of adolescents present unique challenges for those adolescents who are gifted.

GIFTED ADOLESCENTS' SPECIAL PSYCHOSOCIAL NEEDS

In addition to the psychosocial needs of every developing adolescent, the gifted also have unique needs to deal with at this time in their life. Buescher (1985) posited the following six needs of gifted adolescents: ownership, dissonance, risk taking, others' expectations, impatience, and identity.

Ownership of Giftedness. In adolescence the power of peer pressure and conformity can lead a gifted adolescent to deny being gifted. Ownership of advanced ability, of course, is necessary for one to effectively use such talent. It is especially common for gifted females to deny their ability in order to be accepted by others, especially males. In order to develop an accurate sense of their new identity, gifted adolescents need to incorporate the idea of being intellectually advanced into their evolving self-concept.

Dissonance. It is common for gifted adolescents to experience dissonance between what they do and how well they think they should have done. The propensity to expect more of oneself than can actually be developed appears to be a typical carryover trait from middle childhood (Buescher, 1985). Adults' understanding of the dynamic aids in developing more sensitivity to how severely these gifted individuals judge themselves. They are frequently more critical of themselves than others are of them.

Risk Taking. While most average adolescents increase risk-taking behaviors at this age compared with their childhood years, gifted adolescents typically take more risks in childhood and fewer risks in adolescence. Gifted adolescents are more aware of the repercussions of risky behavior (Seeley, 1984). Gifted adolescents also tend to weigh the advantages and disadvantages of certain activities, choosing those in which they will be successful. Gifted adolescents like to be in control of as many aspects of their life as possible. They tend to choose security over risk-taking.

Others' Expectations. Gifted adolescents feel conflicted in trying to respond to the expectations of others versus their own expectations. The multiple options available to them only intensify this conflict. Gifted adolescents report difficulty in responding to their parents' expectations. It is often like trying to hit a moving target, because parents of the gifted often have ambivalent feelings about their children—cherishing them on the one hand but becoming frustrated and energy depleted by them on the other hand. In addition to parents, siblings, friends, relatives, and teachers also express their expectations to the gifted. Thus gifted adolescents experience the "push" from others' expectations and the "pull" of their own expectations (Delisle, 1985). The result can be a low tolerance for ambiguity, stress, and impatience.

Impatience. The predisposition of gifted adolescents for impulsive decision making, coupled with exceptional talent, makes them intolerant of ambiguous, unsolved situations (Buescher, 1985). This impatience influences gifted adolescents to seek answers where none exist. They expect quick resolution of even the most complex problems. Lacking such resolution, gifted adolescents often feel angry and disappointed.

Identity. The concept of the "patchwork selves" described by Elkind (1980) is characteristic of gifted adolescents. "Patchwork selves" can be defined as the type of identity or self that develops due to premature development. The tendency to reach a premature sense of identity as a means of coping with societal pressure to reach an early adulthood is evident in gifted adolescents (Buescher & Higham, 1984, 1985; Delisle, 1985). The result of this premature identity formulation is the closing of important doors to opportunities for the development of full potential. Early identity closure brings considerable stress to later stages of adolescent development and early adulthood.

Sexuality. As noted in Chapter 1, Havighurst (1972) identified several tasks of adolescence that are related to the attainment of social skills, appropriate adult sex roles, and the acceptance of physiological changes. Therefore, it is somewhat surprising that a search of literature on gifted adolescents and sexuality yields little information. For most adolescents, even with the best of guidance, the development of mature sexuality is not an easy task. It can be speculated that the dysplasic lag of social skills behind intellectual skills further complicates the attainment of mature sexual behavior for the gifted. What little research-based information exists about intimate relationships (e.g., Frey, 1988) may not be readily available to gifted adolescents. Since the gifted are seldom taught much about their emotions in a systematic way, a strong feeling of love may leave them very confused. If their intimate relationship is homosexual rather than heterosexual, that confusion may be magnified. Making the development of mature sexuality even more difficult for the gifted is that adolescents, in naming the qualities they regard most desirable in prospective mates, usually emphasize character traits more than intelligence or physical appearance (Jersild, Brook, & Brook, 1978). Thus the very trait for which the gifted receive most attention and reinforcement is devalued in the dating and mate selection process.

While girls may begin physical maturity earlier than boys, sex differences in physical development appear to have little relationship to the ages of initial dating. Dating is a social relationship that is culturally rather than biologically defined. Generally nongifted girls are first interested in boys their own age and then become interested in older boys. Gifted girls are usually interested in friendships with those older than themselves and also prefer dating older boys. Nongifted boys generally turn to younger girls for dating. Since most friendships are built on, among other factors, similar intellectual levels, gifted boys would be expected to be more interested in older girls, who are usually interested in boys older than themselves. The problems resulting from this pattern are numerous for the gifted.

The difficulty that the gifted may have in interpreting nonverbal behavior also adds to the frustration and insecurity of developing relationships. Discerning the true meaning of the subtle signals of the "dating game" may be even more difficult for the gifted given their extreme sensitivity to interpersonal relationships and greater intensity of feelings. Discussing the importance of these issues with gifted adolescents becomes most critical because of the current concern and apparent prevalence of "date rape."

As described earlier, since most gifted adolescents take fewer social risks than their nongifted peers, their sexual-relationship skills are usually delayed. While conforming gifted students might adopt the nongifted peer norms for this task, nonconforming and rebellious gifted students usually experience adjustment to this task much later in early adulthood. As is evident, much confusion exists for the gifted in discovering their sexual pattern.

GENDER DIFFERENCES IN PSYCHOSOCIAL NEEDS

Gifted adolescents experience psychosocial needs differently depending on their gender. Leroux (1986) reported numerous findings on sex differences influencing gifted adolescents. While other chapters in this book discuss this topic more completely, it is important to emphasize here certain patterns specifically related to psychosocial needs. Leroux (1986) found that gifted females are more academically oriented than are gifted males, thus utilizing more of their energy in academics than in psychosocial tasks. An additional finding indicated that gifted males take fewer risks than females in social interaction and in new situations. Gifted females were found to moderate behavior in class due to external influences and to seek access to female teachers and female counselors. Gifted males perceived themselves as more conforming in social settings. Females felt more anxiety over impulse control and familial relationships, whereas gifted males felt more anxiety over personal appearance, social interactions, and ability to adapt to external expectations. Males displayed more sex-stereotyped behavior in public, but in private, among other gifted adolescents, displayed more androgynous behavior.

In addition to these findings, male–female differences exist with regard to gifted adolescents and self-esteem. Gifted adolescent females envision their ideal self as being androgynous (Hollinger & Fleming, 1985). The more the real self is like the ideal, the better self-esteem one obtains (Frey & Carlock, 1989). To this extent it seems that gifted adolescent girls derive social self-esteem from sources that transcend gender-specific behaviors.

COPING STRATEGIES

Given the variety and complexity of psychosocial issues facing the gifted, what coping strategies do they report using? Strop (1985) revealed that gifted adolescents feel competent in cognitive areas but less competent in social and physical areas. Common coping styles reported by gifted adolescents were (1) going off to be alone, (2) looking for a solution, and (3) trying to relax. Females were more likely to talk to a friend when worried; males did not report this as a strategy. Gifted adolescents were least likely to use drugs or talk to a counselor when worried.

When facing disagreements with friends, teachers, and family members, gifted adolescents selected different coping mechanisms (Strop, 1985). In disagreements with friends, gifted adolescents chose a more direct approach such as talking about the problem and disclosing angry feelings to the friend. They were least likely to choose indirect approaches in these situations. In disagreements with teachers, more passive approaches were selected; that is, talking to someone else or letting it work itself out. In disagreements with a family member, gifted adolescents most often chose to go somewhere alone to ponder the situation.

Gifted adolescents infrequently brought personal concerns to counselors, as reported by Strop (1985). When discussing other topics such as information gathering or scheduling with a counselor, gifted adolescents reported having the highest preference for helping professionals who ask students for their opinions. Gifted adolescents preferred that counselors give them enough information and encouragement to enable them to come to a decision on their own. The lowest preference for counseling approaches was a structured contract in which the gifted adolescent agreed to change some aspect of behavior (Strop, 1985).

Strop's (1985) findings are supported by several studies on learning styles that have indicated that a majority (usually cited as 60%-70%) of the gifted prefer "intuitive" ways of processing information rather than directly thinking about and interpreting the facts involved in a problem they might be experiencing (Hoehn & Bireley, 1988; Mills, 1984; Myers & McCaulley, 1985). Intuiters are further described as those who look for possibilities and relationships and like creative solutions. Some of these same studies (Hoehn & Bireley, 1988; Myers & McCaulley, 1985) found that a similar percentage of the gifted are more likely to be introvertive than extravertive (these percentages are reversed in the average population). Those who are introverts tend to prefer approaches that can help them discover solutions in an independent, nondirective manner. As a consequence of these styles, a majority of gifted adolescents may prefer to direct their own discoveries with minimal guidance from others.

PSYCHOSOCIAL INTERVENTIONS

Teachers and counselors can use several interventions to help gifted adolescents meet the variety of psychosocial needs previously discussed in this chapter.

Prevention. Preventive efforts in the form of educating the gifted about their affective needs should begin very early—in the primary grades, not high school. Curriculum materials and affective education can be very helpful in attaining the goal of a smooth transition from childhood to adulthood for gifted adolescents. Materials that can be obtained from American Guidance Services (Circle Pines, Minnesota) are an example of some of the excellent affective materials available. *On Being Gifted* (American Association for Gifted Children, 1978) is also a good resource for understanding the experience of being gifted. For older students, *Guiding the Gifted Child* (Webb, Meckstroth, & Tolan, 1982) can also be insightful.

Decision-Making Skills. Kaplan (1983) reported that gifted adolescents often compound the variety of socioemotional issues facing them by exercising poor decision making. Gifted adolescents exclude the affective domain from the decision-making process, believing that emotions should not play an integral role in cognitive processes (Kaplan, 1983). The tendency to overvalue the cognitive can result in very unsatisfactory decisions. Teaching gifted adolescents decision-making skills can greatly aid them in becoming less impulsive and more holistic in their decisions. Some excellent resources in this area are Arnold (1978), Bergman and Rudman (1985); Clabby and Elias (1987); Gelatt, Varenhorst, Carey, and Miller (1973); Heath and Weible (1983); Heiman and Slomianko (1985); and Stewart (1988).

Self-esteem Enhancement. Self-esteem enhancing activities that help gifted adolescents feel better about themselves socially can greatly assist these individuals. Numerous books and curriculum materials are available on this topic. Some helpful resources in this area are Canfield (1986), Clarke (1983), Frey and Carlock (1989), Fugit (1983), Helmstetter (1986), Krawetz (1984), McDaniel and Bielen (1986), Reasoner (1982), and Stanish (1982).

Socialization Skills. Socialization skills training can also help gifted adolescents. Although the gifted like to appear as if they have mastered these skills, they frequently have not, for the reasons discussed earlier in this chapter. Social skills deficits in the gifted usually consist of lack of information about social skills, of the ability to implement such information, and/or of the ability to evaluate and generalize about social skills. Some helpful resources for teachers and counselors in social skills development are Cartledge and Milburn (1980); Field, Roopnarine, and Segal (1984); LeCroy (1982); Sheppard, Shank, and Wilson (1975); and Stephens (1978).

Stress Management, Suicide Prevention, and Perfectionism Reduction. Stress-management strategies, suicide-prevention activities, and perfectionism-reduction exercises are all discussed in other chapters of this book. It is evident that the combined universal and specific needs that impinge on the gifted adolescent can result in much stress underscoring the need for specific training in these important areas.

Cognitive Relabelling. Frequently, gifted adolescents are their own worst enemy by the nature of the self-talk they engage in about socioemotional concerns. Helping gifted adolescents do cognitive relabelling and thought stopping can put them in control of their thoughts in a productive way. (The process of thought stopping involves first saying "stop" out loud, then progressing to saying "stop" to oneself.) Since the gifted mind is so active, much mind chatter ordinarily exists. If gifted adolescents spend the day telling themselves they are inadequate and worthless, this can easily have a negative effect on their self-esteem.

Eliminating these thoughts and substituting more positive ones can effect a change in attitude. Some helpful resources on this topic are Helmstetter (1986) and Simon (1977, 1978).

Assertiveness Training. Assertiveness training can also help gifted adolescents. Since the gifted may face stereotypical labels, they need to learn how to assert their rights and articulate their need for empathic understanding. Many high schools are beginning to teach assertiveness skills to students. *When I Say "No" I Feel Guilty* (Smith, 1986) is probably the classic resource in this area. Self-help books such as *Managing the Social and Emotional Needs of the Gifted* (Schmitz & Galbraith, 1985) can also be helpful.

Nonverbal Behavior Interpretation. As discussed earlier, gifted adolescents are keen observers of others' behavior. Many psychosocial difficulties occur for them, however, because they tend to be poor interpreters of the behavior they observe. Helping the gifted to learn to interpret nonverbal behavior can facilitate a greater understanding of others and themselves.

SUMMARY

Lester and Anderson (1981) reported that by the time a gifted child has reached the fourth grade, many critical life decisions have been made. Many elementary schools do not, however, have a counselor available for students. Increasing counselor availability for the gifted could be very helpful in preventing many of the psychosocial issues discussed here. Having other supportive adults to serve as role models, provide guidance, and offer understanding could also be very beneficial in prevention efforts.

If the psychosocial needs of the gifted are better understood and effective coping mechanisms provided, perhaps gifted adolescents will not need to respond as they did to the question, What do you want people to understand most about gifted children?

"I would like others to know that we are not geeks, but an interesting varied people." Girl, age 17, Florida

"The gifted child is not a walking, talking computer. Sure academics should be encouraged, but there is a lot more to life than knowing facts. Whether children are learning the alphabet or algebra, they need to be told, 'I love you, not for what you do, but for who you are. You are special.'" Girl, age 14, Michigan. (Delisle, 1989, p. 3)

Others would then understand them, and gifted adolescents would better understand themselves.

REFERENCES

American Association for Gifted Children. (1978). *On being gifted.* New York: Walker.

Arnold, J. D. (1978). *Make up your mind! The seven building blocks to better decisions.* New York: AMACOM.

Barnette, E. (1989). A program to meet the emotional and social needs of gifted and talented adolescents. *Journal of Counseling and Development, 67,* 525–528.

Bergman, S., & Rudman, G. J. (1985). *Decision-making skills for middle school students.* Washington, DC: National Education Association.

Betts, G. (1986). Development of the emotional and social needs of gifted individuals. *Journal of Counseling and Development, 64,* 581–589.

Betts, G., & Neihart, M. (1985). Eight effective activities to enhance the emotional and social development of the gifted and talented. *Roeper Review, 8,* 18–23.

Buescher, T. (1985). A framework for understanding the social and emotional development of gifted and talented adolescents. *Roeper Review, 8,* 10–15.

Buescher, T., & Higham, S. (1984, April). *Young gifted adolescents: Coping with the strain of feeling different.* Paper presented at the 61st Annual Meeting of the American Orthopsychiatric Association, Toronto.

Buescher, T., & Higham, S. (1985, March–April). *Young gifted adolescents' strategies for coping with sources of stress.* Paper presented at the Annual Meeting of the American Educational Research Association, Chicago.

Canfield, J. (1986). *Self esteem in the classroom.* Pacific Palisades, CA: Self Esteem Seminars.

Cartledge, G., & Milburn, J. F. (Eds.). (1980). *Teaching social skills to children.* New York: Pergamon.

Clabby, J., & Elias, M. (1987). *Teach your child decision making.* Garden City, NY: Doubleday.

Clarke, J. I. (1983). *OUCH. That hurts!: A handbook for people who hate criticism.* Plymouth, MN: Daisy Press.

Colangelo, N., & Pfleger, L. (1979). Academic self-concept of gifted high school students. In N. Colangelo & R. Zaffran (Eds.), *New voices in counseling the gifted* (pp. 188–193). Dubuque, IA: Kendall/Hunt.

Coleman, J. (1980). Friendship and the peer group in adolescence. In J. Adelson (Ed.), *Handbook of adolescent psychology* (pp. 408–431). New York: Wiley.

Delisle, J. (1985). Vocational problems. In J. Freeman (Ed.), *The psychology of gifted children* (pp. 367–378). London: Wiley.

Delisle, J. (1989). 2001: An education odyssey. *Gifted Children Monthly, 10*(5), 1-3.

Elkind, D. (1980). Strategies, interactions in early adolescence. In J. Adelson (Ed.), *Handbook of adolescent psychology* (pp. 432-444). New York: Wiley.

Field, T., Roopnarine, J., & Segal, M. (Eds.). (1984). *Friendships in normal and handicapped children.* Norwood, NJ: Ablex.

Fox, L. H., Brody, L., & Tobin, D. (Eds.). (1980). *Women and the mathematical mystique.* Baltimore: Johns Hopkins University Press.

Frey, D. (1988). *Intimate relationships, marriage, and family.* New York: Macmillan.

Frey, D., & Carlock, J. (1989). *Enhancing self esteem* (2nd ed.). Muncie, IN: Accelerated Development.

Fugit, E. (1983). *He hit me back first.* Rolling Hills Estates, CA: Jalmar Press.

Gelatt, H. B., Varenhorst, B., Carey, R., & Miller, G. P. (1973). *Decisions and outcomes: A leader's guide.* New York: College Entrance Examination Board.

Havighurst, R. (1972). *Developmental tasks and education.* New York: Longman.

Heath, P., & Weible, T. D. (1983). *Developing social responsibility in the middle school. A unit teaching approach.* Washington, DC: National Education Association.

Heiman, M., & Slomianko, J. (1985). *Critical thinking skills.* Washington, DC: National Education Association.

Helmstetter, S. (1986). *What to say: When you talk to yourself.* New York: Simon & Schuster.

Hoehn, L., & Bireley, M. (1988). Mental processing preferences of gifted children. *Illinois Council for the Gifted Journal, 1,* 28-31.

Holahan, W., & Brounstein, P. (1986, April). *The acceleration into college and emotional adjustment of the academically gifted adolescent: A synthesis and critique of recent literature.* Paper presented at the convention of the American College Personnel Association, New Orleans.

Hollinger, C., & Fleming, E. (1985). Social orientation and the social self-esteem of gifted and talented female adolescents. *Journal of Youth and Adolescence, 14,* 389-399.

Horowitz, F., & O'Brien, M. (1986). Gifted and talented children. *American Psychologist, 41,* 1147-1152.

Janos, P., & Robinson, N. (1985). Psychological development in intellectually gifted children. In F. Horowitz & M. O'Brien (Eds.), *The gifted and talented: Developmental perspectives* (pp. 180-187). Washington, DC: American Psychological Association.

Jersild, A., Brook, J., & Brook, D. (1978). *The psychology of adolescence.* New York: Macmillan.

Kaplan, L. (1983). Mistakes gifted young people too often make. *Roeper Review, 6,* 73-77.

Krawetz, M. (1984). *Self esteem passport* (2nd ed.). New York: Holt, Rinehart & Winston.

LeCroy, C. (Ed.). (1982). *Social skills training for children and youth.* New York: Haworth Press.

LeResche, L., Strobino, D., Parks, P., Fischer, P., & Smeriglio, V. (1983). The relationship of observed maternal-behavior to questionnaire measures of parenting knowledge, attitudes and emotional states in adolescent mothers. *Journal of Youth and Adolescence, 12,* 19–31.

Leroux, J. (1986, April). *Sex differences influencing gifted adolescents: An ethnographic study.* Paper presented at the Annual Meeting of the American Educational Research Association, San Francisco.

Lester, C. P., & Anderson, R. S. (1981). Counseling with families of gifted children: The school counselor's role. *School Counselor, 29,* 147–151.

Levine, E., & Tucker, S. (1986). Emotional needs of gifted children: A preliminary, phenomenological view. *The Creative Child and Adult Quarterly, 11,* 156–165.

McDaniel, S., & Bielen, P. (1986). *Project self esteem.* Rolling Hills Estates, CA: B. L. Winch & Associates.

Mills, C. (1984, April). *Sex differences in self-concept and self-esteem for mathematically precocious adolescents.* Paper presented at the Annual Meeting of the American Educational Research Association, New Orleans.

Myers, I., & McCaulley, M. (1985). *Manual: A guide to the development and use of the Myers-Briggs Type Indicator.* Palo Alto, CA: Consulting Psychologists Press.

Powell, P., & Haden, T. (1984). The intellectual and psychosocial nature of extreme giftedness. *Roeper Review, 6,* 13–15.

Reasoner, R. W. (1982). *Building self esteem: Teacher's guide and classroom materials.* Palo Alto, CA: Consulting Psychologists Press.

Roedell, W. (1984). Vulnerabilities of highly gifted children. *Roeper Review, 6,* 127–129.

Schmitz, C., & Galbraith, J. (1985). *Managing the social and emotional needs of the gifted.* Minneapolis, MN: Free Spirit.

Seeley, K. (1984). Perspectives on adolescent giftedness and delinquency. *Journal for the Education of the Gifted, 8,* 59–72.

Sheppard, W. C., Shank, S. B., & Wilson, D. (1975). *Teaching social behavior to young children.* Champaign, IL: Research Press.

Silverman, I. K. (1983). Issues in effective development of the gifted. In J. VanTassel-Baska (Ed.), *A practical guide to counseling the gifted in a school setting* (pp. 6–21). Reston, VA: Counsel for Exceptional Children.

Simon, S. (1977). *Vulture.* Niles, IL: Argus Communications.

Simon, S. (1978). *Negative criticism.* Niles, IL: Argus Communications.

Smith, M. (1986). *When I say "no" I feel guilty: How to cope using the skills of systematic assertive therapy.* New York: Bantam.

Stanish, B. (1982). *Connecting rainbows.* Benton Harbor, MI: Patterson Printing.

Stephens, T. (1978). *Social skills in the classroom.* Columbus, OH: Cedar Press.

Stewart, W. J. (1988). *How to teach decision-making skills to elementary and secondary students.* Springfield, IL: Charles C. Thomas.

Strop, J. (1985, April). *A profile of the characteristics, needs and counseling preferences of talent search summer institute participants.* Paper presented at the Annual Meeting of the American Educational Research Association, Chicago.

Webb, J., Meckstroth, E., & Tolan, S. (1982). *Guiding the gifted child.* Columbus: Ohio Psychological Publishing.

CHAPTER 4

Eating Disorders
in the Gifted Adolescent

David M. Garner

It is widely recognized that the incidence of both *anorexia nervosa* and *bulimia nervosa* have increased over the past several decades. It is also evident that both disorders pose serious health risks and are psychologically debilitating. These observations are of particular concern because both *anorexia nervosa* and *bulimia nervosa* frequently affect adolescents who have significant academic and interpersonal strengths before the onset of the eating disorder. The increased prevalence of the eating disorders as well as their devastating consequences have stimulated interest among a wide range of health professionals and have led to the development of effective treatment methods. The aims of the current chapter are to review the literature that has examined the relationship between eating disorders and intellectual functioning, to examine possible setting conditions that may lead to gifted individuals' vulnerability to eating disorders, and to consider therapeutic interventions that may be effective with those who develop eating disorders.

NATURE AND SCOPE OF THE PROBLEM

Competitive Settings

There is reason to believe that eating disorders may be overrepresented in more competitive educational settings that may selectively attract or foster gifted children. Crisp, Palmer, and Kalucy (1976) studied the prevalence of *anorexia nervosa* in private and public schools and found that the disorder was much more common in the private settings. Severe cases were identified in one in every 100 schoolgirls over 15 years old from the private schools compared with one in every 250 in the public institutions. In groups of dance students, who have been found to be

50

predisposed to *anorexia nervosa*, it has been shown that those from the most competitive settings have the greatest risk of developing eating disorders and extreme dieting concerns (Garner & Garfinkel, 1980).

Social Class

Early reports indicated that *anorexia nervosa* was skewed toward the upper social classes, where the pressures to achieve may be more intense (Dally & Gomez, 1979; Kalucy, Crisp, & Harding, 1977; Kendell, Hall, Haily, & Babigan, 1973; Morgan & Russell, 1975; Theander, 1970). However, there is evidence that the disorder has tended to become more common in lower social classes in recent years (Garfinkel & Garner, 1982; Gowers & McMahon, 1989). This may reflect a change in referral patterns, or it may indicate a shift in the social class variation in expectations for achievement, control, and thinness, which are thought to predispose to *anorexia nervosa*.

Intellectual Functioning

It has been a common clinical observation that *anorexia nervosa* patients and to a lesser degree those with *bulimia nervosa* tend to be intelligent; however, it has also been suggested that those with eating disorders are overachievers. Bruch (1978) has made the clinical observation that "anorexics usually excel in their school performance, and this has been interpreted as indicating high intelligence and giftedness . . . [however] the excellent academic achievements are not uncommonly the results of great effort" (p. 46).

The intellectual functioning of eating disorder patients has been examined in a number of empirical studies, and the findings are not uniform. Several investigators have reported that *anorexia nervosa* patients display deficits on measures of certain neuropsychological and intelligence tests (Fox, 1981; Holleman, 1985). These contrast with findings from other studies indicating that many patients score in the superior range on measures of intelligence. Dally and Gomez (1979) found that 90% of their patients with an age on onset of between 11 and 14 had an IQ of 130 or greater. Rowland (1970) reported an average IQ of 113 in his sample, with about one-third having an IQ above 120. He concluded that "the most striking thing about the school behavior of these patients is that they tended to be very good scholars" (Rowland, 1970, p. 109). Touyz, Beumont, and Johnstone (1986) assessed both IQ and parameters of school performance in *anorexia nervosa* and *bulimia nervosa* patients. They found that, although the eating disorder patients had IQ scores comparable to earlier studies (mean for *anorexia nervosa* was 108, range 92–132; for *bulimia nervosa*, 113, range 102–132), the means did not differ significantly from the theoretical distribution on full-scale IQ. However, the eating disorder patients scored significantly higher than age-corrected norms on most tests of academic achievement such as reading, spelling, and arithmetic.

Thus, from these studies, it may be concluded that some eating disorder patients display superior intelligence, but that *anorexia nervosa* and *bulimia nervosa* are also common in those of average intelligence or below. There are at least two possible connections between eating disorders and adolescents characterized as gifted. First, an eating disorder may develop in an adolescent identified as gifted on the basis of exceptional school performance, and it may become evident that the academic achievements have been the result of extraordinary effort rather than intellectual superiority. In these cases, the discrepancy between intellectual functioning and performance levels tends to become evident in later years when subject material becomes more demanding and competition more intense. Second, an eating disorder may develop in an individual who is truly intellectually gifted, and this may relate to particular risk factors associated with the giftedness or its identification. In both of these instances it is important to understand the particular setting conditions that may lead to the development of the disorder and to be able to recommend interventions that may be effective.

SETTING CONDITIONS

Most theorists recognize that eating disorders are heterogeneous and multidetermined in the sense that various predisposing factors can precipitate symptoms in vulnerable individuals (cf. Garner & Garfinkel, 1985). Slade (1982) has proposed a model for the development of *anorexia nervosa* and *bulimia nervosa* that specifies low self-esteem, need for control over some aspect of the life situation, and perfectionism as setting conditions for the development of eating disorders. He has suggested that these setting conditions predispose the individual to an eating disorder, which may be triggered by apparently innocuous psychosocial events. Other authors have identified a range of possible setting conditions related to individual, familial, or cultural factors that can lead to the expression and maintenance of an eating disorder (cf. Garfinkel & Garner, 1982). Potential predisposing factors that seem particularly relevant to those who may be identified as gifted will be briefly reviewed.

Cultural Values Related to Thinness

It is imperative to understand eating disorders within the cultural context. It is well recognized that women are exposed to intense pressure to diet in order to conform to unrealistic cultural standards in which thinness in women is equated with beauty, personal success, and happiness. There is a natural resistance to accepting the view that dieting and the emphasis on thinness have negative consequences, since these attitudes are so deeply woven into our health-conscious culture. It is disconcerting that the norm for women in our society is to feel dissatisfied with their shape and to feel guilty about eating what could be considered reasonable amounts of food (Garner, Rockert, Olmsted, Johnson, & Coscina, 1985; Polivy & Herman, 1987; Rodin, Silberstein, & Striegel-Moore, 1985). Huon, Brown, and Morris (1988) have reported that many of the attitudes displayed by *anorexia nervosa* and *bulimia nervosa* patients are viewed as neither uncommon or abnormal in a survey of adult men and women. Nevertheless, these values have become personally destructive for those who develop eating disorders and must be addressed in treatment.

Eating Disorders in Otherwise Healthy Individuals

Eating disorders may develop in individuals without underlying personality disturbance or family dysfunction, but by the time the individual presents for an assessment, there are secondary disruptions in both of these areas of functioning. The typical scenario in these instances is that the diligent adolescent interprets quite literally the cultural message that weight control is another area for displaying personal competence, and embarks on stringent dieting as part of a program of overall self-improvement. Initial weight loss is deceptively easy and the physical barriers to long-term maintenance are neither obvious nor well publicized by the multi-billion-dollar-a-year weight loss industry. Most adolescents (and some psychotherapists) are unaware that dieting and weight suppression can have adverse consequences, including binge eating and mood changes (Garner et al., 1985; Polivy & Herman, 1985). Particularly for the gifted adolescent who has applied exceptional skills and self-discipline to overcome other adversities, weight control may present itself as simply another challenge to be conquered.

Frustration encountered because of the biological resistance to weight suppression is met with intensified efforts at mastery. Self-induced vomiting and other drastic weight control methods usually begin as temporary measures to deal with failure to control appetite, but they become firmly entrenched as weapons in a battle against appetite. They are seductive since they allow the individual to satisfy food cravings (resulting from deprivation), ostensibly without paying the caloric consequences. Moreover, they undo the tremendous guilt and self-reproach following bouts of overeating. Vomiting, in particular, leads to a relaxation of controls over eating, and this prompts the escalation of the vicious cycle of binging and purging. The metabolic effects of dietary disruption create or further exacerbate serious psychological systems. Thus, in an eating disorder with this type of genesis, the psychological disturbance is a secondary feature related to the chronic dietary chaos, rather than a consequence of true underlying emotional disturbance. It is significant that differentiating these individuals from those with more fundamental personality or family disturbances may be very difficult at presentation (Garner, Olmsted, Davis, Rockert, Goldbloom, & Eagle, 1990). In these instances, brief treatment may be the best diagnostic tool since exposure to the variety of misconceptions about dieting, weight regulation, nutrition, and the social context of the disorder typically leads to complete recovery.

Low Self-esteem

It was Bruch (1962) who first described overwhelming feelings of ineffectiveness as fundamental to eating disorders. The relevance of low self-esteem to the development of eating disorders has been identified as important by most contemporary writers in the field; however, a range of different conceptual vantage points have been offered to account for the deficits in self-concept (for reviews see Garner & Bemis, 1985; Garner & Garner, 1986). Theories that emphasize developmental deficits, family disturbances, cultural pressures, and individual belief systems almost invariably culminate with the manifestation of low self-esteem. Regardless of the derivation of low self-esteem, within the context of the cultural valuation of thinness in women, it is not difficult to understand how an insecure adolescent girl would turn to dieting and weight control as solutions to personal unhappiness. Dieting and weight control begin as means of gaining mastery in other life situations, feeling more competent, improving personal appearance, or addressing family or other interpersonal concerns (Slade, 1982). In the case of the gifted adolescent, it is important to be cognizant that exceptional academic performance does not protect against feelings of inadequacy in other areas of functioning. Low self-esteem must be dealt with directly in treatment, and if there are more fundamental developmental deficits or family problems, these become the focal point of the intervention.

Perfectionism

Bruch (1978) has repeatedly emphasized that the struggle to live up to excessive achievement standards is a characteristic theme in *anorexia nervosa*. She interprets patients' typical superior academic performance as an "overcompliant adaptation" that breaks down in the face of increasing pressures to succeed. Perfectionism has been described as part of the dichotomous thinking style attributed to eating disorders (Garner & Bemis, 1982; Garner, Garfinkel, & Bemis, 1982). As indicated earlier, Slade (1982) has suggested that perfectionism is a prominent setting condition for the development of eating disorders. The families of eating disorder patients have been described as highly achievement-oriented (Bruch, 1973; Dally, 1969; Kalucy et al., 1977), and it could be speculated that perfectionism is particularly germane to a discussion of eating disorders in gifted adolescents, where heightened achievement expectations might be applied to many areas of performance.

Burns (1980) has described perfectionism in terms of a cognitive style characterized by dichotomous thinking and overgeneralization. He depicts "pathological perfectionists" as "those people who strain compulsively and unremittingly toward impossible goals and who measure their own worth entirely in terms of productivity and accomplishment" (Burns, 1980, p. 34). He contends that this thinking style is shaped by current cultural values and then is reinforced by religion, the media, and our educational system, which place excessive emphasis on perfectionism. Perfectionism may be broken down into at least two components that have psychological risks. The first is related to the tendency of the individual to place a premium on superior accomplishments and error-free performance. This value is consistent with the philosophy of many educational institutions and may be intensified in special or accelerated programs aimed at gifted adolescents. The second component is the proclivity for the individual to measure personal worth in terms of performance. Many individuals may rely to some degree on external frames of reference in making self-evaluations, and this formula is reinforced by current cultural values; however, it becomes crystallized in the thinking of many eating disorder patients. The inclination of eating disorder patients to view themselves primarily in terms of weight and shape is simply another expression of a more general tendency to use external standards to judge self-worth (Garner & Bemis, 1982, 1985). Academic goals may be pursued not because of intrinsic interest but because they provide a means of self-verification or acceptance from parents. In this sense, perfectionism in the scholastic arena becomes a means of trying to compensate for feelings of inadequacy in other areas.

In Chapter 5 Miriam Adderholdt-Elliott elaborates on this perfectionistic behavior and discusses it in a variety of areas of functioning.

Super Woman/Wise Woman Contrast

Based on the writings on female psychological development by Gilligan (1982), Chodorow (1978), and others, Steiner-Adair (1989) has suggested that eating disorders may also reflect role conflicts experienced by some young women. Many women experience relationships as integral aspects of their identity formation and self-esteem, yet perceive this need as devalued in light of prevailing cultural expectations for success and independence. In a study of teenage girls attending a private school, Steiner-Adair (1986) divided participants into two groups based on their perception of contemporary cultural ideals for women. The "super women" group identified autonomy, success, and mastery as the ideal traits for women, and thinness was viewed as a marker for these characteristics. In contrast, the "wise woman" was able to identify the expectations for achievement and autonomy as the cultural model but reject these values in favor of a personal ideal in which relationships assumed a central role. None of those in the "wise women" group had high scores on the Eating Attitudes Test (EAT) as compared with those in the "super women" group, who all had high scores. According to Steiner-Adair (1989) these findings support the view that eating disorders involve "the perceived conflict of having to give up feminine (relational) and female (bodily) parts of oneself in order to grow up and be valued as an adult in this culture" (Steiner-Adair, 1989, p. 158).

Programs for gifted adolescents that place a premium on performance, mastery, and the attainment of vocational goals may unwittingly neglect or even devalue the unique role that relationships, nurturance, and caring have had in female psychological development. Although this emphasis may place some women at risk for eating disorders, there is an even more fundamental message. There needs to be greater recognition that empowerment, maturity, and success may be defined within the context of relationships. This may provide a meaningful path for a large group of gifted women who have assumed that expression of their competence means renouncing fundamental elements of their psychology.

Family Involvement

The possible role of the family in the development of *anorexia nervosa* and *bulimia nervosa* has been described by writers from a range of theoretical orientations (cf. Root, Fallon, & Friedrich, 1986; Vandereycken, Kog, & Vanderlinden, 1989), and gifted adolescents may be particularly vulnerable to some of the interactional patterns that have been associated with eating disorders. The early labelling of a child as "gifted" may create heightened parental expectations for performance, which may be met by the child adopting a perfectionistic stance of defining personal worth in terms of performance standards. The gifted child may be overvalued by the parents, and the intense expectations to meet parental needs can create difficulties, particularly in adolescence, when there are greater demands for autonomy. Finally, there may be a tendency to assume that a child with superior intelligence is equally advanced in emotional development. The bright child may be pushed into the role of the "little adult," which can result in blurred parent–child boundaries or an enmeshed interactional style, both of which have been implicated in the development of eating disorders (Minuchin, Rosman, & Baker, 1978).

Positive Stereotyping of Eating Disorders

It has been suggested that *anorexia nervosa* has actually acquired a favorable connotation because the media has repeatedly emphasized its association with positive attributes such as superior intelligence, perfectionism, self-discipline, exercise, and upper class affiliation (Bruch, 1978; Garner et al., 1985; Wooley & Wooley, 1982). Indeed, as indicated earlier, many symptoms required for a diagnosis of an eating disorder are not viewed as unusual or abnormal by members of the general public (Huon et al., 1988). Bruch (1985) has actually suggested that social contagion may be responsible for cases of "me too *anorexia nervosa*," and there is evidence that some patients begin self-induced vomiting after reading about the symptom in media accounts of *bulimia nervosa* (Chiodo & Latimer, 1983). The favorable stereotype applied to eating disorders may be a factor determining symptom choice for some individuals. Particularly within the context of the heightened pressures to perform, certain gifted but emotionally vulnerable adolescents may view an eating disorder as an "acceptable" disqualification from the stresses of competition.

THERAPEUTIC CONSIDERATIONS

Since the treatment of both *anorexia nervosa* and *bulimia nervosa* can be complex, it would be naive to assume that a brief overview could equip a therapist, teacher, or parent to intervene in an effective manner. Extensive reading and specific training in the treatment of eating disorders are the minimum standards for competence (Yager & Edelstein, 1987). Treatment of eating disorders in gifted adolescents should follow the general guidelines for management that have been described in detail elsewhere (Fairburn, 1985; Garner & Garfinkel, 1985; Garner et al., 1982; Johnson & Connors, 1987; Mitchell, 1985). It is generally agreed that a multidimensional approach to treatment is an effective starting point for the integration and sequencing of various interventions based on an analysis of a particular patient's history and present functioning (Garner, Garfinkel, & Irvine, 1986). While there are a number of general principles that apply to all patients, certain specific themes may differentially apply to specific patient subgroups.

General Principles for Treatment

A crucial element in treating both *anorexia nervosa* and *bulimia nervosa* is achieving a balance between addressing psychological issues that may have predisposed the individual to an eating disorder and confronting the aberrant eating patterns that have produced a wide range of secondary symptoms. Throughout all stages of treatment, a "two-track" approach is recommended (Garner et al., 1986). The first track pertains to issues related to weight, binging, vomiting, and other drastic measures designed to control weight. The second track involves the psychological context of the disorder and includes underlying developmental, personality, and family themes. Throughout treatment, there is an explicit focus on both tracks, but early sessions tend to emphasize first-track issues since the psychological picture may change quite remarkably once eating behavior and weight begin to normalize.

In general the sequencing of treatment begins with approaches that are relatively brief and educational in content (Garner et al., 1985). For some patients with *bulimia nervosa* without underlying personality disorder, an educationally oriented group may be sufficient for recovery. It may also be a valuable base for more disturbed patients who require additional intensive individual or group therapy. *Anorexia nervosa* patients usually require more than education because of their intense desire to maintain certain focal symptoms and because of their deteriorated physical state (Garner & Bemis, 1982). Cognitive-behavioral treatment has proven effective in *bulimia nervosa* (cf. Garner, Fairburn, & Davis, 1987) and has been recommended for *anorexia nervosa* (Edgette & Prout, 1989; Garner & Bemis, 1982, 1985). Pharmacotherapy may be considered for *bulimia nervosa* patients who fail to respond to psychosocial interventions (Mitchell, 1988). Family therapy should be considered as the treatment of choice if the patient is young and living at home

(Vandereycken et al., 1989). If the disorder is long-standing or if the symptoms are severe, inpatient treatment should be considered as an initial step; however, outpatient follow-up is essential to reduce the likelihood of relapse. Within this general context, there may be certain themes that are common in the treatment of gifted adolescents with eating disorders.

Challenging Cultural Imperatives for Weight Control

Challenging the cultural imperatives related to dieting and weight control is difficult because they are so consistently a part of current society. It may be further complicated because these values may be shared by therapists, teachers, parents, and others who are confronted by the adolescent with an eating disorder. Patients can be encouraged to gently challenge the validity and the practical implications of their idea that self-worth can be measured in terms of thinness; however, care must be taken to avoid a brazen frontal attack on these values since they may have become central to the patient's identity (Garner & Bemis, 1982). Excellent resource material on eating disorders is now available to help the school counselor and teacher challenge inappropriate cultural values related to thinness (Levine, 1987).

Reframing Perfectionism

As Mahoney (1974) has pointed out, perfectionism is a destructive mental trap that involves catapulting from one end of the self-evaluative continuum to the other following even the slightest deviation from perfect self-control. This pattern of thinking is particularly self-defeating since it involves establishing ever higher standards for performance that become more unrealistic over time. One helpful strategy may be to encourage patients to recognize that perfectionism is a highly ineffective thinking style since it actually decreases the quality and quantity of accomplishments. Several other strategies are discussed in detail in Chapter 5. While all perfectionists apply high performance standards to themselves, eating disorder patients make the additional error of applying rigid performance standards to body weight as if it were highly malleable, when in fact it appears to be under rather tight metabolic or biological control. The eating disorder patient requires repeated reinforcement of the distinction between competence and perfection. Moreover, the fallacies of inferring competence from control of body weight must be emphasized. Additional techniques for addressing these self-defeating thinking styles have been elaborated elsewhere (Garner & Bemis, 1982, 1985; Garner & Rosen, 1990).

Resolution of the Super Woman Image

According to Steiner-Adair (1989), resolution of the two contrasting images and definitions of female adulthood is the primary mission in the treatment of eating disorders. One image is of the slender, independent, professional woman who commands respect and power because of her achievements in traditional male roles. The other is that of the fat, nurturing, traditional female who is dependent on relationships but de-valued and powerless in contemporary society. The dilemmas posed by the conflicting definitions of female adulthood may be extraordinarily potent for the gifted adolescent within educational settings that encourage competitiveness and the acceptance of traditional male values related to achievement. Resolving the conflicts may require a perspective that focuses on (1) recognizing family and cultural factors that may have contributed to conflicting definitions of female adulthood, (2) valuation of relationship needs, and (3) integration of these with rational goals for fulfillment (Steiner-Adair, 1989; Wooley & Wooley, 1980, 1985).

Family Involvement

As indicated earlier, gifted adolescents may be particularly vulnerable to certain types of interactional patterns that could lead to the expression of an eating disorder. Family treatment focuses heavily on challenging enmeshment, overprotectiveness, and performance expectations that are insensitive to the adolescent's needs (Minuchin et al., 1978; Root et al., 1986; Schwartz, Barrett, & Saba, 1985; Vandereycken et al., 1989). Pressures for achievement may simply become too intense for some gifted adolescents. For others, there is overwhelming guilt at disappointing parents and a growing recognition that performance expectations have more to do with parental needs than personal interests. For still others, the demands for increasing autonomy associated with adolescence are frightening, and the eating disorder temporarily halts psychobiological development, thus providing a temporary solution to the conflict (Crisp, 1980). Involvement of the family does not automatically imply that they have had an etiological role in the development of the eating disorder; many of the observed patterns of behavior could be expected as normal adaptations to the development of a life-threatening illness of a family member. The interactional themes that can emerge differ remarkably across families with an eating disordered adolescent, and exceptional skill is required to identify and address the relevant issues.

SUMMARY

Gifted adolescents may be more vulnerable to the development of both *anorexia nervosa* and *bulimia nervosa* because those youngsters possess many of the traits that have been identified as risk factors for these eating disorders. Treatment considerations for gifted adolescents with eating disorders do not differ from those that have been described in the literature; however, there may be certain themes that are more commonly represented in this population. Recent advances in the treatment of eating disorders give reason for considerable optimism regarding outcome.

Acknowledgments. I would like to thank Barbara Rood and Peggy Parker for their assistance in preparing this chapter.

REFERENCES

Bruch, H. (1962). Perceptual and conceptual disturbances in *anorexia nervosa*. *Psychosomatic Medicine, 24*, 187–194.

Bruch, H. (1973). *Eating disorders: Obesity, anorexia nervosa and the person within*. New York: Basic Books.

Bruch, H. (1978). *The golden cage*. Cambridge, MA: Harvard University Press.

Bruch, H. (1985). Four decades of eating disorders. In D. M. Garner & P. E. Garfinkel (Eds.), *Handbook of psychotherapy for anorexia nervosa and bulimia* (pp. 7–18). New York: Guilford Press.

Burns, D. (1980, November). The perfectionist's script for self-defeat. *Psychology Today*, pp. 34–54.

Chiodo, J., & Latimer, P. R. (1983). Vomiting as a learned weight-control technique in bulimia. *Journal of Behavior Therapy and Experimental Psychiatry, 14*, 131–135.

Chodorow, N. (1978). *The reproduction of mothering*. Berkeley: University of California Press.

Crisp, A. H. (1980). *Anorexia nervosa: Let me be*. New York: Academic Press.

Crisp, A. H., Palmer, R. L., & Kalucy, R. S. (1976). How common is *anorexia nervosa*? A prevalence study. *British Journal of Psychiatry, 128*, 549–554.

Dally, P. J. (1969). *Anorexia nervosa*. New York: Grune & Stratton.

Dally, P. J., & Gomez, J. (1979). *Anorexia nervosa*. London: Heinemann.

Edgette, J. S., & Prout, M. F. (1989). Cognitive and behavioral approaches to the treatment of *anorexia nervosa*. In A. Freeman, K. M. Simon, L. E. Beutler, & H. Arkowitz (Eds.), *Comprehensive handbook of cognitive therapy* (pp. 367–384). New York: Plenum.

Fairburn, C. G. (1985). Cognitive-behavioral treatment for *bulimia*. In D. M. Garner & P. E. Garfinkel (Eds.), *Handbook of psychotherapy for anorexia nervosa and bulimia* (pp. 160–192). New York: Guilford Press.

Fox, C. F. (1981). Neuropsychological correlates of *anorexia nervosa*. *International Journal of Psychiatry in Medicine, 12*, 285–290.

Garfinkel, P. E., & Garner, D. M. (1982). *Anorexia nervosa: A multidimensional perspective*. New York: Brunner/Mazel.

Garner, D. M., & Bemis, K. M. (1982). A cognitive-behavioral approach to *anorexia nervosa*. *Cognitive Therapy and Research, 6*, 123–150.

Garner, D. M., & Bemis, K. M. (1985). Cognitive therapy for *anorexia nervosa*. In D. M. Garner & P. E. Garfinkel (Eds.), *Handbook of psychotherapy for anorexia nervosa and bulimia* (pp. 107–146). New York: Guilford Press.

Garner, D. M., Fairburn, C. G., & Davis, R. (1987). Cognitive-behavioral treatment of *bulimia nervosa*: A critical appraisal. *Behavior Modification, 11*, 398–431.

Garner, D. M., & Garfinkel, P. E. (1980). Socio-cultural factors in the development of *anorexia nervosa*. *Psychological Medicine, 10*, 647–656.

Garner, D. M., & Garfinkel, P. E. (1985). *Handbook of psychotherapy for anorexia nervosa and bulimia*. New York: Guilford Press.

Garner, D. M., Garfinkel, P. E., & Bemis, K. M. (1982). A multidimensional psychotherapy for *anorexia nervosa*. *International Journal of Eating Disorders, 1*, 3–46.

Garner, D. M., Garfinkel, P. E., & Irvine, M. M. (1986). Integration and sequencing of treatment approaches for eating disorders. *Psychotherapy and Psychosomatics, 46*, 67–75.

Garner, D. M., & Garner, M. V. (1986). Self-concept deficiencies in eating disorders. In L. M. Hartman & K. R. Blankstein (Eds.), *Perception of self in emotional disorder and psychotherapy* (pp. 133–156). New York: Plenum.

Garner, D.M., Olmsted, M. P., Davis, R., Rockert, W., Goldbloom, D., & Eagle, M. (1990). The association between bulimic symptoms and reported psychopathology. *International Journal of Eating Disorders, 9*, 1–15.

Garner, D.M., Rockert, W., Olmsted, M. P., Johnson, C. L., & Coscina, D. V. (1985). Psychoeducational principles in the treatment of *bulimia* and *anorexia nervosa*. In D. M. Garner & P. E. Garfinkel (Eds.), *Handbook of psychotherapy for anorexia nervosa and bulimia* (pp. 513–572). New York: Guilford Press.

Garner, D. M., & Rosen, L. W. (1990). Cognitive-behavioral treatment of *anorexia nervosa* and *bulimia nervosa*. In A. S. Bellack, M. Hersen, & A. E. Kazdin (Eds.), *International handbook of behavior modification and therapy* (pp. 805–817). New York: Plenum.

Gilligan, C. (1982). *In a different voice.* Cambridge, MA: Harvard University Press.

Gowers, S., & McMahon, J. B. (1989). Social class and prognosis in *anorexia nervosa. International Journal of Eating Disorders, 8,* 105–110.

Holleman, J. L. (1985, September). A pattern of neuropsychological impairment in *anorexia nervosa. Proceedings of the Eighth World Congress of the International College of Psychosomatic Medicine,* Chicago.

Huon, G. F., Brown, L., & Morris, S. (1988). Lay beliefs about disordered eating. *International Journal of Eating Disorders, 7,* 239–252.

Johnson, C., & Connors, M. E. (1987). *The etiology and treatment of bulimia nervosa: A biopsychosocial perspective.* New York: Basic Books.

Kalucy, R. S., Crisp, A. H., & Harding, B. (1977). A study of 56 families with *anorexia nervosa. British Journal of Medical Psychology, 50,* 381–395.

Kendell, R. E., Hall, D. J., Haily, A., & Babigan, H. M. (1973). The epidemiology of *anorexia nervosa. Psychological Medicine, 3,* 200–203.

Levine, M. P. (1987). *How schools can help combat student eating disorders: Anorexia nervosa and bulimia.* Washington, DC: National Education Association.

Mahoney, M. J. (1974). *Cognitive and behavior modification.* Cambridge: Ballinger.

Minuchin, S., Rosman, B., & Baker, L. (1978). *Psychosomatic families: Anorexia nervosa in context.* Cambridge, MA: Harvard University Press.

Mitchell, J. E. (1985). *Anorexia nervosa and bulimia: Diagnosis and treatment.* Minneapolis: University of Minnesota Press.

Mitchell, P. B. (1988). The pharmacological management of *bulimia nervosa:* A critical review. *International Journal of Eating Disorders, 7,* 29–41.

Morgan, H. G., & Russell, G. F. M. (1975). Value of family background and clinical features as predictors of long-term outcome in *anorexia nervosa:* Four year follow-up of 41 patients. *Psychological Medicine, 5,* 355–371.

Polivy, J., & Herman, C. P. (1985). Dieting and binging: A causal analysis. *American Psychologist, 40,* 193–201.

Polivy, J., & Herman, C. P. (1987). Diagnosis and treatment of normal eating. *Journal of Consulting and Clinical Psychology, 55,* 635–644.

Rodin, J., Silberstein, L. R., & Striegel-Moore, R. H. (1985). Women and weight: A normative discontent. In T. B. Sonderegger (Ed.), *Nebraska Symposium on Motivation: Vol. 32. Psychology and Gender* (pp. 267–307). Lincoln: University of Nebraska Press.

Root, M. M. P., Fallon, P., & Friedrich, W. N. (1986). *Bulimia: A systems approach to treatment.* New York: Norton.

Rowland, C. V. (1970). *Anorexia nervosa:* Survey of the literature and review of 30 cases. *International Psychiatry Clinics, 7,* 37–137.

Schwartz, R. C., Barrett, M. J., & Saba, G. (1985). Family therapy for *bulimia.* In D. M. Garner & P. E. Garfinkel (Eds.), *Handbook of psychotherapy for anorexia nervosa and bulimia* (pp. 280–310). New York: Guilford Press.

Slade, P. D. (1982). Towards a functional analysis of *anorexia nervosa* and *bulimia nervosa*. *British Journal of Clinical Psychology, 21*, 167–179.

Steiner-Adair, C. (1986). The body politic: Normal female adolescent development and development of eating disorders. *Journal of the American Academy of Psychoanalysis, 1*, 95–114.

Steiner-Adair, C. (1989). Developing the voice of the wise woman: College students and *bulimia. Journal of College Student Psychotherapy, 3*, (2/3/4), 151–165.

Theander, S. (1970). *Anorexia nervosa. Acta Psychiatrica Scandinavica* (Suppl. 213).

Touyz, S. W., Beumont, P. J. V., & Johnstone, L. C. (1986). Neuropsychological correlates of dieting disorders. *International Journal of Eating Disorders, 5*, 1025–1034.

Vandereycken, W., Kog, E., & Vanderlinden, J. (1989). *The family approach to eating disorders*. New York: PMA Publishing.

Wooley, O. W., & Wooley, S. C. (1982). The Beverly Hills eating disorder: The mass marketing of *anorexia nervosa* (Editorial). *International Journal of Eating Disorders, 1*, 57–69.

Wooley, S. C., & Wooley, O. W. (1980). Eating disorders, obesity, and *anorexia*. In A. Brodsky & R. Hare-Mustin (Eds.), *Women and psychotherapy* (pp. 135–159). New York: Guilford Press.

Wooley, S. C., & Wooley, O. W. (1985). Intensive outpatient and residual treatment for *bulimia*. In D. M. Garner & P. E. Garfinkel (Eds.), *Handbook of psychotherapy for anorexia nervosa and bulimia* (pp. 391–430). New York: Guilford Press.

Yager, J., & Edelstein, C. K. (1987). Training therapists to work with eating disorder patients. In P. J. V. Beumont, G. D. Burrows, & R. C. Casper (Eds.), *Handbook of eating disorders: Part 1. Anorexia and bulimia nervosa* (pp. 379–392). New York: Elsevier.

CHAPTER 5

Perfectionism and the Gifted Adolescent

Miriam Adderholdt-Elliott

Perfectionism is often stressed by our very competitive society. Academia, business, industry, the arts, religion, and social circles all contribute to this phenomenon. Perfectionism has been studied historically from philosophical, literary, and religious perspectives; recently, the study has been brought into the psychoeducational arena. As noted by Garner in Chapter 4, Burns (1980b) cites dichotomous (all-or-nothing) thinking, the setting of unreasonable standards, compulsive reaching toward impossible goals, and the equation of self-worth with productivity and accomplishment as the most notable characteristics of the perfectionist.

Several authors distinguish between perfectionism and a healthy pursuit of excellence (Adderholdt-Elliott, 1987; Burns, 1980b; Leman, 1985). One example I have used to distinguish between the two is that perfectionism equals "doing three drafts, staying up two nights in a row, and handing your paper in late because you had to get it right and still feeling bad about it" (Adderholdt-Elliott, 1987, p. 5). The healthy pursuit of excellence, on the other hand, would be "doing the research necessary for a term paper, working hard on it, turning it in on time, and feeling good about it" (Adderholdt-Elliott, 1987, p. 4). The quality of the product may be the same. Much of the difference is in the student's attitude and perception of the situation.

We can observe perfectionism occurring in all areas of life, including academics, career, interpersonal relationships, and emotional, moral, and sexual relations. Observing and describing perfectionism is easier than measuring it. Attempts have been made to develop scales that measure various types of perfectionism (Burns, 1980a; Jenkins-Friedman, Bransky, & Murphy, 1986). I used operational definitions adapted from the Burns scale for my research on perfectionism in undergraduate women (Adderholdt, 1984). None of these efforts, however, can be described as totally successful. While our methodology remains inexact, we do know that high personal standards characterize many students of superior intellect and make them vulnerable to the perfectionistic cycle. It is important that we use our existing knowledge to avoid the possible negative consequences of perfectionism that is not controlled before adulthood. In this discussion, I will elaborate on the reasons for and behaviors associated with perfectionism, and propose strategies to help the gifted adolescent break the perfectionistic cycle.

REASONS FOR PERFECTIONISM

Birth Order. Seven major reasons exist for the development of perfectionism. One is birth order. First born or only children are around adults so much that they measure their own behavior in terms of adult standards. Parents may be unsure about raising a first child. They often reward "eager beaver" behavior, which, in turn, reinforces their own belief that they are good parents. First born characteristics may be magnified in only children who experience the attention of grandparents as well as parents. Two books that elaborate on these issues are *The Birth Order Book: Why You Are the Way You Are* (Leman, 1985) and *The Only Child: Being One, Loving One, Understanding One, Raising One* (Sifford, 1989).

Perfectionistic Parents. Perfectionistic children have perfectionistic parents. Usually such families are very high achievers. While this naturally raises the hereditary/environment issue, Rowell (1986) calls this a "generation to generation psychological inheritance as opposed to genetic inheritance" (p. 8). I tend to agree with this assessment.

Media Influences. Perfectionism is a very strong message in the media. Teenagers grow up watching unrealistic role models on television. Most contemporary family shows (e.g., *The Cosby Show, Growing Pains*) solve all of their problems in 30 minutes. Parents who were raised on *Ozzie and Harriet, Leave It to Beaver*, and *My Three Sons* may feel inadequate if their home life does not measure up to these television ideals (Procaccini & Kiefaber, 1983).

Pressure from Teachers and Peers. The fourth major reason for perfectionism is pressure from friends and teachers. Gifted students and teachers of the gifted often share similar traits, and they may tend to reinforce each other. Perfectionism is very prevalent in these populations, which increases the probability that enrollment in any type of gifted education program will bring together people with perfectionistic tendencies. In these instances, perfectionistic traits may seem to be "the norm" and will not be recognized as problems.

Developmental Dysplasia. Mental age is greater than chronological age in gifted children and adolescents. Because of this gap, teenagers may have an image of things they want to achieve but may not have the social or emotional skills to carry them out. This discrepancy, in turn, may lead to undue pressure on oneself, a typical part of the perfectionistic pattern.

"Hothousing." The super baby syndrome, or "jumpstarting" toddlers by giving them intensive, early academic training, is often referred to as "hothousing" because children are force fed lessons in much the same way plant growth is encouraged by putting young plants in hothouses. Proponents of this approach (primarily Glen Doman, 1975, 1979, 1984) believe that such practices take advantage of the rapid intellectual growth of the preschool child. Others vigorously disagree. A respected and vocal opponent of too much early pressure, David Elkind (1981), believes that we are raising a generation of "hurried" children who "are forced to take on the physical, psychological, and social trappings of adulthood before they are prepared to deal with them" (p. xii). Elkind contends that parents, school, and the media must share the responsibility for this phenomenon. He predicts that many hurried children will become troubled children or will develop the chronic psychosomatic complaints recognized as stress indicators in adults.

Dysfunctional Families. A final contributing reason for perfectionism is the dysfunctional family. Adult children of alcoholics usually cite the parental drinking problem as the reason for their own perfectionism. As children, they may not have control over their home life. Thus, they put much time and energy into school and, eventually, work because those are areas that can be controlled. One such person (Robinson, 1989) put his energy into writing to escape the chaos. Now the author of 13 books and more than 70 journal articles, he recognized that work addiction, like any other, may be helpful in the workplace but may destroy personal relationships and family life.

MIND GAMES PERFECTIONISTS PLAY

Perfectionists are their own worst enemies. One destructive behavior is the playing of mind games, which can lead to depressive thinking patterns.

Moodswinging. Perfectionists often put their self-esteem into what they are doing. A perfectionist who sets a goal of all A's and makes it will feel great, but if even one B is received, it will result in the individual feeling terrible. Tying self-esteem to achievement can be damaging to mental health because it leads to a "roller coaster" existence (Adderholdt-Elliott, 1987).

The Numbers Game. In childhood, the numbers game can be played by counting the number of dolls, bottle caps, trains, models, or trophies collected. In adulthood, this phenomenon can be translated into the number of operations performed, dollars earned, articles written, or awards accumulated. The person playing the numbers game cares more about the quantity of collections rather than the quality. It is the "number of dollars, not the dollars themselves, that appease" (Friedman & Rosenman, 1974, p. 91). The use of extrinsic rewards instead of intrinsic measures of self-worth or self-satisfaction appears to be common among perfectionists and those described as Type A personalities (Friedman & Rosenman, 1974).

Telescopic Thinking. An analogous way of viewing perfectionism is described as telescopic thinking. Perfectionists use both ends of the telescope when viewing their achievements. When looking at unmet goals, they use the magnifying end, and these goals appear larger than they really are. When looking at met goals, they use the "minifying" end, so that the goals appear minute and insignificant (Adderholdt-Elliott, 1987). I observed an excellent example of this in a graduate student who was upset the day she received her master's degree because she did not have her doctorate. Another example would be a state tennis champion who was disappointed because the championship was not Wimbledon.

Pining over the Past. Perfectionists have a hard time forgetting past mistakes. Many can remember specific test questions they missed many years earlier. Assisting perfectionists should include helping them focus on a commitment to the future rather than belaboring the past (Adderholdt-Elliott, 1987).

Putting Academic or Work Goals First. When work or school takes precedence over friends, family, or health, some of these ingredients of a happy, healthy life will be lost. Often work goals are more tangible than personal relationships and more rewarding to the person who needs extrinsic rewards. Unfortunately, this may result in behavior such as taking steroids to compete better in sports, because winning becomes more important than keeping one's health. Perfectionists often do not appreciate the intangibles of friendship or the joys of a healthy body until these gifts are lost.

MAJOR TRAITS OF PERFECTIONISM

Procrastination. A common trait of perfectionism is procrastination. The procrastinator buys into the belief system that "self-worth = ability = performance" (Burka & Yuen, 1982, p. 32). Because of this equation, they believe that they lose part of themselves when they fail. Since earthly perfection is unattainable, they set themselves up for failure and negative feelings.

Perfectionists have a built-in insurance policy when they use procrastination. The insurance policy reads, "If I would have had more time I could have done better, but since I didn't, I just did the best that I could." Interestingly, perfectionists probably would not have started any earlier even if they had had the time.

"All-or-Nothing Thinking." Burns (1980b) described "all-or-nothing" or dichotomous thinking as another major perfectionistic trait. There is nothing between success and failure, and an event such as one's first "B" equates to "total" failure. Other terms that have been used to describe this same behavior include "the saint-or-sinner syndrome" (Barrow & Moore, 1983), "the God/scum phenomenon" (Pacht, 1984), and the "Icarus Complex" (Murray, 1955). Like Icarus, perfectionists may fall into a psychological sea because they have aimed for an unattainable sun (Knaus, 1979). "Because the perfectionist pursues this pernicious strategy for self-control in a wide variety of activities, he or she experiences an uncontrollable roller coaster effect characterized by emotional lability, extreme fluctuation in motivation and inconsistent effort (Burns, 1980a, p. 38). Binge behavior and both overachievement and underachievement may result from this dichotomous thinking.

Chronic Fear of Failure. Many perfectionists avoid new experiences, especially if they are being graded, because they cannot tolerate less than top grades even during the learning phase. Baldwin (1982) called this gap between what was achieved and what could have been achieved "the failure gap." Perfectionists are terrified of this gap. Baldwin (1982) described the individual as zeroing in on the gap between "what is" and "what could have been if only a little more time had been taken," or "if other people had only met their responsibility" (p. 11).

The failure gap is the source of paradoxical behavior for the perfectionist because it is a reason for high motivation and also the "basis for accepting other people. The inevitable result is severe interpersonal problems because no one can ever really 'make it' in the perfectionist's book. Family and friends suffer from constant negativity and a consistently critical attitude" (Baldwin, 1982, p. 11). Thus, perfectionists have a great deal of trouble with trial and error learning; for example, learning to play the piano or how to balance chemistry equations. Many skills and much knowledge may be lost because of impatience with the intermediate steps of learning.

Paralyzed Perfectionism. Both Riggs (1982) and Delisle (1982c) wrote about the problems of the paralyzed perfectionist. Riggs described such persons as those "who avoid new experiences for fear of failure and who cheat themselves out of fun by choosing only those activities they can do near perfection" (p. 4). She further suggested that they may need counseling to overcome this psychological paralysis.

Delisle (1982a) equated paralyzed behavior with inertia or lack of risk taking resulting from a fear of failure. Inertia may lead to problems with decision making. A perfectionist waiting for the perfect decision may not do anything, because the perfect decision does not exist. On a narrower scale, one may delay turning in a term paper, because the perfect paper does not exist.

Workaholic Syndrome. As previously described, dysfunctional families may encourage workaholic behavior because work is an arena in which the individual can exert control. While other factors may also result in such behavior, the outcomes are likely to be the same. Workaholics exhibit such traits as high burnout rates and limited social relationships. They have a hard time saying no, have trouble with delegation, have lost a sense of balance in life, and often become depressed. Overcoming workaholism necessitates returning to a life that balances play and recreation, family and friends, work and/or school (Brophy, 1986).

PERFECTIONISM IN THE GIFTED POPULATION

While perfectionism can occur at any intellectual level, it appears to be more of a problem in the gifted population. Clark (1988) attributed the frequent lower self-concept of gifted individuals to the unusually high expectations they place upon themselves. Setting personal standards so high that they are unattainable tends to result in self-defeating, mentally unhealthy lifestyles. Terman (1925) also noted these high expectations in the subjects of his longitudinal study. Clark (1988) further stated that such thinking can result in compulsive behavior that, unless dealt with adequately, can persist throughout a lifetime.

Whitmore (1980) described perfectionism as one of the most often overlooked and influential of the traits distinctly associated with individuals of superior intelligence. She noted that vulnerability is increased in those individuals who, although they may be of high intelligence, are socially immature or have a physical disability.

Delisle (1982b) cited perfectionism as a possible cause of teenage suicide. In the gifted, greater expectations may lead to more devastating responses to failure or perceived failure.

BREAKING THE PERFECTIONISTIC CYCLE

Several approaches exist to help break perfectionism. Some can be used by teachers or parents, but others need the skill of trained counselors. Both teachers and counselors can develop teaching units to help students learn more about this mindset through systematic study. Such units can be delivered in several formats, such as learning centers or games as well as traditional classroom teaching. For example, a unit on values clarification would be beneficial since many of the concerns of the perfectionist involve valuing. Children might enjoy playing a perfectionism game involving "go" and "procrastinate" cards, with the situations adapted for different developmental levels.

Group counseling and workshop techniques seem to be the most beneficial approach to this problem. Barrow and Moore (1983) suggested the use of several therapeutic techniques, such as self-talk, relaxation, and imagery. They further provide role-playing exercises and worksheets that help counter the perfectionistic mindset.

Parents can initiate some of the available techniques as early as the preschool years if it appears warranted. I believe that teaching relaxation, creative visualization (picturing changes in behavior in one's mind as a step toward changing that behavior), and coping strategies would be the most beneficial. Ultimately, the concerns of perfectionists are value judgments, which only the individual can decide, but parental support can be of great help. The tape *Magic Friends and Places* (Alvino, 1984) provides guidance in relaxation and visualization for children aged 2–8. Parents, however, need to realize that undue emphasis on this topic may combine with the child's self-imposed concerns and add to, rather than eliminate, the burden.

Books on creative visualization for adolescents and adults have existed for many years. Wiehl's (1958) *Creative Visualization* is an early example, which continues to be used and cited. The widespread use of this technique in sports psychology and Olympic training has served to introduce it to the general public and maintain its popularity. It is particularly useful for extremely rigid perfectionists, who are upset by changes in routine. Prescribing creative visualization as a means of coping with anticipated changes may help to contain their anxiety.

Reality therapy is another effective counseling approach for perfectionists, many of whom use "I should have" statements. Reality therapy assists the person in dealing with past mistakes and then focusing on future possibilities (Glasser, 1975a). Glasser believes that individuals with emotional problems tend to deny the reality of the world around them when, instead, they should accept the reality they cannot change and look to the future. This is particularly applicable to the perfectionist who continues to anguish over past mistakes. Other appealing features of this approach are its emphasis on persistence, assuming responsibility for one's own behavior, and establishing meaningful relationships (Borgers, 1980).

Bibliotherapy often helps perfectionists learn more about themselves. Two resources that specifically address their problems are *Gifted Kids Survival Guide* (Galbraith, 1983) and *Perfectionism: What's Bad About Being Too Good?* (Adderholdt-Elliott, 1987). Burns (1983, 1989) suggests that guided reading as homework between counseling sessions can be of great assistance to the growth process. Libraries have reference lists available on specific topics, which could provide additional reading resources.

Developing the ability to laugh at one's mistakes is useful in combatting perfectionism. Cousins (1979) has popularized the notion that the process of laughter is therapeutic from a physiological standpoint in helping to cure both mind and body. Since humor is often a strength of the gifted and creative (Clark, 1988), it is a natural ability that can be used to good advantage. Torrance (1977) contended that humor is an integral part of our well-being without which much of life would be unbearable. Developing humor in a depressed perfectionist may take some time. However, laughing with someone about mistakes can become catching if it is done in a friendly and nonjudgmental manner. *Humor: Lessons in Laughter for Learning and Living* (Bleedorn and McKelvey, 1984) provides a good source of humor units (grades 3–12) for teachers who wish to use them preventively or to assist specific children who need additional laughter in their lives.

Perfectionists often rely on the praise of others for reinforcement. Assistance in changing their outlook to an internal locus of control may help break this need. Persons with an internal focus rely on their own ability to evaluate their performance and become their own primary reinforcers. Instead of saying, "That's perfect, I got straight A's," it is important for the individual to include self-evaluations such as "How do I feel about my performance?" Adults should encourage and praise the self-evaluation to the same extent that they praise the accomplishment.

When perfectionists are changing, it is particularly important that they develop creative outlets. Most people have this need, but with this group, it is imperative. A perfectionist should have at least one activity that can be completed without self-criticism. This activity may become what Glasser (1975b) described as "a positive addiction." Two other techniques that give concrete guidance to the "recovering" perfectionist are to break major goals into smaller, more reachable steps (for example, writing a research paper section by section rather than approaching it holistically; Lakein, 1973) and to consciously select certain areas in which they will do well while they are "letting go" in others.

Finally, school personnel and parents need to look at their own behavior that encourages perfectionism. In *Mindstorms*, Papert (1980) addresses the need to "debug" schools from the idea that students either "got it" or "got it wrong." In computer technology, Papert says, "The question to ask about the programming is not whether it is right or wrong but if it is fixable" (p. 23). Translating Papert's concept to all academic disciplines would help alleviate perfectionistic tendencies that are exacerbated by well-meaning educators. This would be a great service to future generations.

SUMMARY

In conclusion, this discussion supports the contention of the ancient Greeks, who believed that there should be a harmonious balance between the faculties of both mind and body. What makes an act excellent and in what portion balance is achieved is a value judgment each of us has to make as an individual.

REFERENCES

Adderholdt, M. (1984). *The effects of perfectionism upon the self concepts of undergraduate women at the University of Georgia.* Unpublished doctoral dissertation, University of Georgia, Athens.

Adderholdt-Elliott, M. (1987). *Perfectionism: What's bad about being too good?* Minneapolis: Free Spirit.

Alvino, J. (Ed.). (1984, April). Relaxation adventures to ease the stressful ones. *Gifted Children Newsletter*, p. 5.

Baldwin, B. (1982, July/August). Perfectionists: Professional anatomy of failure, prescription for recovery. *Piedmont Pace Magazine*, pp. 11–18.

Barrow, J., & Moore, C. (1983). Group interventions with perfectionistic thinking. *Personnel and Guidance Journal, 61*, 612–615.

Bleedorn, B., & McKelvey, S. (1984). *Humor: Lessons in laughter for learning and living.* Buffalo: DOK Publishers.

Borgers, S. (1980). Using reality therapy in the classroom with gifted individuals. *Gifted Child Quarterly, 24*, 167–168.

Brophy, B. (1986, April 7). Workaholics beware: Long hours may not pay. *U.S. News and World Report*, p. 60.

Burka, J., & Yuen, L. (1982, January). Mind games procrastinators play. *Psychology Today*, p. 44.

Burns, D. (1980a). *Feeling good: The new mood therapy.* New York: New American Library.

Burns, D. (1980b, November). The perfectionist's script for self-defeat. *Psychology Today*, pp. 34–54.

Burns, D. (1983). The spouse who is a perfectionist. *Medical Aspects of Human Sexuality, 17*, 219–230.

Burns, D. (1989). *The feeling good handbook: Using the new mood therapy in everyday life.* New York: Morrow.

Clark, B. (1988). *Growing up gifted* (3rd ed.). Columbus, OH: Merrill.

Cousins, N. (1979). *Anatomy of an illness as perceived by the patient.* New York: Bantam.

Delisle, J. (1982a, August). Gifted children learn to underachieve. *Gifted Child Newsletter*, p. 5.

Delisle, J. (1982b). Striking out: Suicide and the gifted adolescent. *G/C/T, 24*, 16–19.

Delisle, J. (1982c). Learning to underachieve. *Roeper Review, 4*, 16–18.

Doman, G. (1975). *How to teach your baby to read: The gentle revolution.* Garden City, NY: Doubleday.

Doman, G. (1979). *Teach your baby math.* New York: Simon & Schuster.

Doman, G. (1984). *How to multiply your baby's intelligence.* Garden City, NY: Doubleday.

Elkind, D. (1981). *The hurried child: Growing up too fast too soon.* Reading, MA: Addison-Wesley.

Friedman, M., & Rosenman, R. (1974). *Type A behavior and your heart.* New York: Ballantine.

Galbraith, J. (1983). *The gifted kids survival guide.* Minneapolis: Free Spirit.

Glasser, W. (1975a). *Reality therapy.* New York: Harper & Row.

Glasser, W. (1975b). *Positive addiction.* New York: Harper & Row.

Jenkins-Friedman, R., Bransky, P., & Murphy, D. (1986). *Empowering gifted students.* Unpublished perfectionism scale, University of Kansas, Lawrence.

Knaus, W. (1979). *Do it now: How to stop procrastinating.* Englewood Cliffs, NJ: Prentice-Hall.

Lakein, A. (1973). *How to get control of your time and your life.* New York: Peter Wyden.

Leman, K. (1985). *The birth order book: Why you are the way you are.* Old Tappan, NJ: Fleming H. Revell.

Murray, H. (1955). American Icarus. In A. Burton & R. Harris (Eds.), *Clinical studies in personality* (pp. 615–641). New York: Harper & Row.

Pacht, A. (1984). Reflections on perfection. *American Psychologist, 39,* 386–390.

Papert, S. (1980). *Mindstorms: Children, computers, and powerful ideas.* New York: Basic Books.

Procaccini, J., & Kiefaber, M. (1983). *Parent burnout.* Garden City, NY: Doubleday.

Riggs, G. (1982, August). Paralyzed learners need counseling. *Gifted Child Newsletter,* p. 4.

Robinson, B. (1989). *Work addiction: Hidden legacies of adult children.* Deerfield Beach, FL: Health Communications.

Rowell, J. (1986, Spring). Who says perfect is best? *Growing Up Magazine,* pp. 8–9.

Sifford, D. (1989). *The only child: Being one, loving one, understanding one, raising one.* New York: Putnam's.

Terman, L. (1925). *Genetic studies of genius: Vol. 1. Mental and physical traits of a thousand gifted children.* Stanford: Stanford University Press.

Torrance, E. P. (1977). *Discovery and nurturance of giftedness in the culturally different.* Reston, VA: Council for Exceptional Children.

Whitmore, J. (1980). *Giftedness, conflict, and underachievement.* Boston: Allyn & Bacon.

Wiehl, A. (1958). *Creative visualization.* St. Paul, MN: Llewellyn.

CHAPTER 6

Stress Management
with the Gifted Adolescent

Judy Genshaft
Jim Broyles

Gifted adolescents have unique personality characteristics that may make them more susceptible to stress than their peers are. For example, Hollingworth (1942) discusses the gap between intellectual capability and the level of social functioning found in the highly gifted child. While these children are advanced in their intellectual abilities, they may not necessarily be as advanced socially and emotionally. For a number of reasons this imbalance may produce stress for the gifted individual.

THE CONCEPT OF STRESS

Origins of Theories on Stress

Hans Selye (1956) pioneered most of the early research on stress and is often credited with borrowing the term from physics to refer to the human reaction to danger signals. Selye defined stress as "the nonspecific response of the body to any demand" and as "the rate of wear and tear on the body" (p. 84). According to his work, any external stimulus that evokes a stress response is a stressor. Examples of these stimuli might be the death of a loved one, changing schools, or even less evident external stressors such as too much sugar or caffeine intake. Selye noted that individuals may interpret or react to stimuli differently, but his original definition of stress was interpreted in a more normative sense and has guided much of the recent literature.

Taking an expanded view, Lazarus and Folkman (1985) emphasize transactions between people and the environment, and hypothesize that cognitive variables and mediational processes are central to the experience of stress. From this point of view, stress results when events or situations are perceived by individuals as threatening or as placing demands on them that exceed their ability to cope. The term *cognitive appraisal* is used to describe how the individual perceives the stressful situation. At a very general level, cognitive appraisal is the process that enables a person to evaluate a potential stressor in terms of its significance for well-being (Johnson, 1986).

Stress and Physical Illness

Many people wonder about the link between stress and illness. In the past 10 years a number of studies have shown that stress can negatively affect the immune system (Coddington & Troxell, 1980; Holmes & Masuda, 1974). Certain illnesses seem to be associated with specific stages of the stress reaction. Tension headaches, asthma attacks, or chest pains are more likely to strike during the "alarm reaction" or first stage when the body reacts to the stressor. If the stressor is not overwhelming, the second stage sets in. During this stage, called the resistance phase, the body begins to adapt and either fight or avoid the stress as it repairs itself. The third stage, or exhaustion phase, results if there is chronic exposure to the same stressor. The ability to adapt is eventually exhausted, and the signs of the first stage (alarm reaction) reappear (Kuczen, 1987).

Sources of Stress

Within the context of Lazarus' theory outlined above (Lazarus & Folkman, 1985), any stimulus that is personally threatening to an individual is a stressor. Sometimes the stressor is physical such as heat, cold, or unpleasant weather, but the most common sources of stress are sociological and psychological (Copeland, 1987). For example, most adolescents report school problems as the most common source of stress in their lives (Andreasen & Wasek, 1980). In addition, family disruption and discord have been found to have a detrimental effect on adolescents, with males even more vulnerable than females (Rutter, 1970; Wolkind & Rutter, 1973). As the erosion of family, school, and community continues in our society, potential sources of stress for adolescents increase.

Sources of stress are frequently defined in terms of major life changes, but only recently have researchers begun studying the effect of life change on children. Several scales have been developed to measure the stressfulness of a child's environment. Among them is a test, entitled Events and Life Change Units for Use with Four Age Groups, which appeared in the *Journal of Pediatrics* (Heisel, Ream, Raitz, Rappaport, & Coddington, 1973). This instrument is designed to identify and measure stressful events that children are more likely to experience. The following are examples of the life events listed on the scale:

> Beginning nursery school, first grade, or high school
> Birth or adoption of a brother or sister
> Death of a parent
> Change of a parent's financial status
> Discovery of being an adopted child
> Failure of a year in school

No questionnaire has been developed to date that attempts to identify all forms of adolescent stress, particularly with gifted adolescents. Although Copeland and Kelly (1986) have developed an adolescent stress questionnaire to link adolescent stress with illness, delinquency, and school problems, their questionnaire has not yet met the essential standards of test construction on such issues as norming, validity, and reliability, which would permit its recommendation at this time. A strong need for research still exists in this area.

Signals of Stress

In addition to identifying potential sources of stress, Dirkes (1983) believes it is important to recognize symptoms of anxiety in gifted adolescents.

> The following patterns could be symptoms of undesirable levels of anxiety: decreased performance; expressed desire to be like age-peers; reluctance to work in a team; expressions of low self-concept; excessive sadness or rebellion; repetition of rules and directions to make sure that they can be followed; reluctance to make choices or suggestions; avoidance of new ventures unless certain of the outcome; extremes of activity or inactivity, noise or quietude; and other marked changes in personality. (p. 68)

The most critical and destructive result of stress and anxiety among gifted students is suicide. Delisle (1986) lists the following warning signals of suicidal behavior:

1. Self-depreciation
2. Shift in school performance
3. Increased absorption with school
4. Frequent mood shifts

These stress signals may result from dissatisfaction with their work, fear of failure, or feelings of inadequacy. Delisle (1986) points out that often until this critical point is reached, the gifted child receives little, if any, help in dealing with stress and anxiety.

VULNERABILITY TO STRESS

Though our traditional concepts of stress are very strongly associated with specific life events and circumstances, the definitions of stress discussed earlier in this chapter reveal that individual perceptions, characteristics, and resources play a crucial role. These intrapersonal factors are perhaps the most pertinent to our concept of stress since they are the primary targets of the remedial efforts described later. This discussion of personal characteristics that increase a gifted adolescent's vulnerability to stress will focus on three major factors: beliefs that facilitate the stress reaction, personality differences that predispose individuals to stress, and coping skills that can minimize feelings of stress. Since they are integral to our understanding of stress within the framework of Lazarus' cognitive theory, this discussion will begin with beliefs that facilitate the stress reaction.

Individual Perceptions

From the point of view of many cognitive therapy theorists, all individuals' perceptions of reality are filtered through their thoughts and beliefs about reality (Ellis & Greiger, 1977). An individual's emotional reaction, then, including the subjective experience of stress and anxiety, has as much to do with his or her thoughts and beliefs about reality as with the events in the environment themselves. For example, gifted adolescents may become depressed or despondent when they fail to make the football team or lose the election for president of the accounting club. An initial analysis of these situations may suggest that the events are directly responsible for the subsequent negative emotions. However, within the framework of cognitive therapy it becomes apparent that these adolescents believe that if they are not able to achieve their desired goal they are worthless, or at the very least less likable people. This dysfunctional belief, then, is more directly responsible for the feeling of depression experienced.

This method of analyzing emotional experience may be just as easily applied to feelings of stress, and Barbara Kuczen (1987) provides a description of commonly held beliefs that are likely to lead to stressful reactions. The following is a summary of these:

- *I am obligated to you.* Frequently, parents attempt to teach their children responsibility by pointing out their obligations to others. Unfortunately, some children begin to feel overly obligated to a large number of people in their lives, and as a result feel stressed when they cannot meet these obligations adequately.
- *I must be the best all the time.* A number of environmental circumstances may lead children to believe they must always be among the most competent, highest achieving individuals in their peer group. Parents and teachers may unwittingly contribute to the development of this belief by overemphasizing achievement, such as an adolescent's grade point average, or even the number of points scored in the last basketball game. Since always being the best is an unrealistically high standard for anyone to attain, it is easy to see how this belief may lead to considerable stress. In fact, studies of gifted adolescents reveal that most of these young people are prone to setting up impossibly high standards for themselves (Altman, 1983; Karnes & Oehler-Stinnet, 1986).
- *The world is a terrible place to live.* Though the world is far from perfect, some adults tend to overemphasize its shortcomings. They tend to allow world problems to affect them personally to the point that it interferes with their daily functioning. This view is easily transferred to children and adolescents, and the subsequent stress it causes may be even greater for younger people, given their innate sense of helplessness and dependency on adults. A study by James Delisle (1986) suggests that young people with advanced ability may be significantly more sensitive than their peers to the problems of the adult world. Gifted adolescents, then, may be especially likely to hold this negative point of view.
- *I deserve the very best no matter what.* Sometimes parents and teachers understandably come to believe that their children deserve the very best in life. Unfortunately, in their enthusiastic effort to provide for youngsters, they forget that children must also learn that to obtain the very best requires work. Children who have all their desires granted may grow up with the belief that "I deserve the very best in life, and very little effort, work, or sacrifice is required of me to get it." Children who hold this belief may experience considerable stress when the world does not accommodate their views. Delisle (1983) points out that a significant number of gifted children are rewarded in the classroom for very little effort, simply because their ability is so much greater than that of their peers. When they enter college, however, they find that many of their

minimal efforts are received with less enthusiasm, and they become immediately frustrated.

● *I can do anything.* In an effort to instill self-confidence, teachers and parents frequently tell students, "You can accomplish anything." While this encouragement may at times be appropriate, particularly with children who are working below their ability in a certain area or who are overly intimidated by specific circumstances, it may at times lead to stress, particularly for the gifted. Many gifted adolescents strive for perfection (Karnes & Oehler-Stinnet, 1986; Leroux, 1986), and those who hold this belief may use it to justify their efforts. They may eventually come to react to any failure, no matter how small or insignificant, as disastrous since it is regarded as proof of their imperfection. Adolescents who take this belief to an extreme may open themselves to significantly high levels of stress.

This list by Kuczen provides an excellent description of mediating ideas that may make everyday circumstances stressful for the adolescents who hold them. Other, more obvious faulty beliefs mentioned by Kuczen are "I'm not as good as everyone else"; "Stress is something that noble, good, hard working people experience"; "The world is a dangerous place"; and "I should be concerned about myself and no one else."

Personality Differences

A discussion of intrapersonal factors that contribute to stress would be incomplete without including some of the recently emerging research on personality types. From this frame of reference, individuals are predisposed to react to a wide variety of life circumstances in ways that are typical for them. Though the means of classifying personality types may be slightly oversimplified, researchers in this area generally identify two or three broad personality types, which are quite useful in describing patterns of reaction that can lead to the experience of stress. Kuczen (1987) describes these categories for young people as "hot reactors" and "cool reactors" (p. 39), and points out that they are very similar to the more familiar Type A and Type B personality categories defined by cardiologists Meyer Friedman and Ray Rosenman in 1959. Kuczen describes the Type A, or "hot reactor," individual as "impatient, competitive, insecure, hostile, aggressive, and hurried" (p. 42), while "cool reactors," or Type B individuals, are just the opposite. Kuczen offers a number of examples of Type A characteristics in children and adolescents. These include having a short fuse; attempting to do two things at once, such as homework and talking on the phone; hating to wait in line; eating too fast; experiencing rage over minor frustrations; being leaders; enjoying arguing; and performing better when competition is involved. This summary of the research points out that not only are these Type A individuals more prone to stress reactions, but they are more likely as a result to experience ill health at some point in their lives.

Coping Skills

In response to the identification of these personality characteristics, a number of researchers have attempted to discover coping strategies that help individuals increase their resistance to stress. Kuczen (1987) discusses important research conducted by Kobasa and Maddi at the University of Chicago, which identified specific characteristics possessed by individuals who cope unusually well with circumstances normally perceived as stressful. The three primary characteristics identified have important implications for gifted adolescents. The first is *control:* Individuals who handle difficult situations particularly well have a strong sense that they can have an impact on the events in their environment. Several researchers in the area of gifted education (Blackburn & Erickson, 1986; Delisle, 1983) have found that gifted students frequently feel the need to control and direct their own learning experiences, while many school curricula seldom offer this opportunity to students. The manner in which the directive tendency is handled may have important implications for how well this coping strategy develops for the gifted student.

The second coping skill identified was *challenge:* Individuals who remain relatively immune to stress are able to see new and potentially difficult circumstances that arise in life as challenging rather than threatening. They view these circumstances as an opportunity for new growth. While many gifted adolescents appear to possess this optimistic outlook on life, a significant number hold extremely high standards for themselves, and may as a result view events that require new effort as a challenge to their self-esteem and consequently as threatening (Altman, 1983; Karnes & Oehler-Stinnet, 1986; Leroux, 1986).

The third important coping strategy that appeared to reduce stress was *commitment:* Individuals who cope well realize that it is through their efforts alone that stressful circumstances are dealt with. While adolescents who possess this quality draw on a number of resources for help and comfort, including parents, teachers, and counselors, they realize that it is ultimately their own responsibility to face and negotiate challenging circumstances. Again, many gifted adolescents are recognized for this initiative and commitment to self. However, Perrone (1986) points out that a subgroup of gifted students enter school only to discover that their special talents and abilities are unappreciated, while at the same time they are required to continually perform tasks they perceive as boring and insignificant. The result, Perrone states, is the development of an external locus of control, or the idea that the events of one's life are controlled entirely by factors outside oneself. It becomes clear, then, that gifted adolescents in this category may feel no responsibility for themselves at all and may, as a result, come to rely on the interventions of others when challenging circumstances arise.

INTERVENTIONS

Since stress is an individualized matter, its control must also be individualized. A particular control technique may work for one person yet be totally ineffective for another. Different mechanisms will need to be tried to determine the best approach for the gifted adolescent. The interventions, support, and relaxation recommendations reviewed here have been researched and proven effective for adolescents and adults (Kuczen, 1987).

It is important to first help gifted adolescents become aware of themselves and the signals of stress they experience. This technique may be particularly effective with gifted adolescents because they are hypersensitive to feelings about themselves and others. With proper guidance and understanding they can learn how to deal with this awareness (Gridley, 1987). As pointed out earlier in this chapter, mental and emotional stress creates a tension that often appears as a physiological symptom, such as sleepiness, stomach aches, or mood changes. Encouraging gifted adolescents to become aware of their own bodies and how stress affects them can be beneficial. For example, do they have different symptoms when the level of stress is low versus high, or are their manifestations simply more intense? It may be helpful for them to develop a "warning signs" checklist of their own reactions, so that something can be done before the stress becomes greater.

It was pointed out at the beginning of the chapter that stress is a personal interpretation of an event. Thus, fear of receiving a "B" on a mathematics examination may be terribly distressing for one person and not for another. A gifted adolescent's coping strategy also may be quite personal. Maladaptive coping strategies, such as use of drugs, nervous mannerisms, or lying to others, are individual reactions. These may delay successful coping processes and often create additional stress. A second important step in stress management, then, is to encourage a gifted adolescent to become aware of and change beliefs and attitudes that may magnify stress, as well as to teach the adolescent the alternative, positive responses to stress, mentioned previously, so that balance or equilibrium can be regained.

Relaxation techniques have proven to be among the most successful methods of stress reduction (Richter, 1984). They may be particularly effective with gifted children since "highly gifted children frequently suffer from body tension as they tend to become so excited, are so active, and tend to overextend themselves in a number of activities" (Whitmore, 1980, p. 314). There are several different "packages" or formats for producing relaxation, but they basically have similar goals—to release muscle tension and create a quieting response. For example, Kuczen (1987) suggests a four-step process:

1. Recognize physical signs, especially shallow breathing
2. Relax facial muscles, concentrate on feeling calm
3. Breathe in deeply four counts and out four counts
4. Exhale and imagine heaviness and warmth throughout the body

A more extensive muscle relaxation approach has been proposed by Herbert Benson (1975). His six-step method includes

1. Lie in a comfortable position
2. Close eyes
3. Breathe deeply through the nose
4. Tense and relax each muscle grouping (feet, ankles, legs, hips, fingers, wrist, arms, back, shoulders, buttocks, neck, jaws, and face) for 5 seconds to become aware of tension in your own body; concentrate on each totally relaxed position for at least 20 seconds
5. Sit quietly for a few minutes
6. Breathe normally for 2 or 3 minutes before getting up

Again, these are only two examples of the many successful relaxation techniques available. Creative daydreaming, creative imagery, and meditation are other forms of relaxation that have proven effective.

Other approaches, such as focusing on problems, pinpointing the stressor, and developing effective problem-solving techniques, may be classified under the broader categories of cognitive-behavioral strategies. Here the first step is to help the gifted adolescent get the facts or analyze what has happened to produce a stressful situation. After the problem has been clarified, a plan for reducing, eliminating, or controlling the stress will be developed. Several alternative approaches or choices should be outlined to help the gifted adolescent understand the different options. Regularly evaluating the gifted adolescent's choice of strategy is an essential final step. This method of problem solving will increase the person's ability to handle pressure as well as anticipate stressful situations in the future and plan accordingly.

One major task of socialization is teaching gifted adolescents how to control and use the energy that has built up internally from stress. Researchers suspect that both crying and laughing cause biochemical changes that are related to feelings of pain relief or pleasure. Similarly, physical exercise has been shown to increase calm, produce more resilience, and increase energy. Stress increases the body's flow of adrenaline, while exercise dissipates it. Another approach, writing, has been shown to give vent to fears and emotions. Simply writing about a stressor, such as science or math anxiety, helps the adolescent bring inner feelings out into the open. For this reason, diaries or journals are often recommended for stress reduction.

The last and perhaps most important stress management technique is to provide support for the gifted adolescent under stress. This can be achieved by accentuating the positive and helping the youngster work toward realistic goals. Often adolescents look for help in the wrong places or take poor advice. It is important, then, to help the adolescent seek assistance early and from appropriate sources, whether family or professionals. Keeping the adolescent's self-esteem strong and positive is critical at this time.

SUMMARY

Although the term is used easily and often today, stress has proven difficult to define and study precisely. The concept, however, continues to be useful in helping us understand an aspect of human experience. Understanding sources and manifestations of stress may be especially important when considering gifted adolescents, since they may possess specific characteristics or be exposed to unique circumstances that lead to feelings of stress.

Attempts to define stress have focused on both the bodily reactions to stress as well as the role of an individual's specific thoughts and attitudes in promoting stressful feelings. This approach has revealed that life events that are perceived as threatening to an individual's well-being cause stress. These life events are frequently associated with life changes that are not uncommon in the lives of most gifted adolescents. A number of symptoms, including excess sadness or anxiety, may signal undesirable levels of stress.

Gifted adolescents who possess certain personal characteristics may experience an increased vulnerability to stress. These characteristics include specific thoughts and beliefs held, individual personality differences, and the inner resources available to the adolescent. The specific stress-inducing characteristics in each of these categories have been described in this chapter.

Approaches to managing stress vary depending on its source and the individual gifted adolescent. In general, approaches to managing stress include teaching the individual to be aware of bodily responses to stress, identifying faulty beliefs that may exacerbate stress, developing positive coping strategies, and practicing relaxation techniques. Individuals working with gifted adolescents experiencing stress also may find it helpful to teach positive problem-solving strategies or increase certain daily activities such as physical exercise or writing. Perhaps the most important assistance may be in the form of emotional support from a close adult.

REFERENCES

Altman, R. (1983). Social-emotional development of gifted children and adolescents: A research model. *Roeper Review, 6*, 65–68.

Andreasen, N. C., & Wasek, P. (1980). Adjustment disorder in adolescents and adults. *Archives of General Psychiatry, 37*, 1166–1170.

Benson, H. (1975). *The relaxation response.* New York: Morrow.

Blackburn, A., & Erickson, D. (1986). Predictable crises of the gifted student. *Journal of Counseling and Development, 64*, 552–555.

Coddington, R., & Troxell, J. (1980). The effect of emotional factors on football injury rates: A pilot study. *Journal of Human Stress, 6*, 3–5.

Copeland, E. P. (1987). Children and stress. In A. Thomas & J. Grimes (Eds.), *Children's needs: Psychological perspectives* (pp. 586–594). Washington, DC: National Association of School Psychologists.

Copeland, E. P., & Kelly, M. (1986). *Stress, locus of control, and perceived abusive parenting styles as predictors of adolescent delinquency.* Paper presented at the annual conference of the Rocky Mountain Psychological Association, Denver, CO.

Delisle, J. (1983). Counseling the gifted: What we know, and how it can help. *Gifted Education International, 2*, 19–21.

Delisle, J. (1986). Death with honors: Suicide among gifted adolescents. *Journal of Counseling and Development, 64*, 558–560.

Dirkes, M. (1983). Anxiety in the gifted: Pluses and minuses. *Roeper Review, 6*, 68–70.

Ellis, A., & Greiger, R. (1977). *Handbook of rational emotive therapy.* New York: Springer.

Gridley, B. E. (1987). Giftedness. In A. Thomas & J. Grimes (Eds.), *Children's needs: Psychological perspectives* (pp. 234–241). Washington, DC: National Association of School Psychologists.

Heisel, J., Ream, J., Raitz, R., Rappaport, M., & Coddington, R. (1973). The significance of life events as contributing factors in the disease of children. *Journal of Pediatrics, 83,* 119–123.

Hollingworth, L. (1942). *Children above 180 IQ Stanford-Binet: Origin and development.* Yonkers, NY: World Book.

Holmes, T. H., & Masuda, M. (1974). Life change and illness susceptibility. In B. S. Dohrenwend & B. P. Dohrenwend (Eds.), *Stressful life events: Their nature and effect* (pp. 45–72). New York: Wiley.

Johnson, J. H. (1986). *Life events as stressors in childhood and adolescence.* Beverly Hills, CA: Sage.

Karnes, F., & Oehler-Stinnet, J. (1986). Life events as stressors with gifted adolescence. *Psychology in the Schools, 23,* 406–414.

Kuczen, B. (1987). *Childhood stress.* New York: Delta.

Lazarus, R. S., & Folkman, S. (1985). *Stress, appraisal, and coping.* New York: Springer.

Leroux, J. (1986). Suicidal behavior and gifted adolescents. *Roeper Review, 9,* 77–79.

Perrone, P. (1986). Guidance needs of gifted children, adolescents, and adults. *Journal of Counseling and Development, 64,* 564–565.

Richter, N. C. (1984). The efficacy of relaxation training with children. *Journal of Abnormal Child Psychology, 12,* 319–344.

Rutter, M. (1970). Sex differences in children's responses to family stress. In E. J. Anthony & C. Koupernick (Eds.), *The child in his family* (pp. 165–196). New York: Wiley.

Selye, H. (1956). *The stress of life.* New York: McGraw-Hill.

Whitmore, J. R. (1980). *Giftedness, conflict, and underachievement.* Boston: Allyn & Bacon.

Wolkind, S. N., & Rutter, M. (1973). Children who have been "in care": An epidemiological study. *Journal of Child Psychology and Psychiatry, 14,* 97–105.

PART II

EDUCATIONAL ISSUES

A discussion of the educational needs of the gifted often includes consideration of those administrative "containers" in which we place gifted students (e.g., enrichment or acceleration options) or the type of curriculum we should deliver (e.g., content, process/product, thematic, or compacted/accelerated). These are important topics, but they have been thoroughly discussed in many other places.

Our emphasis is on the gifted adolescent as a learner. Chapters 7–9 of this part outline the outcomes of successful education. We hope that all capable students can develop the skills of critical and creative thinking and can apply those skills in a variety of leadership roles. This, of course, is not always the case. Underachieving students and those whose talents may be hidden by disability have special needs and present special challenges, as explored in Chapters 10 and 11. We have emphasized the need to identify such students and have provided specific approaches for awakening hidden or underrated talent.

Finally, we realize that specific programs for gifted adolescents are rare or nonexistent in many school systems. To continue the pleasures and payoffs provided by the differentiated curricula available in many elementary programs, gifted adolescent students may need to look beyond in-school opportunities. In Chapter 12 information on the history and current status of a number of such programs is provided for those who wish to participate in these enrichment options.

The educated person is a product of opportunity and experience, of natural ability and learned skills. As educators, counselors, and parents, it is our task to identify and deliver the processes, opportunities, and skills that can enhance learning and result in gifted young adults who are problem solvers and decision makers as well as storehouses of factual knowledge.

CHAPTER 7

Encouraging Higher Level Thinking in the Gifted Adolescent

Susan R. Amidon

With the increasing concern in recent years about the many issues facing all young people in America's middle schools, change seems imminent. "The early adolescent years are crucial in determining the future success or failure of millions of American youth," requiring a focus on making this a "time of purposeful exploration and preparation for constructive adulthood" (Carnegie Council on Adolescent Development, 1989, p. 10). Further, the educational response must go beyond the traditional curriculum, as emphasized by the National Science Board Commission on Pre-College Education in Mathematics, Science, and Technology (1983) when it declared in its summary report that education must return to the basics, but the basics of the twenty-first century cannot be limited to reading, writing, and arithmetic. The basics must include communication, higher problem-solving skills, and scientific and technological literacy. Development of students' capacities for problem solving and critical thinking in all areas of learning must drive our future educational goals.

When considering gifted adolescents, one cannot assume that critical thinking, creativity, and autonomy are inherent. Those working with such students have found that often they want only to find the one "right" answer and may display dependency, rigidity, intolerance for ambiguity, inability to take cognitive risks, and anxiety (Wassermann, 1982). Glaser (1985) has said that a student does not tend "naturally" to develop a general disposition to thoughtfully consider the subjects and problems that he or she experiences. In addition, Glaser asserts that there is little evidence that students acquire critical thinking merely through the study of a particular subject. As we begin to accept that the ability to think critically and creatively is imperative for young people in the twentieth and twenty-first centuries (Halpern, 1984), the special strengths and needs of the gifted adolescent must be specifically addressed.

CRITICAL AND CREATIVE THINKING

Gifted students may use many thinking processes, such as problem solving, scientific inquiry, and ethical decision making, as well as an array of strategies including observing, encoding, identifying patterns, and summarizing. These processes and strategies utilize both critical and creative thinking, which are seen as complementary.

In *Dimensions of Thinking: A Framework for Curriculum and Instruction* (Marzano, Brandt, Hughes, Jones, Presseisen, Rankin, and Suhor, 1989), the authors suggest that all good thinking involves both quality assessment (critical thinking) and the production of novelty (creative thinking). The difference in the kind of thinking used then becomes only one of degree and emphasis.

Ennis (1985) has defined critical thinking as "reasonable reflective thinking that is focused on deciding what to believe or do" (p. 10). A question has arisen about the appropriateness of instruction in the middle grades in this area—in other words, can adolescents engage in critical thinking? In a recent review of the literature, Daniel Keating (1988) found no evidence of developmental constraints on the ability of early adolescents to engage in critical thinking. Thus, critical thinking processes can be taught, and "improving students' performance on essential skills and maximizing their interaction in the complex process of decision making becomes, then, a central focus of secondary school instruction" (Presseisen, 1987, p. 28).

Halpern (1984) has said that "creativity can be thought of as the ability to form new combinations of ideas to fulfill a need" (p. 324). Perkins (1981) further emphasizes creative production and risk taking as essential elements of creative thinking. John Gowan (1977) summarized the need for instruction in this area for the gifted and talented, when he stated, "If we learn to domesticate creativity—that is, to enhance rather than to deny it in our culture—we can increase the number of creative persons in our midst by about fourfold" (p. 89).

VIEWS ON THINKING AS DEMONSTRATED BY THE GIFTED AND TALENTED

Gifted students are distinguished from their peers by many characteristics, including the following:

- Curiosity covering a wider than usual range of interests and a memory that more thoroughly retains the information gained as a result (Clark, 1988)

- Greater complexity in thinking, in combination with the capability to synthesize information from disparate fields (Bruch, 1975)
- Demonstrated need for classroom emphasis on higher levels of thinking (Maker, 1982)
- Preference for complex tasks (Terry, 1984)
- Qualitatively different and exceptional insight abilities (Sternberg & Davidson, 1984)

These observed strengths have led to some interesting theories about the way gifted students are said to think "differently."

Cognitive Information Processing

Flavell (1985) addresses the changing developmental capacity of the human cognitive system to process information. The general idea is that children of younger ages may find it difficult to engage in mental activities that require them to interrelate more pieces of information than their memory can handle. This capacity is said to increase with age. The "why" of this increasing capacity is still under study but may be related to both the *structural* ("hard-wired," biological) capacity and the *functional* (attention span, speed, organization, computer access) capacity of the individual.

As discussed in Chapter 1, Sternberg (1986) has proposed a triarchic theory of intellectual giftedness that elaborates three specific subtheories. The componential subtheory "relates intelligence to the internal world of the individual, specifying the mental mechanisms that lead to more and less intelligent behavior" (p. 223). The experiential subtheory describes intelligent behavior in terms of how effectively one can solve problems related to novelty and automatization of experience. Finally, the contextual subtheory relates "intelligent behavior to one's adaptation to, shaping of, and selecting real world environments of importance to the individual" (p. 223).

Insight

Renzulli and Reis (1985) contend that above average (but not necessarily superior) intelligence, creativity, and task commitment should be the prerequisites for identification of the gifted. However, these traits may also be viewed as highly contextual and dependent on individual information processing of specific task requirements (Flavell, 1985). Sternberg and Davidson (1984) agree with these prerequisite characteristics, and suggest five further generalizations about the gifted, without regard to any specific domain:

1. Higher general intelligence and exceptional specific ability
2. Exceptional capitalization upon patterns of abilities
3. Exceptional environmental-shaping abilities
4. Exceptional problem-finding ability
5. Exceptional ability to conceive higher order relations

Renzulli (1990) further elaborates that the development of gifted behaviors is a developmental process resulting from the application of cognitive, motivational, and affective processes to domain specific areas that place a high premium on creative production.

In addition to the above abilities, insight as demonstrated by the gifted may be particularly useful for identification and programming (Sternberg & Davidson, 1984). This "suddenness of solution" (Simon, 1979, p. 141) is demonstrated by the gifted individual applying knowledge-acquisition components in novel ways. The processes demonstrated in the following examples of historical scientific insight, as cited by Sternberg (1986), have been found to be utilized by gifted students engaged in problem solving:

- *Selective encoding*—sifting relevant from irrelevant information, as shown in the discovery of penicillin by Sir Alexander Fleming when he noticed that an errant mold had killed bacteria in a culture dish
- *Selective combination*—creating a unified whole from isolated ideas, as demonstrated by Darwin's formulation of the theory of evolution from seemingly isolated observations
- *Selective comparison*—relating new ideas to past information, as shown through the famous example of Kekule's discovery of the benzene ring, after his dream of a snake dancing around and then biting its tail

Studies with gifted individuals (Sternberg & Davidson, 1982, 1984, 1987; Wisnyai, 1988) may serve as the basis for future training to enhance these skills.

Problem Solving

Halpern (1984) observed that "much of everyday thinking is like the scientific process of hypothesis testing" (p. 111). This sort of deductive problem solving has been studied in great detail, especially as it relates to novice and expert performance (Ericsson & Simon, 1984; Harmon &

King, 1985; Hayes-Roth, Waterman, & Lenat, 1983; Larkin, 1980; Schoenfeld & Herrman, 1982). Presseisen (1986) further suggests that "expertise develops gradually and is very much related to prior knowledge acquired and to the quality of experience in 'playing with' that knowledge" (p. 9). Since problem-solving behavior is a complex cognitive skill that is a major aspect of intelligent human activity (Chi & Glaser, 1984; Resnick & Glaser, 1977), it is imperative that we offer educational activities to allow gifted adolescents to benefit from varied expert problem-solving techniques.

Problem Finding

Problem finding (discovery) can be thought of as a special case of problem solving (Langley, Simon, Bradshaw, & Zytkow, 1987). In its simplest sense, it is seen as induction, or movement from a set of facts to an accepted, quantified generalization. Discovery may also focus on the irregular side of nature and the order to be found in the chaos (Gleick, 1987). Discovery is said to occur when a single mind perceives in disorder a deep new unity (Bronowski, 1958). The "facts" may be familiar ones that turn up in a new environment or, conversely, one may observe new phenomena in a familiar environment. Pasteur said that "accidents favor the prepared mind" (Langley et al., 1987); gifted adolescents trained in thinking skills and processes may be able to more often *find* the significant problems.

THEORY INTO PRACTICE

Many strategies may be utilized to teach the concepts and processes of critical and creative thinking. But before one can concentrate on these, an environment that encourages "thinking" must be set by the teacher, counselor, psychologist, or parents. Some questions that one may ask to determine if such a setting exists are the following (adapted from Barrell, 1985):

- If a student poses an unusual or divergent question, how often do I ask, "What made you think of that?"
- How often do students give reasons for making statements?
- Do I stress *how* to think, rather than *what* to think?
- How often do students set objectives for their own learning?
- Do I frequently encourage students to seek alternative answers?

- How often do students actively listen to each other?
- How often do students relate subject matter to experiences in other subjects or in their personal lives?
- Can most of the questions I pose be answered with short answers or do they elicit longer responses?
- Do children automatically accept whatever the text (authority) says is the right answer, or do they feel free to question it?

Teaching Strategies

An educator may develop a repertoire of practical strategies for the teaching of thinking skills. These most often may be classified as directive, mediative, generative, and collaborative (Costa, 1985). These strategies may further be applied to specific cognitive instruction in the content areas and may utilize such diverse applications as composition, discovery, valuing, and computers to facilitate student learning (Tiedt, Carlson, Howard, & Watanabe, 1989).

Inductive/Directive Instruction. A framework for introducing a new thinking skill can be either inductive or directive (Beyer, 1987). An inductive introduction involves students in immediate execution of the new strategy, and is most useful with average to above average students with considerable content-area background. However, instructors may be more comfortable and feel more effective when the introduction is teacher directed. Lesson organization should be in terms of a five-stage framework:

1. Several examples of the skill should be given.
2. The teacher should introduce, present, and demonstrate the skill.
3. Instructive practice should follow.
4. Review and transfer to another type of content should be demonstrated.
5. Additional opportunities to apply the skill should be provided. It is also suggested that students apply the skill in both individual and paired situations, and be given time to reflect on the use of the particular thinking strategy (Beyer, 1985).

Mediative Instruction. Mediative strategies seek to promote students' expression of opinions with evidence to support positions, as well as their application of critical and creative thinking to novel situations. Mediative techniques are sometimes referred to as "Socratic" methods because the teacher mediates through questioning and dilemma discussions. Open-ended discussion, inquiry-based instruction, value awareness, and concept development are examples of teacher-mediated activities (Costa, Hanson, Silver, & Strong, 1985).

Generative Instruction. Generative instruction is most often referred to as creative problem solving or divergent production, and occurs through the use of brainstorming about an ill-defined problem, and then moves through the stages of fact finding, problem finding, idea finding, and solution finding, to acceptance finding (Parnes, 1967). Use of the scientific method, synectics (Gordon, 1961), analogical thinking, right-brain instruction, and metaphor are only some of the techniques available to address creativity.

Collaborative Instruction. Collaborative strategies have been strongly enhanced through the positive outcomes of the research on cooperative learning, and such learning is emphasized as imperative for adolescents (Carnegie Council, 1989). Structured student groups for positive interaction may range from large quality circles to paired problem solving (Whimby & Lockhead, 1986). In all of these groupings, the focus is on enhancing the self-concept of the student as a problem solver, through positive interdependence, verbal interaction, communication, and the use of social as well as cognitive skills.

Learning Strategies

Prior to embarking on a thinking-skills classroom focus with gifted adolescents, it is important for an educator to consider "why" the chosen instructional methods, learning strategies, and materials are important. Any strategies should be related to a strong theoretical basis with outcomes that can be evaluated. The activities should be developmentally appropriate for adolescents, especially in the areas of motivation, self-concept, and real-world application. Content area thinking skills and processes must be well defined; good examples of strategies that are especially appropriate for gifted learners follow.

Protocol Analysis. Protocol analysis, the study of the strategies used by field experts in solving problems, has been used as the basis for programming artificial intelligence computer systems (expert systems) and may serve as the basis for "think aloud" problem-solving approaches with gifted students (Anderson, 1986; Larkin, 1983; Resnick & Glaser, 1977). Such a process would allow the actual processes used by the learner to be examined, because the educator would record the steps used in problem solving as the student encountered a novel situation. Such methodology goes beyond the pencil and paper tests by which we usually attempt to measure thinking. Verbal reports may also offer some additional information about the metacognition (thinking about thinking) of the learner and could result in the development of more appropriate individualized learning activities.

Graphic Organizers. The purpose of graphic organizers is to help integrate thinking skills into content instruction. These visual metaphors allow a student to convert ideas to something concrete, so that they can be restructured, shaped, refined, and controlled. Inductive thinking (e.g., spider maps, network trees, fishbone maps) as well as deductive thinking (e.g., problem solution frames, comparison matrixes) may be shown through these media.

Analogical Reasoning. Reasoning by analogy has long been perceived as having a close relationship with intelligence, especially as defined and measured by Spearman and Raven (Sternberg, 1977). Through this general learning strategy, in which unfamiliar terms are introduced by reference to more familiar ones, students learn to express their ideas in terms that are easily understood. It is suggested that activities that focus on third-order analogies (the degree of analogy between two analogies) can result in further strategy development and higher order reasoning in adolescence (Alexander, 1984; Sternberg & Downing, 1982).

Reflective Thinking. In using strategies to enhance reflective thought, thinking becomes the search for meaning (Barrell, 1984). Content materials are selected because of their complexity and presentation of real-life dilemmas. Creating metaphors to capture the essence of the ideas and experiences is seen as the challenge. The universal, transdisciplinary themes of such issues as leadership, power, identity, and ethics are the sources of the conflicts requiring decisions to be made.

Thinking-Skills Programs

Several thinking-skills programs are available that offer comprehensive teacher training materials and program materials for student use. In selecting an appropriate program, the same suggestions apply as are relevant in the selection of instructional and learning strategies. The program should have a sound theoretical basis, materials and methods should be appropriate for the intended audience, and evaluation methods should be delineated. Some comprehensive sources for program summaries include *Developing Minds: A Resource Book for Teaching Thinking* (Costa, 1985), *Thinking in the Classroom* (Chance, 1986), and *Educational Programs That Work* (National Diffusion Network, 1989). A thinking-skills program should meet the needs of the school district, classroom teacher, and individual students. There is no one program that meets the needs of all users, and educators should carefully research any program or combination of programs being considered.

Additionally, it should be noted that there is some concern about the value of programs which divorce thinking-skills training from content. Renzulli (1977) forcefully warns against relying too heavily on thinking-skills activities and policies to the exclusion of content. While most of the recent programs are more than a collection of isolated activities, each should be evaluated with Renzulli's admonition in mind:

> Our preoccupation with process objectives has caused us to forget that *process is the path rather than the goal of learning,* and unless we view processes in this manner, there is a danger of trying to ram them down students' throats in much the same way that we force-fed youngsters with facts and figures. (p. 8; emphasis in original)

The controversy over the value of thinking skills programs is far from resolved.

EVALUATION

Evaluation of the success of a program in developing thinking processes and skills is one of the most challenging aspects of introducing a thinking-skills program. In the current rush for educational accountability, higher order thinking skills should not be forgotten because "if higher order or critical thinking is not being assessed, teachers are less likely to demand it of students" (Carnegie Council, 1989, p. 48).

Evaluation must encompass both assessment of basic thought processes and higher order, more complex processes. Teachers must strive to develop criterion-referenced tests that deal with the potential patterns of error in the specific content areas and must become familiar with ways to remediate insufficient learning of thinking skills. Multifaceted information about student performance will be required for a complete diagnostic assessment (Presseisen, 1987).

One instrument in this assessment could be a thinking-skills test, such as the New Jersey Test of Reasoning Skills, Cornell Critical Thinking Test, or Watson-Glaser Critical Thinking Appraisal (Costa, 1985). These tests are considered to be norm-referenced and thus test only thinking skills that adhere to the theoretical basis of the individual test. Another indicator of growth in thinking skills would be enhanced student self-concept as a problem solver.

Some general behavioral indicators of "better thinking" have been offered by Arthur Costa (1984), including persevering when the solution to a problem is not immediately apparent, decreasing impulsivity, flexibility in thinking, metacognition (the ability to know what one does not know), checking for accuracy, problem posing, drawing on past knowledge and experiences, transference beyond the learning situation, precision of language, and enjoyment of problem solving.

CONCLUSION

Through emphasis on excellence in education and the enhancement of thinking, we must also address the ultimate curriculum for the gifted adolescent. We must, as Harry Passow (1988) has said, "attend to another dimension of giftedness: the development of caring, concerned, compassionate, committed individuals who develop and use their giftedness for society's benefit as well as for self-fulfillment" (p. 13). Compassionate, thinking individuals are needed to address the problems of peace, ethics, and global problem solving demanded by the modern world.

REFERENCES

Alexander, P. A. (1984). Training analogical reasoning skills in the gifted. *Roeper Review, 6*, 191–193.

Anderson, M. (1986, Winter). Protocol analysis: A methodology for exploring the information processing of gifted students. *Gifted Child Quarterly, 30*, 28–32.

Barrell, J. (1984). Reflective thinking and education for the gifted. *Roeper Review, 6*, 194–196.

Barrell, J. (1985). Classroom observation checklist. In A. L. Costa (Ed.), *Developing minds: A resource book for teaching thinking* (p. 314). Alexandria, VA: Association for Supervision and Curriculum Development.

Beyer, B. (1985). Practical strategies for the direct teaching of thinking skills. In A. L. Costa (Ed.), *Developing minds: A resource book for teaching thinking* (pp. 145–150). Alexandria, VA: Association for Supervision and Curriculum Development.

Beyer, B. (1987). *Practical strategies for the teaching of thinking.* Boston: Allyn & Bacon.

Bronowski, J. (1958). The creative process. In *Readings from Scientific American: Scientific genius and creativity* (pp. 2–9). New York: Freeman.

Bruch, C. B. (1975). Children with intellectual superiority. In J. J. Gallager (Ed.), *The application of child development research to exceptional children* (pp. 245–261). Reston, VA: Council for Exceptional Children.

Carnegie Council on Adolescent Development. (1989). *Turning points: Preparing America's youth for the 21st century*. New York: Carnegie Corporation.

Chance, P. (1986). *Thinking in the classroom*. New York: Teachers College Press.

Chi, M., & Glaser, R. (1984). Problem solving ability. In R. H. Sternberg (Ed.), *Human abilities: An information processing approach* (pp. 227–250). New York: Freeman.

Clark, B. (1988). *Growing up gifted* (3rd ed.). Columbus, OH: Merrill.

Costa, A. (1984). Thinking: How do we know students are getting better at it? *Roeper Review, 6*, 197–198.

Costa, A. L. (Ed.). (1985). *Developing minds: A resource book for teaching thinking*. Alexandria, VA: Association for Supervision and Curriculum Development.

Costa, A. L., Hanson, R., Silver, H., & Strong, R. (1985). Mediative strategies. Generative strategies. In A. L. Costa (Ed.), *Developing minds: A resource book for teaching thinking* (pp. 171–172). Alexandria, VA: Association for Supervision and Curriculum Development.

Ennis, R. H. (1985). Goals for a critical thinking curriculum. In A. L. Costa (Ed.), *Developing minds: A resource book for teaching thinking* (pp. 54–57). Alexandria, VA: Association for Supervision and Curriculum Development.

Ericsson, K. A., & Simon, H. A. (1984). *Protocol analysis*. Cambridge, MA: MIT Press.

Flavell, J. H. (1985). *Cognitive development* (2nd ed.). Englewood Cliffs, NJ: Prentice-Hall.

Glaser, E. M. (1985). Critical thinking: Educating for responsible citizenship in a democracy. *National Forum, 65*, 24–27.

Gleick, J. (1987). *Chaos: Making a new science*. New York: Penguin.

Gordon, W. (1961). *Synectics*. New York: Harper Brothers.

Gowan, J. C. (1977). *The development of the creative individual*. San Diego, CA: Knapp.

Halpern, D. F. (1984). *Thought and knowledge: An introduction to critical thinking*. Hillsdale, NJ: Lawrence Erlbaum.

Harmon, P., & King, D. (1985). *Expert systems*. New York: Wiley.

Hayes-Roth, F., Waterman, D. A., & Lenat, D. B. (1983). *Building expert systems*. Reading, MA: Addison-Wesley.

Keating, D. P. (1988, November). *Adolescents' ability to engage in critical thinking*. Madison, WI: National Center on Effective Secondary Schools.

Langley, P., Simon, H. A., Bradshaw, G. L., & Zytkow, J. M. (1987). *Scientific discovery: Computational exploration of the creative process*. Cambridge, MA: MIT Press.

Larkin, J. (1980). Teaching problem-solving in physics: The psychological laboratory and the practical classroom. In D. T. Tumas & F. Reif (Eds.), *Problem solving and education: Issues in teaching and research* (pp. 111–127). Hillsdale, NJ: Lawrence Erlbaum.

Larkin, J. (1983). The new science education. In A. Lesgold & F. Reif (Eds.), *Computers in education: Realizing the potential* (pp. 95–108). Pittsburgh, PA: U.S. Department of Education.

Maker, C. J. (1982). *Curriculum development for the gifted.* Rockville, MD: Aspen Press.

Marzano, R. J., Brandt, R. S., Hughes, C. S., Jones, B. F., Presseisen, B. Z., Rankin, S. C., & Suhor, C. (1989). *Dimensions of thinking: A framework for curriculum and instruction.* Alexandria, VA: Association for Supervision and Curriculum Development.

National Diffusion Network (1989). *Educational programs that work.* Longmont, CO: Sopris West.

National Science Board Commission on Pre-College Education in Mathematics, Science, and Technology. (1983). *Educating Americans for the 21st century: A plan of action for improving mathematics, science and technology education for all American elementary and secondary students so that their achievement is the best in the world.* Washington, DC: National Science Foundation.

Parnes, S. (1967). *Creative behavior guidebook.* New York: Scribner's.

Passow, A. H. (1988). Educating gifted persons who are caring and concerned. *Roeper Review, 11,* 13–15.

Perkins, D. N. (1981). *The mind's best work.* Cambridge, MA: Harvard University Press.

Presseisen, B. (1986, April). *Critical thinking skills: State of the art definitions and practice in public schools.* Paper presented at the Annual Meeting of the American Educational Research Association, San Francisco.

Presseisen, B. (1987). *Thinking skills throughout the curriculum.* Bloomington, IN: Pi Lambda Theta.

Renzulli, J. S. (1977). *The enrichment triad model.* Mansfield Center, CT: Creative Learning Press.

Renzulli, J. (1990). "Torturing data until they confess": An analysis of the analysis of the three-ring conception of giftedness. *Journal for the Education of the Gifted, 13,* 309–331.

Renzulli, J. S., & Reis, S. M. (1985). *The schoolwide enrichment model: A comprehensive plan for educational excellence.* Mansfield Center, CT: Creative Learning Press.

Resnick, L. B., & Glaser, R. (1977). Problem solving and intelligence. In R. V. Kail & J. W. Hagen (Eds.), *Perspectives on the development of memory and cognition* (pp. 205–229). Hillsdale, NJ: Lawrence Erlbaum.

Schoenfeld, A., & Herrman, D. (1982). Problem perception and knowledge structure in expert and novice mathematical problem solvers. *Journal of Experimental Psychology—Learning, Memory and Cognition, 8,* 484–494.

Simon, H. (1979). *Models of thought.* New Haven, CT: Yale University Press.

Sternberg, R. J. (1977). Component processes in analogical reasoning. *Psychological Review, 84,* 353–378.

Sternberg, R. J. (1984). *Human abilities: An information processing approach.* New York: Freeman.

Sternberg, R. (1986). A triarchic theory of giftedness. In R. Sternberg & J. Davidson (Eds.), *Conceptions of giftedness* (pp. 223–243). Cambridge: Cambridge University Press.

Sternberg, R. J., & Davidson, J. E. (1982, June). The mind of the puzzler. *Psychology Today,* pp. 37–44.

Sternberg, R. J., & Davidson, J. E. (1984, Spring). The role of insight in intellectual giftedness. *Gifted Child Quarterly, 28,* 58–64.

Sternberg, R. J., & Davidson, J. E. (1987). Teaching thinking to college students: Some lessons learned from experience. *Teaching Thinking and Problem Solving, 9,* 1–2, 10.

Sternberg, R. J., & Downing, C. J. (1982). The development of higher-order reasoning in adolescence. *Child Development, 53,* 209–221.

Terry, P. (1984). *How to use microcomputers with gifted students: Creative microcomputing in a differentiated curriculum.* Manassas, VA: The Reading Tutorium.

Tiedt, I. M., Carlson, J. E., Howard, B. E., & Watanabe, K. (1989). *Teaching thinking in K–12 classrooms.* Boston: Allyn & Bacon.

Wassermann, S. (1982, May). The gifted can't weigh that giraffe. *Phi Delta Kappan, 63,* 621.

Whimby, A., & Lockhead, J. (1986). *Problem solving and comprehension.* Hillsdale, NJ: Lawrence Erlbaum.

Wisnyai, S. A. (1988). *Effect of insight training on the critical thinking skills of gifted students in biology.* Unpublished dissertation, Ohio State University.

CHAPTER 8

Encouraging Creativity and Talent in Adolescents

Jane Piirto

If one were to drive up Amsterdam Avenue behind Lincoln Center in New York City early in the morning just before the schoolday begins, one would see hundreds of teenagers lounging, talking to each other in groups, crossing the street. These are students at Fiorello H. LaGuardia High School of Music and Art and Performing Arts, the school whose predecessor on West 43rd Street was the prototype for the television show, *Fame*. These are talented adolescents from all five boroughs of New York City, admitted to the school by competitive audition. Of both sexes and all races and socioeconomic backgrounds, they have one thing in common—their potential for achievement in the visual or the performing arts (dance, drama, and vocal and instrumental music).

The attention of the casual passerby near LaGuardia High School is immediately drawn to one characteristic of these visual and performing arts students. Their mode of dress and hairstyles reflect a departure from those of other high school students. LaGuardia adolescents, and the adolescents at other high schools for the performing arts elsewhere in our nation, dress and wear their hair in styles that will reach the rest of the country's youngsters a year or two later. In this sense, adolescents who study the arts could be called avant garde. To recognize this, one need only drive by a high school for athletes, a high school in a rural town, a high school for the children of diplomats, a high school for intellectually gifted students, or a high school in the suburbs of any large city. Each of these groups projects a value system and a unique "flavor," which is defined for other adolescents through their manner of dress. The students of LaGuardia clearly value individuality and novelty.

This chapter will discuss this attitude and other characteristics of adolescents in the visual and performing arts who are often called creative, as well as those of young people who are scientifically and mathematically creative. *Creative* is defined here as producing novel products; that is, *creativity* implies production. Both *intellective* characteristics

104

(mental powers and the processes used to master ideas) and *nonintellective* (social, behavioral, and emotional) characteristics will be described with an emphasis on the latter. Tannenbaum (1983) made these differentiations, which I have found useful in describing creatively gifted adolescents. The chapter will discuss their childhood experiences, as well as situational factors that block or enhance creativity. The effectiveness of creativity training for the development of creative products will be explored; gender differences will be discussed. Finally, suggestions will be offered for enhancing creativity in young people.

Adolescents with science or mathematics talent may dress more conservatively, though they are certainly creative, and perhaps more intellectually gifted. In the terminology of gifted education, *intellectually gifted* students have high *IQs*, defined as above 130 or two standard deviations above the mean, while *creatively gifted* students have above-average *IQs*, one standard deviation above the mean. This difference is noted in several states' definitions of giftedness. For example, the State of Ohio, which has one of the most liberal definitions of gifted children in the United States, and which was in the top 20% in amount of state funding in 1986–87 (Mitchell, 1988), requires that students be identified in the "Creative Thinking" category. Students gifted in creative thinking ability are identified by a group or individual intelligence test with "performance one standard deviation above the mean, minus the standard error of measurement" and either an "individual or group test of creative ability" or "a checklist of creative behaviors" (Ohio Department of Education, 1984, p. 3).

NONINTELLECTIVE CHARACTERISTICS
OF CREATIVE STUDENTS

Arts Students

Artistically talented youth are often tradition breakers (Halkitis, 1989). As noted, students at LaGuardia show their difference from students attending the regular high schools by the way they dress. This is one of their nonintellective characteristics. Studies of visual artists indicate that, compared to nonartists, art students demonstrate more autonomy, independence, and flexibility; are more androgynous; have more access to primary processes; and show more sensitivity to their environment and to others (Getzels & Csikszentmihalyi, 1976). Males, especially, showed high motivation with regard to production in their talent dimension. Both males and females had a high degree of aesthetic sensitivity and critical judgment. Compared with other adolescents, both preferred more complexity to simplicity and more ambiguity to emphasis on the right answer (Barron, 1968, 1972; MacKinnon, 1978). They were more "friendly, outgoing, curious, attentive to detail, interested in and self-confident of their own creativity and intelligence" and also possessed ambition, drive, and a desire for education in their domain of creativity (Walberg, 1988, p. 356).

Arts students showed personality types on the Myers-Briggs Type Indicator (described in Chapter 13; Myers, 1962) that tended to emphasize intuition and perception rather than judgment and thinking (Myers & Myers, 1980). They were risk takers and were unconventional, nonconformist, imaginative, and idealistic. They were not shy about showing their emotions. They preferred to work alone if they were visual artists, writers, and musicians. While often impulsive in behavior, they were able to delay closure in their judgments about morality, politics, and social phenomena. They were often experimenters with the new, from lifestyle to food (Barron, 1968, 1972; Bloom, 1985; Dellas & Gaier, 1970; Getzels & Csikszentmihalyi, 1976; Guilford, 1977; MacKinnon, 1978; Torrance, 1987).

A study of 20 artistically talented adolescents by Clark and Zimmerman (1988) confirmed many of these traits, but the researchers found that these young artists made art when "stimulated by pleasurable experiences" (p. 345) and not, as Getzels and Csikszentmihalyi (1976) reported, when inspired by emotional crises. Clark and Zimmerman also found that about half of their subjects favored working alone, and the others liked to work in groups. These students liked school and did well, where Getzels and Csikszentmihalyi's subjects had mixed reactions to their earlier schooling. These students also had support from both parents, where Getzels and Csikszentmihalyi's male subjects reported supportive mothers and harsh fathers.

Science and Math Students

The construct of creativity exists not only in students involved in the arts. Creative adolescents may be gifted in science, mathematics, or other fields as well. Whether creativity can be manifested without emphasis on a product is often debated, and whether the quantity or quality of that product should be emphasized in young creative people is also at issue (Runco, 1987). The point here is that the product is the emphasis of the process undertaken by these manifestly talented young people.

Studies of Westinghouse winners (Subotnik, 1988), the Study of Mathematically Precocious Youth (Fox, 1974; Stanley & Benbow, 1982), and studies of accelerated students or students who have moved rapidly through particular subject matter have shown that the nonintellective factors mentioned above were, to some extent, present in these students as well. Independence and autonomy, field independence, single-mindedness, and motivation to achieve in their chosen field, were especially obvious in mathematically and scientifically creative adolescents.

Simonton (1988) noted that many of the most successful and productive scientific creators were precocious, which means they began their career productivity earlier than other scientists. This holds true for other creative people as well, including artists, writers, and musicians. A rule of thumb could be that the earlier a person begins to be productive, the more productive that person will be. Simonton (1988) said, "Early productivity is one of the single best predictors of later productivity in all domains of creativity" (p. 75). In fact, the statistics are so compelling, that "the odds that 'late bloomers' will establish a scientific reputation are minuscule" (p. 75).

John-Steiner (1985), in her discussion of scientific thinking as revealed by interviews, biographies, autobiographies, and the notebooks of scientists, artists, and other creative people, said that young creative scientists had "informal apprenticeships of the mind" (p. 176) as well as patience, imagination, and determination "to go beyond the simple collection of facts" in their work (p. 179).

Young mathematicians and young scientists differ a little (Tannenbaum, 1983). Both need a certain threshold of general intelligence. Scientifically and mathematically creative youth usually have IQ's in the high, rather than the above-average ranges. Both think visually rather than verbally, having good spatial relations ability, and both have a certain interest in mathematics, but the scientist uses mathematics as a tool, and the mathematician uses mathematics as an art. The passion of young scientists is science; of young mathematicians, mathematics.

Young scientists may also have personal problems. Roe (1964) said that among the personal problems of young scientists were (1) the lack of ingroups, or groups where they will be accepted; (2) the conflict between their values and family values, if they are selected for potential and their families devalue science; (3) the development of their verbal abilities in the early grades; (4) and the attitudes of the schools, where teachers often dismiss off-the-wall and nonconforming ideas. These problems are similar to those that all creative youth suffer.

Walberg (1988) said that young scientists were "preoccupied with things and ideas" rather than with humans and emotions (p. 357). This goes along with the findings of Myers and Myers (1980) about young scientists, who overwhelmingly were introverted, scoring high on the introversion dimension. Young scientists did not have many dates, or they dated many people (or "girls" as Walberg said, indicating that most of the young scientists were male). They read more biography than they did fiction, were not very involved in school activities, and expressed more confidence in their intelligence, while the young artists expressed more confidence in their creativity.

DEVELOPMENT OF THE CREATIVE PERSON

The creatively gifted adolescent differs from the intellectually gifted adolescent not only in the above mentioned nonintellective traits, but in the presence or absence of several factors in the environment. The optimum environment for the enhancement of personal soundness among intellectually gifted males (and perhaps gifted females) contains several factors, including health, home stability, respect for father, closeness with mother, positive relations with siblings, and opportunities for competitive play (Barron, 1968). MacKinnon (1978) pointed out that highly creative individuals did not report all the factors mentioned above, but that something affecting any one of the factors has happened in the childhood of the person who becomes a creative person. Guilford (1977) said that creative people have had some trauma in their childhoods: "There was often lack of parental harmony, of closeness with a parent, or there was the death of a parent. The most creative individuals were likely to be the first-born, or among the early children in the family" (p. 168).

However, Freud (1938) said that the genesis of creativity is in conflict, and what motivates creativity in some people is what, in others, motivates neurosis. Miller (1990) stated it more firmly. Childhood trauma can either lead to creative production or to destructiveness. Whether the traumatized child will grow up, as Hitler, to be destructive, or, as Picasso, to be creative, depends on the warmth of adult figures towards the developing child. Perhaps creative expression and the need for it is an attempt to seek equilibration, to make sense out of life (Lubeck & Bidell, 1988).

A developmental sequence of creativity was proposed by Lessner and Hillman (1983). They saw childhood and adolescent creativity as essentially narcissistic, selfish, and of value only to the creator. Combining the theories of Freud, Erikson, Piaget, and Kohlberg, they called this first stage of creative development creative internal enrichment. This stage is followed by creative external enrichment (late adolescence to middle-age), when a person develops an external focus for his or her creativity.

Biographical studies suggest a contrasting approach to understanding the development of creative adolescents. Biographical studies of creative adults have confirmed that something going askew in childhood is common among creative adults. For example, Tennessee Williams and Dylan Thomas had sickly childhoods. Thomas Wolfe's father deserted the family, and John Berryman's father committed suicide. The creative adolescents formed extremely close attachments to their doting and demanding mothers (Piirto, 1989a, 1989b). Many artistically creative males were not athletic in school, though a disproportionate number of them, especially writers, seem to have a passion for baseball. This is perhaps because there are no size requirements in baseball, so every child can get into neighborhood games.

The danger of using a biographical approach to the question of what enhances creativity and what blocks it is that biographical data are necessarily specific to the individual being discussed, with different authors suggesting different causes for the adult creative production and behavior. What is a typical biography? What is a typical experience for a person in expressing creativity during adulthood? Utilizing the Goertzels' data (1962, 1978), Simonton (1986, 1987, 1988) extrapolated biographical typicality in creative people: For example, writers and poets were apt to be from the city and have nonreligious, small families, with nonsupportive fathers and unhappy home environments. Artists and performers had less formal education than scientists and politicians, but were more likely to have gone to special schools, and were often precocious. Not surprisingly, the writers were also voracious readers.

Piechowski and Cunningham (1985) postulated that there are three different patterns of response in creative artists (as opposed to the intellectually gifted), and that each of these types of creative artist has different kinds of *overexcitability*. According to Dabrowski's theory of emotional development, an overexcitability may be defined as "enhanced and intensified mental activity distinguished by characteristic forms of expression which are above common and average" (Piechowski & Silverman, 1989, p. 34). These forms of expression are (1) psychomotor, (2) sensual, (3) intellectual, (4) imaginational, and (5) emotional.

Piechowski and Cunningham (1985) found that only one of the three types had childhoods with trauma. Pattern A had balanced overexcitabilities, and childhoods without trauma. Pattern B had greater emotional overexcitability, as well as "sensitivity, even oversensitivity, feelings of guilt, inadequacy, shame, shyness, or inhibition" (p. 171). They had experienced "rejection, negative criticism, even emotional deprivation" (p. 167) in their childhoods and were prone to depression, anxiety, and feelings of inadequacy. Pattern C came from fundamentalist backgrounds and were characterized by sensual, psychomotor, and imaginational overexcitability, with polarities in emotions, empathy, and inner integration. All three patterns had high intellectual overexcitability, represented as intelligence, curiosity, love of learning, and thinking in both images and words.

In another study, David Willings (1980) identified three types of creatively gifted people. One type were the *adaptive thinkers*, who think in interdisciplinary terms and see relationships among disparate things. These people often choose careers that are unconventional, for example, biomedical literary criticism. A second type of creatively gifted people were the *elaborative thinkers*, or deep researchers. Often shy and reserved, they are frequently ridiculed for their passionate study of topics that engage them. Perhaps this type could be illustrated by the people who never finish their dissertations because they are perfectionistic and can never study a topic deeply enough. The third type of creatively gifted people were the *developmental thinkers*. Preferring to fly by the seat of their pants and play hunches, these people do not want to be confused by facts, by empirical data. They prefer what is satisfying to what is right or wrong.

Utilizing a case study approach, Willings chose people who sought counseling as examples of the three types of creatively gifted. Willings thought the duty of the counselor was to help creatively gifted persons accept their creativity. Although most creatively gifted people don't seek counseling because of their creativity, but because of social problems their creativity has caused, counselors should point out that many of their problems stem from their unwillingness to compromise their creative giftedness. He also said that creatively gifted people can relate best to creatively gifted counselors, who are themselves a different type of creative thinker.

There are few conclusive truths about the development of creatively gifted adolescents, although childhoods that are less than ideal may be a differentiating factor between those who become adult creative producers and those who are less creative. This is especially true of writers, and is less true of mathematicians. Many scientists have experienced the "orphanhood effect," or the death or absence of one parent (Simonton, 1988, p. 110). Another common characteristic is that they use their adolescent years to gain skills in a certain domain (Piirto, 1990). For example, writers intensify their reading and writing; musicians intensify practice, give performances, and take lessons from higher level teachers; visual artists begin intensive studio work; scientists begin serious experimentation; mathematicians begin to work with higher levels of mathematics.

SITUATIONAL FACTORS THAT ENHANCE
OR BLOCK CREATIVE EXPRESSION

Much work has been done on the situational factors that enhance or block creativity. A playful, accepting, warm, humor-filled, nonthreatening atmosphere enhances the incubation process in which creative ideas are nurtured. A critical, rigid, rules-filled, schoolroom-like atmosphere blocks creative expression (Ghiselin, 1952; Navarre, 1979; Wallas, 1926). Lowered metabolism and attention that is permitted to be unfocused seem to encourage creative problem solving (McAleer, 1989). Many people say they get their best ideas after exercising or while driving on a boring highway. Both of these situations lower metabolism and unfocus attention. The increase of endorphins (brain peptides containing amino acids resembling opiates), which produce a feeling of euphoria, and the runner's high that happens after a person has been exercising for about a half an hour, are also called creativity enhancers.

Many biographical reports have emphasized that there really is a creative process, and that creative people tap into some altered state when they are being creative. Ancient Greeks called the process the visitation of the Muse, and it has always been mysterious (Bloom, 1985; Ghiselin, 1952; Koestler, 1964; Osborn, 1963; Parnes, 1981; Rosner & Abt, 1974; Rothenberg & Hausman, 1976). The creative process has been called Janusian (Rothenberg, 1979), "a magic synthesis" (Arieti, 1976), and "satori" (Torrance, 1979).

THE EFFECTIVENESS OF CREATIVITY TRAINING

In the past 40 years, since Guilford's (1950) speech to the American Psychological Association about the construct of creativity, various people have asserted that creativity can be trained in young people and in adults. They have manufactured programs and exercises in divergent production, to encourage people to improve their flexibility, fluency, originality, and ability to elaborate and make transformations (Guilford, 1967). Other trends in creativity training have emphasized guided imagery (Bagley & Hess, 1984); future problem solving (Torrance, 1987), which is based on the Osborn (1963) and Parnes (1967) model of creative problem solving; Odyssey of the Mind competitions (Gourley, 1981; Miklus, 1989); deBono's co*RT* lateral thinking (1978); Meeker's (1973) divergent production exercises; and Torrance's research into the enhancement of divergent production (Torrance, 1974, 1987; Torrance & Myers, 1970), among others.

Torrance (1987), Torrance and Goff (1989), and Feldhusen and Clin-kenbeard (1986) reviewed the research results of over 2,000 studies using the Torrance Tests of Creative Thinking, as well as other studies using other measures such as the Purdue Creative Thinking Program, the creative problem-solving approach, the Productive Thinking Program, Imagi/Craft, and New Directions in Creativity. These tests and programs measure and train *divergent thinking*. Divergent thinking has also been called creative thinking, though this is too simplistic a definition of creative thinking, as Sternberg (1988) so aptly noted: "Such tests [psycho-metric tests of creativity] capture at best only the most trivial aspects of creativity" (p. 246). Gardner (1982) also commented on the studies of adolescent creativity, saying that "the measures on which they have relied in their studies have almost all been brief tasks—learning word lists, mastery of a maze—which can be surmounted in a matter of minutes (and which are even more rapidly forgotten)" (p. 352).

Perkins (1981) tested many of these creative process postulations. He made what he called "propositions" based on the prevailing thought about the creative process, and then refuted or modified the propositions based on experimentation and research, calling these "revised proposi-tions." Perkins, a cognitive psychologist, worked with producing artists and poets. He used what is called the think-aloud technique, interrupting the poets and painters while they were writing poems or painting, to ask them to say what they were thinking. The formation of schemata, making long searches, setting the work aside, knowing what to undo, were a few ways these creative people made their selections while creating.

Cognitive psychologists have come out almost unanimously caution-ing against the use of creativity tests and creativity training. Weisberg (1986, 1988) painstakingly debunked many of the so-called "myths" about genius and creative problem solving, insight and divergent think-ing. He said that "the thought processes involved in great creative acts are no different than those involved in the things we all do every day" (Weisberg, 1988, p. 172). Creative production necessarily takes commit-ment and knowledge of a certain domain; that is not what is emphasized in creativity training. Instead, the training may emphasize that risk-taking is necessary, and the trainer may encourage the trainees to take risks. Weisberg said that such advice is overly simplistic.

Training in divergent thinking also includes such open-ended activi-ties as brainstorming, making up stories, thinking of new and unusual uses for objects, and forcing relationships between unlike objects. In diver-gent thinking there may be many correct answers, whereas with *conver-gent thinking* there is usually only one correct answer. Guilford (1967) used both of these terms in his structure of the intellect. Most school learning is concerned with convergent thinking, though Torrance and Goff (1989) have said that "a quiet revolution" in the classrooms has been taking place, and more divergent thinking is being taught. A look at the teachers' manuals for common reading series is a case in point. The newest ones all contain "enrichment" exercises that encourage divergent thinking. These exercises were not present in older reading series. Divergent thinking has hit the mainstream.

With the concept of divergent thinking as a form of creativity coming under serious attack in the 1980's, divergent-thinking tests such as the Torrance Tests of Creative Thinking (Torrance, 1974) have simultaneously been challenged on a theoretical level. Even earlier, however, independent research efforts have generally failed to confirm Torrance's hypothesis that high scores on such tests were predictive of substantive creative production in later life (Tannenbaum, 1983).

For example, fluency, elaboration, and originality scores on the Just Suppose Test were alleged to be predictive for "young adult creative achievement" but Torrance and Safter (1989) did not say what that achievement was. Perkins (1988) said that "measures of ideational fluency and flexibility apparently do not relate reliably to real-world creative achievement within a discipline" (p. 378) and called such testing "off-center" (p. 380). The issue of whether divergent thinking and creativity are synonymous is yet to be resolved.

Whether divergent thinking is creativity, is at issue. That divergent thinking is an aspect of creativity is evident. It would seem that creative giftedness includes the nonintellective factors described above as well. In fact, Perkins (1988) stated that flexibility, fluency, and general intelligence are not so important in the encouragement of creativity as personality factors such as autonomy, independence, self-reliance, valuing originality, tolerating ambiguity, and being more aesthetically than pragmatically inclined. Intrinsic motivation (Amabile, 1983) is also necessary.

Torrance (1987) also noted other indicators of the success of these training programs for elementary and secondary students, such as (1) a sense of well-being in the participants; (2) improvement in attitude toward school subjects such as mathematics; (3) decisions made by the students to follow creative pursuits or careers; (4) an increase in type and length of creative writing; and (5) improvement in self-concept. Thus, it is evident that formal creativity training has some success in enhancing creative production. However, Perkins (1988) indicated that the positive effects of such training are in the values that are induced as a result of the training. Treating creativity training as the teaching of techniques rather than as the acquisition of attitudes, is to diminish creativity instruction.

He said "efforts to foster creativity should pay at least as much attention to building creative attitudes as imparting technical resources" (p. 381).

The training of techniques such as brainstorming (fluency) and set-breaking (flexibility) has been widely used in gifted child education programs throughout the United States, as a means of differentiating the curriculum. Whether such training is more valuable for gifted students than for nongifted students is also an issue. Some use has been made of the techniques with disadvantaged and minority children as well. Educational publishers have capitalized on the creativity training movement, and have published teachers' guides to aid teachers in creativity training.

There is little evidence that the creative adolescents who attend the specialized schools for the visual and performing arts, or the specialized schools for math and science, have participated in such creativity training in their elementary years. Their acceptance into such specialized schools has had to do with concrete performance on tests, in auditions, and in portfolios, and with assessment by professionals. The curricula in the specialized schools may not include formal creativity training either. A typical 8-period day at LaGuardia High School in New York City contains 3 or 4 periods of intensive study of the art (for example, an instrumental music student studies music theory, has an ensemble period, and then has 1 or 2 periods of band or orchestra), as well as 4 periods of general academic study. Most schools for the arts have similar curricula.

The gifted adolescents are chosen for the schools on the basis of their creative products, and not for their success on tests that measure divergent production. While they attend the school, they practice. Bloom and his colleagues, in their study of talent development, noted that talented children who become successful adult professionals study their field to the point of "automaticity" (Bloom, 1985, 1986). Musicians practice, athletes practice, mathematicians practice, chess players practice. The notion that creativity is separate from the product the gifted adolescent produces, that it springs from exposure to general exercises in fluency, flexibility, brainstorming, and elaboration, without specific nurturing in the field in which the creativity is exhibited, seems not yet to have influenced the curricula of special schools for gifted adolescents.

In fact, the role of parents and specialized teachers in these adolescents' talent development seems more important than the creativity training they have had. As Bloom and his colleagues found (1985), parents often nurture and direct their children in the fields in which the parents themselves have interest and talent. The talented child is then taught by a teacher, who passes on what knowledge he or she can and then hands the child to another, more masterful, teacher. That is the path of creative adult production. In the very depth of their special training, these children develop automaticity.

In their adolescent years, spontaneity in young creatively gifted students often gives way to conformity. Residential schools for young artists make special provisions to deny the stereotypes that young artists are interested in drugs, rock n' roll, and sex. In an interview, an administrator at the North Carolina School of the Arts said, "Peer pressures with our students are more intense than with other students. We try to create an atmosphere for them where they can pursue academic and artistic pursuits without undue pressure" (R. Ussery, personal communication, July, 1989). All adolescents, both traditional and artistic, conform to the image their admired peers project. The truly nonconforming young artist or creative adolescent would probably be the one with the button-down collar and the docksiders, standing outside of LaGuardia High School in the morning.

Studies from Galton's (1869/1976) study of eminence to the present (Bloom, 1985; Goertzel & Goertzel, 1962; Goertzel, Goertzel, & Goertzel, 1978; Simonton, 1987, 1988) have shown that creative adult producers often come from families that themselves are erudite, literate, and encouraging, or at least tolerant, of children's creative expression (Wallace & Walberg, 1987). In adolescence, potential creative writers and visual and performing artists, and creative young scientists and mathematicians and architects acquire the knowledge that they need. The divergent producing of their youth has been shaped by their families and their special teachers; in their adolescent training, they become convergent producers. Music training, for example, is highly convergent and disciplined, as is training in mathematics, science, and sports. The production of novel products, or creativity, is not encouraged until the subject matter has been mastered.

GENDER DIFFERENCES
IN CREATIVE ADOLESCENTS

Most American inventors have been men; most dancers, women. There is a social taboo against boys who participate in dance and other arts, especially in rural areas. At least in the United States, gifted boys who are the most respected are the athletic, Rhodes scholar types (Alvino, 1988; Tannenbaum, 1983). Boys who are highly able creatively fall even more outside the norm of what is expected of them than do girls who are highly able creatively. The stereotype of the nerd or sissy haunts the creatively able boy.

It is somehow more acceptable for high school girls to be highly able creatively, but their problems come when they try to reconcile the paradox of the stereotype of the nurturing, recessive, motherly female with the stereotype of the unconventional artist. What Loeb (1975) called "the 'If-I-haven't-dusted-the-furniture-and-made-the-beds-do-I-have-the-right-to begin-carving?' syndrome" afflicts women (p. 10). Most women artists have gone unrecognized in history. The profession of artist demands an extraordinary commitment in terms of willingness to take rejection, to live in poverty, and to be field independent. Those are traits of committed males, but not of committed females, who usually choose careers as art educators, but not as artists (Harris, 1989).

The early achievement that Simonton (1988) said was necessary for scientific genius to be manifested holds true for males, but it may not hold true for females, whose difficulty in achieving what Nochlin (1988) called "supremely great" (p. 149) art may be due to developmental differences. Females may have a different career and productivity pattern (Belenky, Clinch, Goldberger, & Tarule, 1986; Gilligan, Lyons, & Hanmer, 1990). Females seem to have a developmental pattern of a searching for connectedness, while males have one of searching for separation. Females, because of reproductive and family necessity, may begin their career productivity later. This of course, is to their detriment, since early achievement seems necessary for eminence. Biological and environmental influences affect all people. Gowan (1984) postulated that testosterone had to do with males' superior spatial ability. Higham and Navarre (1984) called for "differential equality" (p. 43) in the education of adolescent gifted girls.

Boys who are able in the creative fields—for example, music, visual arts, design, dance, fashion, theatre—have problems also. Many of them are homosexual, or bisexual, as witnessed by the many deaths of creative men from AIDS recently. Whether homosexuality is biologically engendered in creative men, or societally engendered, is not the question. The fact is that creatively gifted boys seem to tend to go into fields that have norms that are freer and less structured, and expectations that are more accepting and tolerant than other fields. Whether more men in creative fields are homosexual than men in noncreative fields is also not known. Sex role stereotyping affects all boys and girls, including the creatively gifted.

Recent critiques of masculinity/femininity scales and scores on standardized personality tests have shown that social norms and environmental prejudices influence these scales (Harris, 1989). Boys have a particularly difficult time, in Freudian terms, separating from their mothers in order to become like their fathers, and perhaps what might be the sensitivity of creatively gifted boys might give them special problems in this. The caution must be that social values determine the acceptability of any gift at any time, and a person's gender may determine how acceptable his or her creativity is.

CONCLUSION

Adolescence is a stage of life through which all people, creative or not, talented or not, must go. Whether a child will become a scientist or mathematician, an inventor or a visual artist, a dancer or a designer, seems to be determined by early experiences. Talent is nurtured by practice and concentration. An early start is especially necessary in dance and in music performance. Visual artists may start later, though often their talent was evident in their childhood. Composers peak in their 50s (Simonton, 1987). Young scientists have collections and young mathematicians are precocious. Precocity or prodigy is not always necessary for adult achievement (Feldman, 1986), though precocity or prodigy is often predictive, as the biographies of creative people indicate.

To recognize which children have the talent and to nurture that talent is essential. Though family interest and encouragement are essential also, perhaps the school's identification of potential is what will lead to the creation of environments within which the potential can grow. The necessary practice, the quiet places in which to think, the very necessity of solitude to the creative process (Storr, 1988), and the supportive and not overly evaluative atmosphere can all be provided by those who discover adolescents or children with potential, as shown by the quality of their products.

However, since childhood identification is of necessity the identification of potential, it is also essential that more children receive the generalized training that might evoke creative responses, and that creativity training not be limited to only those young children identified as gifted. This is especially important because traditional identification measures, such as IQ tests, may not find disadvantaged or culturally different children. The greatest challenge to gifted education today is the challenge of equity. The addition of creativity training to all early childhood curricula may provide one means to equity in the identification of gifted young people.

REFERENCES

Alvino, J. (1988, September). Snips and snails and puppy dog tails. *Gifted Children Monthly*, pp. 1–3, 15, 23.

Amabile, T. M. (1983). *The social psychology of creativity*. New York: Springer-Verlag.

Arieti, S. (1976). *Creativity: The magic synthesis*. New York: Basic Books.

Bagley, M., & Hess, K. (1984). *200 ways of using imagery in the classroom*. New York: Trillium.

Barron, F. (1968). *Creativity and personal freedom*. New York: Van Nostrand.

Barron, F. (1972). *Artists in the making*. New York: Seminar Press.

Belenky, M., Clinch, B., Goldberger, N., & Tarule, J. (1986). *Women's ways of knowing*. New York: Basic Books.

Bloom, B. (Ed.). (1985). *Developing talent in young people*. New York: Ballantine.

Bloom, B. (1986). The hands and feet of genius. *Educational Leadership, 43*, 70-77.

Clark, G., & Zimmerman, E. (1988). Views of self, family background, and school: Interviews with artistically talented students. *Gifted Child Quarterly, 32*, 340-346.

deBono, E. (1978). *CoRT thinking lesson series*. Blanford Forum, Dorset, UK: Direct Education Services.

Dellas, M., & Gaier, E. (1970). Identification of creativity: The individual. *Psychological Bulletin, 73*, 55-74.

Feldhusen, J., & Clinkenbeard, P. (1986). Creativity instructional materials: A review of research. *Journal of Creative Behavior, 20*, 176-188.

Feldman, D. (1986). *Nature's gambit: Child prodigies and the development of human potential*. New York: Basic Books.

Fox, L. H. (1974). A mathematics program for fostering precocious achievement. In J. Stanley, D. Keating, & L. Fox (Eds.), *Mathematical talent: Discovery, description and development* (pp. 101-125). Baltimore: Johns Hopkins University Press.

Freud, S. (1938). *The basic writings of Sigmund Freud*. (L. Brill, Ed. & Trans.). New York: Random House.

Galton, F. (1976). Genius as inherited. In A. Rothenberg & C. Hausman (Eds.), *The creativity question* (pp. 42-47). Durham, NC: Duke University Press. (Original work published 1869)

Gardner, H. (1982). *Art, mind, & brain: A cognitive approach to creativity*. New York: Basic Books.

Getzels, J. W., & Csikszentmihalyi, M. (1976). *The creative vision*. New York: Wiley.

Ghiselin, B. (Ed.). (1952). *The creative process*. New York: Mentor.

Gilligan, C. (1990, April). *Invited address*. Paper presented at the meeting of the American Educational Research Association, Boston.

Gilligan, C., Lyons, N., & Hanmer, T. (Eds.). (1990). *Making connections: The relational worlds of adolescent girls at Emma Willard School*. Cambridge, MA: Harvard University Press.

Goertzel, V., & Goertzel, M. G. (1962). *Cradles of eminence*. Boston: Little, Brown.

Goertzel, M. G., Goertzel, V., & Goertzel, T. G. (1978). *Three hundred eminent personalities.* San Francisco: Jossey-Bass.

Gourley, T. J. (1981). Adapting the varsity sports model of non-psychomotor gifted students. *Gifted Child Quarterly, 25,* 164–166.

Gowan, J. (1984). Spatial ability and testosterone. *Journal of Creative Behavior, 18,* 187–190.

Guilford, J. P. (1950). Creativity. *American Psychologist, 5,* 444–454.

Guilford, J. P. (1967). *The nature of human intelligence.* New York: McGraw-Hill.

Guilford, J. P. (1977). *Way beyond the IQ.* Buffalo, NY: Creative Education Foundation; Great Neck, NY: Creative Synergetic Associates.

Halkitis, P. (1989, May/June). Gifted students break traditions. *Gifted Children Monthly,* p. 15.

Harris, L. J. (1989). Two sexes in the mind: Perceptual and creative differences between women and men. *Journal of Creative Behavior, 23,* 14–25.

Higham, S. Lynch, & Navarre, J. Piirto. (1984). Gifted adolescent females require differential treatment. *Journal for the Education of the Gifted, 8,* 43–49.

John-Steiner, V. (1985). *Notebooks of the mind: Explorations of thinking.* New York: Harper & Row.

Koestler, A. (1964). *The act of creation.* New York: Macmillan.

Lessner, W. J., & Hillman, D. (1983). A developmental schema of creativity. *Journal of Creative Behavior, 17,* 103–114.

Loeb, K. (1975, November). Our women artist/teachers need our help: On changing language, finding cultural heritage, and building self-image. *Art Education, 28,* pp. 9–11.

Lubeck, S., & Bidell, T. (1988). Creativity and cognition: A Piagetian framework. *Journal of Creative Behavior, 22,* 31–41.

MacKinnon, D. (1978). *In search of human effectiveness.* Buffalo, NY: Creative Education Foundation.

McAleer, N. (1989, April). On creativity: the roots of inspiration. *Omni,* p. 42.

Meeker, M. (1973). *Divergent production sourcebook.* Vida, OR: SOI Institute.

Miklus, S. (1989, April). Forum. *Omni,* p. 16.

Miller, A. (1990). *Unlocking the key: Tracing childhood trauma in creativity and destructiveness.* New York: Doubleday.

Mitchell, B. (1988). The latest national assessment of gifted education. *Roeper Review, 10,* 5–6.

Myers, I. (1962). *Manual: The Myers-Briggs Type Indicator.* Palo Alto, CA: Consulting Psychologists Press.

Myers, I. B., & Myers, P. B. (1980). *Gifts differing.* Palo Alto, CA: Consulting Psychologists Press.

Navarre, J. Piirto. (1979). Incubation as fostering the creative process. *Gifted Child Quarterly, 23,* 192–200.

Nochlin, L. (1988). *Women, art, and power.* New York: Harper & Row.

Ohio Department of Education. (1984). *Rule for school foundation units for gifted children.* Columbus: Author.

Osborn, A. F. (1963). *Applied imagination* (3rd ed.). New York: Scribner's.

Parnes, S. J. (1967). *Creative behavior workbook*. New York: Scribner's.

Parnes, S. J. (1981). *The magic of your mind*. Buffalo, NY: Bearly Limited.

Perkins, D. (1981). *The mind's best work*. Cambridge, MA: Harvard University Press.

Perkins, D. (1988). The possibility of invention. In R. Sternberg (Ed.), *The nature of creativity* (pp. 362–385). New York: Cambridge University Press.

Piechowski, M., & Cunningham, K. (1985). Patterns of overexcitability in a group of artists. *Journal of Creative Behavior, 19*, 153–174.

Piechowski, M., & Silverman, L. (1989). Comparison of intellectually and artistically gifted on five dimensions of mental functioning. *Mensa Research Journal, 27*, 33–41.

Piirto, J. (1989a). Does writing prodigy exist? *Creativity Research Journal, 2*, 134–135.

Piirto, J. (1989b, May/June). Linguistic prodigy: Does it exist? *Gifted Child Monthly*, pp. 1–2.

Piirto, J. (1990). Profiles of creative adolescents. *Understanding Our Gifted, 2*, 1.

Roe, A. (1964). Personal problems and science. In C. Taylor & F. Barron (Eds.), *Scientific creativity: Its recognition and development* (pp. 132–138). New York: Wiley.

Rosner, S., & Abt, L. (Eds.). (1974). *Essays in creativity*. Croton-on-Hudson, NY: North River Press.

Rothenberg, A. (1979). *The emerging goddess: The creative process in art, science, and other fields*. Chicago: University of Chicago Press.

Rothenberg, A., & Hausman, C. (Eds.). (1976). *The creativity question*. Durham, NC: Duke University Press.

Runco, M. (1987). The generality of creative performance in gifted and nongifted children. *Gifted Child Quarterly, 31*, 121–125.

Simonton, D. K. (1986). Biographical typicality, eminence and achievement styles. *Journal of Creative Behavior, 20*, 17–18.

Simonton, D. K. (1987). Genius: The lessons of historiometry. In S. Isaksen (Ed.), *Frontiers of creativity research: Beyond the basics* (pp. 66–76). Buffalo, NY: Bearly Limited.

Simonton, D. K. (1988). *Scientific genius: A psychology of science*. New York: Cambridge University Press.

Stanley, J., & Benbow, C. (1982). Using the SAT to find intellectually talented seventh graders. *College Board Review, 122*, 26–27.

Sternberg, R. (1988). *The triarchic mind: A new theory of human intelligence*. New York: Viking.

Storr, A. (1988). *Solitude: A return to the self*. New York: Free Press.

Subotnik, R. (1988). Factors from the Structure of Intellect Model associated with gifted adolescents' problem finding in science: Research with Westinghouse Science Talent Search winners. *Journal of Creative Behavior, 22*, 42–53.

Tannenbaum, A. (1983). *Gifted children: Psychological and educational perspectives*. New York: Macmillan.

Torrance, E. P. (1974). *Torrance tests of creative thinking: Norms and technical manual.* Lexington, MA: Personnel Press/Ginn-Xerox.

Torrance, E. P. (1979). *The search for satori and creativity.* Buffalo, NY: Bearly Limited.

Torrance, E. P. (1987). Teaching for creativity. In S. Isaksen (Ed.), *Frontiers of creativity research: Beyond the basics* (pp. 190–215). Buffalo, NY: Bearly Limited.

Torrance, E. P., & Goff, K. (1989). A quiet revolution. *Journal of Creative Behavior, 23,* 112–118.

Torrance, E. P., & Myers, R. E. (1970). *Creative learning and teaching.* New York: Dodd-Mead.

Torrance, E. P., & Safter, H. T. (1989). The long range predictive validity of the Just Suppose Test. *Journal of Creative Behavior, 23,* 219–223.

Walberg, H. (1988). Creativity and talent in learning. In R. Sternberg (Ed.), *The nature of creativity* (pp. 340–361). New York: Cambridge University Press.

Wallace, T., & Walberg, H. (1987). Personality traits and childhood environments of eminent essayists. *Gifted Child Quarterly, 31,* 65–69.

Wallas, G. (1926). *The art of thought.* London: C. A. Watts.

Weisberg, R. (1986). *Creativity: Genius and other myths.* New York: W. H. Freeman.

Weisberg, R. (1988). Problem solving and creativity. In R. Sternberg (Ed.), *The nature of creativity* (pp. 148–176). New York: Cambridge University Press.

Willings, D. (1980). *The creatively gifted: Recognizing and developing the creative personality.* Cambridge: Woodhead-Faulkner.

CHAPTER 9

Leadership and Gifted Adolescents

Frances A. Karnes
Suzanne Meriweather-Bean

The challenge of understanding the development of leadership is critical. Leadership is a term that has been in use for fewer than 200 years, but the root word *leader* has been in the literature for more than 6 centuries.

Leadership is sometimes attributed to genetic traits, social or situational conditions, and/or knowledge and skills acquisition. Although ambiguity surrounds the definition and process of developing leaders, the need for more effective leaders is manifest in every level, region, and segment of our society (DeHaan, 1962).

The contemporary expression of a "lack of leadership" signals the importance of the potential for a crisis of leadership to occur, resulting in feelings of aimlessness and purposelessness in society (Hollander & Julian, 1984). Society calls for the intelligence, creativity, and critical judgment of gifted people in almost every aspect of our lives. To maintain and advance our human existence and to face the challenge of the problems of society, gifted persons must be appropriately identified and developed in ways that will ensure their filling the leadership gap (Passow, 1977).

Although leadership has been distinguished as one of the categories of giftedness in definitions sponsored by both federal and state efforts, it remains the least articulated of the curricular areas for gifted students (Foster, 1981). The paucity of investigative studies regarding the development of leadership in gifted young people indicates a need for more attention to this particular field of study.

OVERVIEW OF LEADERSHIP

Definitions of Leadership

Definitional confusion continues to besiege the study of leadership. As many as 130 definitions of leadership can be found in the literature

122

(Foster, 1981). They have evolved from a simplistic, innate-trait definition to a more complex, person-process-situation interactive interpretation.

Leadership has been depicted as a dichotomous concept. Leaders have been categorized as autocratic versus democratic (Lewin & Lippitt, 1938), directive versus participative (Bass & Barrett, 1981), task-oriented versus relations-oriented (Fiedler, 1967), "Theory X" coercive versus "Theory Y" ideologists (McGregor, 1960), and concerned with production versus concerned with people (Blake & Mouton, 1964). Another dichotomy of leadership is that of the active versus the reflective leader. An active leader is one who exerts influence over the group through the force of his or her personality. Politicians or leaders of community service groups are examples of active leaders. A reflective leader is one who is influential through the force of his or her ideas. Aristotle and Einstein are examples of reflective leaders (Addison, 1985).

Gardner (1987) referred to leadership as the process of persuasion and example by which an individual induces a group to take action that is in agreement with the leader's purposes or the shared purposes of all. Most recently, Barr and Barr (1989) proposed this definition of a leader:

> A leader sees the vision, communicates its possibilities, believes in its achievement, inspires others to contribute their best, motivates others to want to belong, stretches and pushes people, and demonstrates the confidence of victorious achievement of the vision. (p. 21)

Theories of Leadership

Schriesheim, Tolliver, and Behling (1984) suggested that theories or models of leadership have moved through distinct phases. Early approaches to leadership from the pre-Christian era to the late 1940s emphasized the examination of leader characteristics in an attempt to identify a set of universal characteristics that would be descriptive of leaders in all situations. Several early researchers (Mumford, 1909; Murphy, 1941; Person, 1928) advanced theories that explained the emergence of a great leader as a result of time, place, and circumstance.

Research from the late 1940s to the early 1960s moved away from trait and environmental theories to investigations of the relationship between leaders' behaviors and subordinates' satisfaction and performance (Jacobs, 1970). Researchers began to move toward a situational treatment of leadership. This approach examines the relationship among leader and subordinate behaviors or characteristics and the situation in which leaders and subordinates find themselves (Blake & Mouton, 1985; Hersey &

Blanchard, 1982; Vroom & Yetton, 1974). The comprehensive works of Stogdill (1974) and Bass (1981) demonstrate that leadership effectiveness is highly dependent on the relationship between leader characteristics and the demands of particular situations.

Currently, researchers are examining the transformational and transactional models of leadership (Bass, 1985). The two models differ with regard to the process by which the leader motivates subordinates, as well as in the types of goals set. Transformational leaders are purported to be responsible for performance beyond ordinary expectations as they transmit a sense of mission, stimulate learning experiences, and encourage new ways of thinking. In contrast, transactional leaders achieve performance as merely required by the use of contingent rewards or negative feedback. Transactional leaders who wish to increase their subordinates' productivity will do so by initiating changes in the structure of the workplace or by instituting merit pay. Money, rather than sense of mission or innovation, drives the relationship of transactional leaders and their workforce.

GIFTEDNESS AND LEADERSHIP

Terman's (1925) classic study of the gifted concluded that gifted students were likely to be leaders in school. In Stogdill's (1948) early review of 30 studies that investigated the relationship between leadership and intelligence, he cited the findings of Hollingworth (1926), which pointed out that leadership was inhibited by extreme discrepancies between the intelligence of leaders and that of the group. Hollingworth found that among a group of children with average intelligence, the IQ of the leaders was likely to fall between 115 and 130. A child with a high IQ, such as 160, would have problems assuming a leadership position in this type of group, but might function as a leader of a group with a mean IQ of 130.

Schakel (1984) conducted a study to determine the differences between the leadership profiles of intellectually gifted and nongifted students. A series of self-report instruments were administered to 136 gifted and nongifted students in grades 9 through 12. The results were that in comparison with nongifted students, gifted students were intuitive rather than sensing, more abstract in their learning, less directing, less desirous of being controlled by others, less likely to include others, more delegating, more desirous of affection, and less likely to express affection. Schakel hypothesized that these differences indicated that gifted students could be characterized as visionary leaders, while nongifted students appeared to be organizational leaders.

Unique parallels exist between the definitions of giftedness and leadership. Both areas are moving toward a broader, more dynamic definition that takes into account cultural and situational factors. The identification and assessment procedures for both giftedness and leadership have expanded to reflect the complexity and multidimensionality of the concepts.

Identification and Characteristics of Leadership Potential

Leadership has undergone and will continue to undergo many transformations. However, the perplexing tasks of identifying leaders and determining the components of effective leadership remain with us. The social utility of gifted education is to provide society with highly trained leaders. Leaders in medicine, technology, education, business and industry, politics, and the arts are thought most likely to emerge from among the ranks of the gifted (Howley, Howley, & Pendarvis, 1986). The role of the school in assisting the larger society in the development of attitudes, concepts, and skills in our gifted youth must go beyond educating them toward followship. The school must include an understanding of the fundamentals of leadership as well as the identification and acquisition of special attitudes and skills necessary for leadership in the young people who are disposed toward seeking and accepting such a level of social involvement and responsibility (Foster & Silverman, 1988).

Education toward leadership is probably the most controversial of all the components of gifted education (Lindsay, 1988). Florey and Dorf (1986) stated that few gifted programs identify students with high leadership potential or incorporate leadership concepts and skills into their present gifted curricula. However, many characteristics of gifted adolescents enable them to profit maximally from leadership development. Most gifted adolescents are thought to be mature enough to internalize their experiences and young enough to be open-minded and curious (Black, 1984). This may be the optimal period of life for identifying and nurturing leadership potential.

Leadership characteristics of gifted adolescents include the desire to be challenged, creative problem-solving ability, critical reasoning ability, initiative, persistence, sensitivity, self-sufficiency, the ability to tolerate ambiguity, the ability to see new relationships, and enthusiasm (Black, 1984; Chauvin & Karnes, 1983; Plowman, 1981).

A multidimensional approach to identifying student leadership potential based on a sound leadership definition and theory is preferred. Conradie (1984) suggested that leadership potential should be identified early so that it can be channeled in a positive direction. He further stated that the identification process should be continuous because often, as children develop, hidden social potential emerges. Olivero (1977) offered three methods for identifying student leadership potential. He proposed parents as excellent identifiers of leadership potential for young students, sociometric devices for early adolescent students, and personality and self-esteem inventories for upper secondary level students.

Addison (1985) and Sisk (1984) reported various methods as useful in identifying student leadership potential. Their composite suggestions included nomination and/or rating by peers, teachers, self, or community group members (i.e., scout, church, or 4–H group leaders); observation of simulation activities; biographical information on past leadership experiences; interviews; personality tests; and leadership styles instruments that may be interpreted to give leadership profiles and behaviorally oriented measurements of leadership.

A study conducted by Friedman, Friedman, and Van Dyke (1984) found that while self-nominations were the single best method for identifying students with leadership potential, no one method of identifying leadership giftedness was found to be empirically superior. Multiple sources of information are needed for identifying gifted adolescents with leadership potential.

Screening and Identification Instruments

The status of screening and identification instruments in the area of leadership can be described as limited and at the infancy stage. Very few measures with standardization data have been reported as available to school personnel. Two instruments that do have standardization benefits are rating scales: the Leadership Characteristics (Part IV) of the Scales for Rating Behavioral Characteristics of Superior Students (SRBCSS) (Renzulli, Smith, White, Callahan, & Hartman, 1976) and the Roets Rating Scale for Leadership (Roets, 1986a). The Eby Gifted Behavior Index (Eby, 1989), although commercially available, has no standardization data on the social/leadership scale. The High School Personality Questionnaire (Cattell, Cattell, & Johns, 1984), the Myers-Briggs Type Indicator (Myers & McCaulley, 1985), and the Murphy-Meisgeier Type Indicator for Children (Meisgeier & Murphy, 1987) have been standardized and may be used for screening and identification.

The SRBCSS (Renzulli et al., 1976) was designed to assist teachers in their nominations of gifted and talented students for specialized programs. The instrument consists of four rating scales: learning, motivation, creativity, and leadership. The items, based on observable characteristics, were derived from a review of the literature in each of the four areas. A criterion accepted early in the development process was that at least three separate studies had to have specified the importance of a specific characteristic in order for it to be included in the instrument.

The field testing of the first experimental edition of the rating scales was undertaken in a variety of school districts offering programs for gifted and talented youth. Counselors, teachers, and other school personnel were asked to offer suggestions, many of which were incorporated.

The Roets Rating Scale for Leadership (Roets, 1986a) was designed as a self-rating instrument for students in grades 5–12 and aged approximately 10–18. The 26-item scale contains statements pertaining to the ability of the student to be self-directed, to assume responsibility, and to exhibit other characteristics of leadership. An investigation of the reliability of this scale with the Leadership Characteristics of the SRBCSS indicated a correlation of $R = .55$.

The Eby Gifted Behavior Index (Eby, 1989) contains six checklists to identify the behavioral processes of elementary and secondary school gifted youngsters in six different talent fields: verbal, math/science/problem solving, musical, visual spatial, social/leadership, and mechanical/technical/inventiveness. In addition, Eby offers a seventh scale developed to provide criteria for the rating of original products developed by students. The teacher, through the use of the Social/Leadership Checklist and a five-point, Likert-type rating format, may rate students on 20 items across the following areas: perceptiveness, active interaction with the environment, reflectiveness, persistence, independence, goal orientation, originality, productivity, self-evaluation, and the effective communication of ideas. No validity and reliability studies for this checklist are reported in the accompanying manual.

The High School Personality Questionnaire (HSPQ) (Cattell et al., 1984) renders a Leadership Potential Score. The HSPQ assesses 14 bipolar traits of personality: warmth, intelligence, emotional stability, excitability, dominance, enthusiasm, conformity, boldness, sensitivity, withdrawal, apprehension, self-sufficiency, self-discipline, and tension. The questionnaire was designed and standardized to be a self-rating instrument for students ranging in age from 12 to 18. It may be given individually or in groups. Numerous studies attesting to the validity and reliability of the instrument with a variety of adolescent samples are described in the manual (Cattell, Cattell, & Johns, 1984).

The Leadership Potential Score (LPS) is predicted from the HSPQ by an equation derived empirically by combining scores on the 14 primary scales using a specific formula (Johns, 1984). The LPS has been employed in several studies with intellectually gifted, creative, and leadership students (Karnes, Chauvin, & Trant, 1984, 1985; Karnes & D'Ilio, 1989b). The mean scores of the subjects in each study were above those of the norming group.

The Myers-Briggs Type Indicator (MBTI) (Myers & McCaulley, 1985) provides psychological type information based on Carl Jung's theory of observable differences in mental functioning. According to Myers and McCaulley (1985), people create their "type" through the exercise of their individual preferences. Type theory provides a model for understanding the nature of difference among leaders (McCaulley et al., 1990). A complete description of this scale can be found in Chapter 13 of this book.

The Murphy-Meisgeier Type Indicator for Children (MMTIC) (Meisgeier & Murphy, 1987) was also developed based on Jung's theory of psychological type. This 70-item instrument for students in grades 2–8 was designed to measure the same preference scales as the MBTI. A further discussion of this test can be found in Chapter 13.

Current Research

The majority of research related to leadership focuses on adults. However, studies on leadership as it relates to gifted adolescents have increased over the last decade.

Karnes, Chauvin, and Trant (1984) conducted a study using the High School Personality Questionnaire with 199 students attending a self-contained high school for the intellectually gifted. While the HSPQ failed to discriminate between those individuals who held an "elected" leadership position and those who did not, elected leaders tended to be more tenderminded (i.e., sensitive, overprotected, intuitive), tense, driven, group dependent, and conscientious than the nonelected group.

Additionally, females scored significantly higher than males on excitability, and males scored significantly higher than females on sensitivity (Karnes, Chauvin, & Trant, 1984). Another study of 95 student leaders with the HSPQ conducted by Karnes and D'Ilio (1989b) revealed that females scored significantly higher than males on emotional stability, dominance, and independence. The Leadership Potential Score did not differentiate between males and females who scored in the high average range.

Several studies indicated that participation in extracurricular/community activities provides unique opportunities for students to belong and contribute to a group as well as to experience success (Bass, 1981; Bennett, 1986; McNamara, Haensley, Lupkowski, & Edlind, 1985; Stogdill, 1974). These studies suggested that extracurricular activities may be more highly correlated with adult leadership than is academic achievement.

Recent studies have shown that psychological type can be a good predictor of leadership style and behavior (Barr & Barr, 1989; Campbell & Velsor, 1985; Lawrence, 1982; McCaulley et al., 1990; Myers & Myers, 1980). Alvino (1989) reviewed data collected with the Myers-Briggs Type Indicator on gifted students and young adults. His analysis revealed that high school student leaders who were not necessarily designated as gifted fell predominantly into a group that could be described as analytical managers of facts and details, practical organizers, imaginative harmonizers of people, and warmly enthusiastic planners of change. Leaders in student government activities fell predominantly into a group that could be described as independent, enthusiastic, intuitive, aggressive, and innovative. (See Chapter 13 for descriptions of the instrument.) These psychological types found among subpopulations of gifted students and student leaders parallel the psychological types found among adults in leadership positions.

A study conducted by Meriweather (1989), involving 176 intellectually gifted students in grades 6–8, examined the relationship between leadership potential and the variables of birth order, elected leadership position(s), gender, grade level, participation in extracurricular activities, the dimensions of psychological type, and a teacher rating of leadership characteristics. A significant relationship was found between the combined group of variables and the leadership potential of the gifted students in this study. Each of the variables of the extroversion/introversion, the thinking/feeling, and the judging/perceiving dimensions of psychological type was found to have the independent power to significantly discriminate between students with high and nonhigh leadership potential, while the other variables did not discriminate between these two groups.

The sex-role stereotyping concepts of leadership positions of intellectually gifted students in grades 4–6 and of student leaders in grades 6–11 have been studied (Karnes & D'Ilio, 1989a). In both groups, boys held more traditional stereotypical views than girls. The girls perceived most of the leadership roles to be suitable for either sex, while the boys were more traditional in their views in over half of the leadership roles. The implications of both studies need to be examined by parents and teachers.

Karnes and D'Ilio (1989c) investigated the perceptions of the home environment of student leaders and those of their parents and found that the two groups view the interactions within the family in different ways. The major differences were that the student leaders rated the dimensions of independence, intellectual/cultural orientation (involvement in intellectual/cultural activities), and expressiveness (family communication) significantly lower than their parents did. Recommendations from the study stressed the importance of discussing these differences and the reasons for them, and developing a variety of activities within the home to enhance and extend the leadership potential of student leaders.

LEADERSHIP PROGRAMS AND CURRICULA

Leadership Instructional Programs and Materials

Programs and materials available in the area of youth leadership development are somewhat limited. However, new instructional aids are currently being developed in this area. Demonstration programs for training young leaders are also being designed and implemented. This section includes a brief description of existing programs and materials.

The Leadership Skills Development Program (Karnes & Chauvin, 1985a, 1985b) emphasizes the acquisition and application of the necessary leadership concepts and skills based on those identified as necessary to function as an adult leader in society. The major components of the diagnostic/prescriptive program are the Leadership Skills Inventory (LSI), the Leadership Skills Inventory Profile Sheet, and the *Leadership Skills Inventory Activities Manual.* The LSI consists of nine subscales: Fundamentals of Leadership, Written Communication, Speech Communication, Values Clarification, Decision Making, Group Dynamics, Problem Solving, Personal Development, and Planning. It was standardized on eight samples of students in grades 4 through junior college in seven states. The process used to determine content validity is reported in the manual (Karnes & Chauvin, 1985a), along with internal consistency reliability data using the Spearman-Brown formula (.80–.93) and the Kuder-Richardson formula (.78–.90) for each of the individual samples and for the total sample. Criterion and content validity studies have been conducted (Karnes & D'Ilio, 1988a, 1988b).

The students are administered the LSI, which is a self-rating and self-scoring instrument, upon entering the program. After they complete the inventory, the students plot their scores on the Leadership Studies Inventory Profile Sheet, which graphically depicts their strengths and weaknesses in leadership concepts and skills on the nine subscales. The students immediately know the concepts and skills that have been acquired and those in need of strengthening. This information provides the teacher with the data needed to assist the students in planning the appropriate instructional activities. For every item on the LSI, the *Leadership Skills Inventory Activities Manual* (Karnes & Chauvin, 1985a) provides one or more instructional strategies. It is not necessary for the teacher to incorporate all the activities in the manual, but only those, based on the student's self-perceived strengths and weaknesses, that will provide the improvement necessary to become an effective leader. The activities are student centered rather than completely teacher directed. Many of the strategies utilize group discussions and simulations as the primary vehicle for learning.

Crucial to the program is the application of the acquired leadership concepts and skills, which is facilitated through developing and executing a "Plan for Leadership." After the completion of the instructional component of the program, each student is asked to identify an area of need or change in his or her school, community, or religious affiliation. The plan should focus on an area in which the student may initiate something new or change an already existing situation. The plan must have two major purposes: (1) to bring about desirable changes in the behavior of otders, and (2) to solve a major problem or effect major improvements. It should be realistic, within the scope of the student's capabilities, and well sequenced and comprehensive. Components of the plan include a statement as to the overall goal, with accompanying objectives, activities, resources, timelines, and methods for evaluation. The plan developed by each student is presented in class for peer review. Karnes and Meriweather (1989) present the types of plans prepared by male and female students, the numbers of plans developed during each year of the program, and an example of a completed plan.

The LSI instrument and materials form the basis of the Leadership Studies Program, a one-week summer residential experience, which has been validated (Karnes, Meriweather, & D'Ilio, 1987). Statistical analysis of the data collected in the program indicates that pre/post assessment gains are significant ($p = .01$) (Karnes, Meriweather, & D'Ilio, 1987). Additional support for the program is given by the students and their parents, and by leaders of the community and university who have assisted with various aspects of it.

The program has direct application for public, private, and parochial schools. After a careful analysis of all the program components, including the nine instructional areas necessary for being a leader and the plan for leadership, teachers and administrative decision makers can readily select the format of the program appropriate for their school. The program may be conducted as a separate class at the junior or senior high school level or as an ongoing component of a resource or pullout enrichment program, or the appropriate components may be included in English, speech, social studies, and other academic courses. Whatever the administrative arrangement, students should be given the opportunity to prepare and implement a plan for leadership development. Appropriate and supportive mentorship and internship provisions for leadership growth should be made readily available to students.

While space limitations do not permit a comprehensive discussion of each, several other leadership programs exist. Gallagher (1982) orchestrated the development of a curriculum unit on leadership for upper elementary and junior high school gifted youth by bringing together teachers of the gifted and content specialists who designed lessons to illustrate particular leadership concepts. The resulting products focus on three types of leaders: traditional, legal-rational, and charismatic. Included in the materials are reproducibles for student use, an annotated bibliography, and evaluation forms for parents and students.

Roets (1986b) developed an instructional program for students, ages 8–18, entitled Leadership: A Skills Training Program. Instructional activities center around the themes of people of achievement, language of leadership, project planning, and debate and discussion. Suggested readings are included for both young people and adults.

Twenty-five strategies for developing leadership have been developed by Magoon and Jellen (1980) for the expressed purpose of assisting future leaders to develop skills for leading and understanding why it is better to lead than to "boss." A discussion checklist for committee work, a group observation scale, and a listing of references are included.

Several books have been published which contain instructional activities for leadership training (Richardson & Feldhusen, 1987; Sisk & Rosselli, 1987; Sisk & Shallcross, 1986). *Leadership Education: Developing Skills for Youth* (Richardson & Feldhusen, 1987) evolved from earlier work by Feldhusen, Hynes, and Richardson (1977). The eleven chapters provide discussions and activities of such components of leadership as communication, parliamentary procedure, and developing group goals. Field testing with both vocational/technical students (Hynes, Feldhusen, & Richardson, 1978) and summer leadership programs (Feldhusen & Kennedy, 1986) elicited favorable evaluation results.

Sisk and Shallcross (1986) consider their book, *Leadership: Making Things Happen*, to be a practical guide to help clarify the meaning of leadership. The ten chapters address such topics as self-understanding, intuitive powers, communication, futuristics, women in leadership positions, and learning styles. Sisk and Rosselli (1987) developed *Leadership: A Special Kind of Giftedness* for the purpose of assisting in the understanding of the concepts of leadership and in applying current theories to personal lives and teaching. The five parts of the book focus on definitions, theories, a model for planning and developing leadership training activities, a summary of teaching/learning models, and a discussion of current issues and trends on this topic. Twenty lessons and a self-rating leadership skills and behavior scale are provided, although no standardization data are given for the latter.

Finally, Parker (1983) developed a Leadership Training Model which includes the components of cognition, interpersonal communication, problem solving, and decision making. Recently, Parker (1989) offered several activities for each of the components of this currently unvalidated model.

One can readily see that, while individual variations exist, these programs generally include information on leaders and leadership, problem solving, communication skills, planning, and decision making.

Incorporating Leadership Concepts and Skills into the Curriculum

Without emphasis on leadership development or special effort on the part of parents, school personnel, and adult leaders in the community, only a few students are likely to emerge as leaders. Learning and applying the concepts and skills of leadership can be, and all too frequently are, accepted and treated as an outcome incidental to the total educational experience. This is a goal of such critical importance to the individual and to society that it should be made central in the school and deliberate efforts to achieve it should be made throughout the educational enterprise.

Immediate responses to questions raised about what the school is doing to promote and provide opportunities for leadership development are likely to include references to such options as student government, club and class officers, and athletic teams. While these traditional experiences are helpful to the selected few, a broader-based curriculum should be considered.

There are several strategies that strengthen the education and broaden the experience gifted youngsters obtain in preparation for leadership roles. Scope and sequences of instructional units on leadership development should be provided at each grade level in resource rooms for the gifted. Secondary schools should offer structured courses on leadership for which credit is granted. The student, with the help of a guiding adult, may devise a personal plan for leadership development, including provisions for obtaining the experiences set forth in the plan. Students can present and share individual plans during conference sessions arranged for that purpose, revise plans if the critique brings forth acceptable suggestions, and then report back to peers on progress made after following the plan for an extended period of time.

One feasible alternative to offering special-credit courses is to give leadership development a strong emphasis throughout the school program and to plan activities, present opportunities for experience, and provide an environment in all phases of school life for the clear purpose of enabling each student to realize his or her potential for leadership. This approach not only serves exceedingly well students of exceptionally high leadership potential, but also meets the leadership development needs of all students.

Leadership mentorships and internship programs provide opportunities for youngsters to work directly with outstanding adult leaders in the community. Teachers, administrators, and parents who join with adult leaders to make this option available go a long way to alleviate concerns about leadership in the future.

For students who are not afforded the opportunity of leadership training in school, a variety of models can be utilized outside school. Youth leadership conferences, seminars, and summer residential programs are offered through various colleges and universities, civic organizations, and businesses and industries across the nation. The *Leadership Network Newsletter*, a biannual publication of the Center for Gifted Studies at the University of Southern Mississippi, disseminates information on leadership training programs for adolescents.

SUMMARY AND FUTURE DIRECTIONS

Leadership development must be afforded much higher priority in homes, schools, and communities. More purposeful approaches to leadership development in young people are needed. Separate courses in leadership should be incorporated into existing courses across the regular school curriculum. More attention should be given to past and current leaders from a variety of domains in order to help students develop a deeper appreciation of characteristics and skills necessary for effective leadership in diverse situations. Internships with school or community leaders is another approach to developing leadership potential in gifted young people that should be explored.

Implementing these programs mandates training in the area of leadership for parents, educators, guidance counselors, and communities, as well as additional research on the identification of leadership potential and longitudinal studies to follow young leaders throughout their adult lives.

Learning the basic concepts and acquiring the skills of leadership will be enhanced by active participation in various leadership roles. Home and community support is vital to the development of the leadership potential of gifted students. That support is much more likely to be achieved when it is widely known that leadership development is a central emphasis in the school.

REFERENCES

Addison, L. (1985). *Leadership skills among the gifted and talented.* 1985 Digest, ERIC Clearinghouse, National Institution of Education (ERIC Document Reproduction Service No. ED 262 511).

Alvino, J. (1989). Psychological type: Implications for gifted. *Gifted Children Monthly, 10*(4), 1–2, 23.

Barr, L., & Barr, N. (1989). *The leadership equation.* Austin, TX: Eakin Press.

Bass, B.M. (1981). *Stogdill's handbook of leadership: A survey of theory and research.* New York: Free Press.

Bass, B. M. (1985). *Leadership and performance beyond expectations.* New York: Free Press.

Bass, B. M., & Barrett, G. V. (1981). *People, work, and organizations: An introduction to industrial and organizational psychology.* Boston: Allyn & Bacon.

Bennett, W. J. (1986). *What works: Research about teaching and learning.* Washington, DC: U.S. Department of Education.

Black, J. D. (1984). *Leadership: A new model particularly applicable to gifted youth.* (ERIC Document Reproduction Service No. ED 253 990).

Blake, R. R., & Mouton, J. S. (1964). *The managerial grid.* Houston: Gulf Publishing.

Blake, R. R., & Mouton, J. S. (1985). *The managerial grid III.* Houston: Gulf Publishing.

Campbell, D., & Velsor, E. V. (1985). *The use of personality measures in the leadership development program.* Greensboro, NC: Center for Creative Leadership.

Cattell, R. B., Cattell, M. D., & Johns, E. F. (1984). *Manual and norms for the High School Personality Questionnaire.* Champaign, IL: Institute for Personality and Ability Testing.

Chauvin, J. C., & Karnes, F. A. (1983). A leadership profile of secondary students. *Psychological Reports, 53,* 1259–1262.

Conradie, S. (1984). The identification of leadership potential. In J. Cawood et al. (Eds.), *Climbing the ladder to leadership: A panel discussion.* Paper presented at the international conference on education for the gifted, Ingenium 2000, Stellenbosch, South Africa. (ERIC Document Reproduction Service No. ED 292 228).

DeHaan, R. F. (1962). *A study of leadership in school age children.* Holland, MI: Hope College Press.

Eby, J. W. (1989). *Eby Gifted Behavior Index (Administration manual)*. East Aurora, NY: D.O.K.

Feldhusen, J., & Kennedy, D. (1986). Leadership training for gifted and talented youth. *Leadership Network Newsletter, 1*(2), 1–2.

Feldhusen, J. F., Hynes, K., & Richardson, W. B. (1977). Curriculum materials for vocational youth organizations. *Clearinghouse, 50*, 224–226.

Fiedler, F. E. (1967). *A theory of leadership effectiveness.* New York: McGraw-Hill.

Florey, J. E., & Dorf, J. H. (1986). *Leadership skills for gifted middle school students.* (ERIC Document Reproduction Service No. ED 273 404).

Foster, W. (1981). Leadership: A conceptual framework for recognizing and educating. *Gifted Child Quarterly, 25*(1), 17–25.

Foster, W. H., & Silverman, L. (1988). Leadership curriculum for the gifted. In J. VanTassel-Baska, J. Feldhusen, K. Seeley, G. Wheatley, L. Silverman, & W. Foster (Eds.), *Comprehensive curriculum for gifted learners* (pp. 356–360). Boston: Allyn & Bacon.

Friedman, P. G., Friedman, R. J., & Van Dyke, M. (1984). Identifying the leadership gifted: Self, peer, or teacher nominations. *Roeper Review, 7*(2), 91–94.

Gallagher, J. J. (1982). *A leadership unit.* New York: Trillium Press.

Gardner, J. (1987). Leadership. In M. B. Clark (Ed.), *The cultivation of leadership: Roles, methods, and responsibilities.* Greensboro, NC: Center for Creative Leadership.

Hersey, P., & Blanchard, K. H. (1982). Leadership style: Attitudes and behaviors. *Training and Development Journal, 36*(5), 50–52.

Hollander, E. P., & Julian, J. W. (1984). Contemporary trends in the analysis of leadership process. *Psychological Bulletin, 71*, 387–397.

Hollingworth, L. S. (1926). *Gifted children: Their nature and nurture.* New York: Macmillan.

Howley, A., Howley, C. B., & Pendarvis, E. D. (1986). *Teaching gifted children: Principles and strategies.* Boston: Little, Brown.

Hynes, F., Feldhusen, J. F., & Richardson, W. B. (1978). Application of a three-stage model of instruction to youth leadership training. *Journal of Applied Psychology, 63*, 623–628.

Jacobs, T. O. (1970). *Leadership and exchange in formal organizations.* Alexandria, VA: Human Resources Research Organization.

Johns, E. F. (1984). The relationship of personality and achievement to creativity and leadership behaviors. In R. B. Cattell, M. D. Cattell, and E. F. Johns (Eds.), *Manual and norms for the High School Personality Questionnaire.* Champaign, IL: Institute for Personality and Ability Testing.

Karnes, F. A., & Chauvin, J. C. (1985a). *Leadership Skills Inventory Activities manual.* East Aurora, NY: D.O.K.

Karnes, F. A., & Chauvin, J. C. (1985b). *Leadership Skills Inventory.* East Aurora, NY: D.O.K.

Karnes, F. A., Chauvin, J. C., & Trant, T. J. (1984). Leadership profiles as determined by the HSPQ of students identified as intellectually gifted. *Roeper Review, 7*(1), 46–48.

Karnes, F. A., Chauvin, J. C., & Trant, T. J. (1985). Validity of the leadership potential score of the High School Personality Questionnaire with talented students. *Perceptual and Motor Skills, 61*, 163–166.

Karnes, F. A., & D'Ilio, V. (1988a). Assessment of criterion-related validity of the Leadership Skills Inventory. *Psychological Reports, 62*, 263–267.

Karnes, F. A., & D'Ilio, V. (1988b). Assessment of concurrent validity of the Leadership Skills Inventory with gifted students and their teachers. *Perceptual and Motor Skills, 66*, 59–62.

Karnes, F. A., & D'Ilio, V. (1989a). Leadership positions and sex role stereotyping among gifted students. *Gifted Child Quarterly, 33*(2), 76–78.

Karnes, F. A., & D'Ilio, V. (1989b). Personality characteristics of student leaders. *Psychological Reports, 64*, 1125–1126.

Karnes, F. A., & D'Ilio, V. (1989c). Student leaders' and their parents' perceptions of the home environment. *Gifted Child Quarterly, 33*(4), 165–168.

Karnes, F. A., & Meriweather, S. (1989). Developing and implementing a plan for leadership: An integral component for success as a leader. *Roeper Review, 11*(4), 214–217.

Karnes, F. A., Meriweather, S., & D'Ilio, V. (1987). The effectiveness of the Leadership Studies Program. *Roeper Review, 9*(4), 238–241.

Lawrence, G. (1982). *People types and tiger stripes: A practical guide to learning styles.* Gainesville, FL: Center for the Applications of Psychological Type.

Lewin, K., & Lippitt, R. (1938). An experimental approach to the study of autocracy and democracy: A preliminary note. *Sociometry, 1*, 292–300.

Lindsay, B. (1988). A lamp for Diogenes: Leadership giftedness and moral education. *Roeper Review, 1*(1), 8–11.

Magoon, R. A., & Jellen, H. G. (1980). *Leadership development: Democracy in action.* Poquoson, VA: Human Development Press.

McCaulley, M. H., & the Staff of the Center for Applications of Psychological Type. (1990). The Myers-Briggs Type Indicator and leadership. In K. E. Clark & M. B. Clark (Eds.), *Measures of Leadership.* New York: Center for Creative Leadership.

McGregor, D. (1960). *The human side of enterprise.* New York: McGraw-Hill.

McNamara, J. F., Haensly, P. A., Lupkowski, A. E., & Edlind, E. P. (1985). *The role of extracurricular activities in high school education.* Paper presented at the annual convention of the National Association for Gifted Children, Denver, CO. (Report prepared at the Gifted and Talented Institute, Texas A & M University, College Station, TX.)

Meisgeier, C., & Murphy, E. (1987). *Murphy-Meisgeier Type Indicator for Children.* Palo Alto, CA: Consulting Psychologists Press.

Meriweather, S. (1989). *A study of leadership potential in middle school gifted students.* Unpublished doctoral dissertation, University of Southern Mississippi, Hattiesburg.

Mumford, E. (1909). *The origins of leadership.* Chicago: University of Chicago Press.

Murphy, A. J. (1941). A study of the leadership process. *American Sociological Review, 6*, 674–687.

Myers, I. B., & McCaulley, M. (1985). *Manual: A guide to the development and use of the Myers-Briggs Type Indicator.* Palo Alto, CA: Consulting Psychologists Press.

Myers, I. B., & Myers, P. B. (1980). *Gifts differing.* Palo Alto, CA: Consulting Psychologists Press.

Olivero, J. L. (1977). Leading leaders. In A. H. Passow (Ed.), *A new generation of leadership.* Ventura, CA: Ventura County Superintendent of Schools.

Parker, J. P. (1983). The Leadership Training Model: Integrated curriculum for the gifted. *G/C/T*, pp. 8–13.

Parker, J. P. (1989). *Instructional strategies for teaching the gifted.* Boston: Allyn & Bacon.

Passow, A. H. (Ed.). (1977). *A new generation of leadership.* Ventura, CA: Ventura County Superintendent of Schools.

Person, H. S. (1928). Leadership as a response to environment. *Education Records Supplement No. 6, 9*, 10–21.

Plowman, P. D. (1981). Training extraordinary leaders. *Roeper Review, 3*, 13–16.

Renzulli, J. S., Smith, F. H., White, A. J., Callahan, C. M., & Hartman, R. K. (1976). *Scales for Rating the Behavioral Characteristics of Superior Students* (SRBCSS). Wethersfield, CT: Creative Learning Press.

Richardson, W. B., & Feldhusen, J. F. (1987). *Leadership education: Developing skills for youth.* New York: Trillium.

Roets, L. (1986a). *Roets Rating Scale for Leadership.* Des Moines, IA: Leadership Publishers.

Roets, L. S. (1986b). *Leadership—A Skills Training Program.* New Sharon, IA: Leadership Publications.

Schakel, L. (1984). *Investigation of the leadership abilities of intellectually gifted students.* Unpublished dissertation, University of South Florida, Tampa.

Schriesheim, C. A., Tolliver, J. M., & Behling, O. C. (1984). Leadership theory: Some implications for managers. In W. E. Rosenbach & R. L. Taylor (Eds.), *Contemporary issues in leadership.* Boulder, CO: Westview Press.

Sisk, D. A. (1984). Leadership as it relates to gifted education. *Gifted International, 2*(2), 130–148.

Sisk, D. A., & Rosselli, H. C. (1987). *Leadership: A special kind of giftedness.* New York: Trillium.

Sisk, D. A., & Shallcross, D. J. (1986). *Leadership: Making things happen.* Buffalo, NY: Bearly Limited.

Stogdill, R. M. (1948). Personal factors associated with leadership: A survey of the literature. *Journal of Psychology, 25*, 35–71.

Stogdill, R. M. (1974). *Handbook of leadership.* New York: Free Press.

Terman, L. M. (1925). *Genetic study of genius: Vol. 1. Mental and physical traits of a thousand gifted children.* Stanford: Stanford University Press.

Vroom, V., & Yetton, P. W. (1974). *Leadership and decision-making.* New York: Wiley.

CHAPTER 10

Patterns of Underachievement Among Gifted Students

E. Susanne Richert

> In every cry of every man,
> In every infant's cry of fear,
> In every voice in every ban,
> The mind-forg'd manacles I hear.
> > William Blake, *London* (1794/1968)

A review of research reveals five major issues in defining underachievement among gifted students:

1. *Confusion about the definition of underachievement.* As Dowdall and Colangelo (1982) have pointed out, definitions of underachievement vary and conflict. Most definitions of underachievement among the gifted do have the common factor of assuming that there is a discrepancy between potential ability and demonstrated achievement.
2. *Confusion about what constitutes gifted potential.* In the literature on gifted underachievers, potential is defined in a variety of ways, but most often it is related to IQ. Almost invariably, underachievement is defined in terms of *academic* achievement and is measured either by a standardized achievement test, grades, or meeting specific teacher expectations.
3. *Absence of clear distinctions between academic and gifted achievement.* Repeated studies (Hoyt, 1965; Taylor, Albo, Holland, & Brandt, 1985) have revealed no correlation, or sometimes even a small negative correlation, between academic achievement (good grades) and adult giftedness in a wide range of fields. This makes it clear that half of gifted adults were high achievers in school—and half were not. Giftedness, or original contribution to a field, requires *nonacademic* abilities unrelated or even inversely related to school achievement, such as creativity, risk taking, and intrinsic motivation. Many of the evaluation criteria for determining grades—such as propensity for convergent thinking, conformity to expectations of teachers or test makers, meeting externally determined deadlines, paper and pencil evaluation—may well be in-

versely correlated with adult eminence or original contributions in virtually all fields. Therefore, research does not support either the use of
academic achievement to measure *gifted* underachievement, or the use
of academic underachievement to predict giftedness in adults. These are
my conclusions, but the debate on this issue is far from over.

4. *Underestimation of the amount and degree of underachievement
   among students with gifted potential.* At least 50% of students identified through IQ have been designated as academic underachievers
   (Gowan, 1957; National Commission on Excellence in Education,
   1984; Raph, Goldberg, & Passow, 1966; Terman & Oden, 1947). Yet the
   50% figure does not include underachievement among students who
   were *not* identified because IQ was used.

5. *Development of counterproductive curriculum objectives for gifted
   underachievers.* There exists confusion between definitions of gifted
   and academic underachievement. It is highly questionable whether
   the goal for "underachieving" gifted students *should* be primarily
   academic achievement and higher standardized test scores. The bias
   that drives such goals has been the pervasive myth that academic
   achievement is always the path to adult giftedness.

DEFINING MAXIMUM GIFTED POTENTIAL

Aspects of Gifted Potential

Gifted potential is not a single-dimensional intellectual phenomenon,
but a complex ability that emerges from the interaction of innate potential, learning, and experience. As Hollingworth (1926), Renzulli (1978),
Tannenbaum (1983), Terman and Oden (1947), and I (Richert, 1982a),
along with many others, have stated, nonintellectual factors are necessary
variables in gifted achievement, for which I will use the operational
definition, *original contribution to a field.*

Figure 10.1 is a schematic depicting the four aspects of gifted potential
necessary for the manifestation of giftedness, or original contribution to a
field.[1] The first circle illustrates the capacities/skills necessary for the
specific kind of giftedness the individual possesses. These types of giftedness may be categorized into the seven "intelligences" defined by

---

1. Renzulli (1978) uses a three-ring schematic but does not define each of the circles,
or their interrelationship, the same way, nor does he distinguish between the manifestation
of giftedness in adults and the gifted potential evident in children, who do not necessarily
develop all the requisite abilities concurrently.

Figure 10.1 Maximum Human Potential

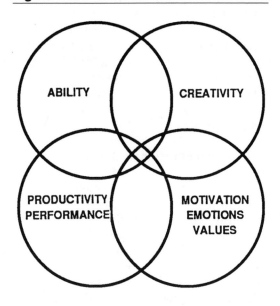

©1990 E. Susanne Richert

Gardner (1983), the three areas Sternberg uses (1985), any of the six areas in the federal definition, or any human ability (Renzulli, 1978; Richert, 1986).

The second circle refers to products or performance as the visible, concrete, or measurable manifestations of giftedness—the solution, product, or performance itself. Renzulli (1978), Tannenbaum (1983), and I as well as others (Richert, 1987, 1991; Richert, Alvino, & McDonnel, 1982) stress the importance of the application of the abilities to specific products, if only to have an observable manifestation of giftedness.

The third circle refers to the criteria for creativity that are used in any society or historical period to assess a product, performance, or solution as original. Creativity, as Torrance (1964, 1972, 1979) and Renzulli (1978), among many others, have insisted, is absolutely necessary for gifted achievement.

The fourth circle depicts the emotional and ethical components of giftedness, which provide the energy to develop an individual's potential giftedness. Without this motivation, neither high achievement nor IQ scores by themselves can guarantee that someone will make an original contribution to any field.

As Gardner (1983) and Sternberg (1985) have emphasized, there is a big difference between school- or test-measured "intelligence" and pragmatic, real-life, or gifted "intelligence." Creative artists and writers who have made the greatest breakthroughs rarely received the approval of either their teachers or the art or literary critics of their time. Yet the majority of the literature on underachieving gifted students deals only with ability as measured by tests (achievement or IQ) or productivity as assessed by indicators of academic achievement such as grades, test scores, and teacher evaluations.

Characteristics of Maximum Human Development

The diverse views of writers who represent Eastern as well as Western philosophical and psychological perspectives were analyzed to formulate a comprehensive conceptualization of the characteristics of maximum intellectual, creative, emotional, and ethical potential. Summarized in Table 10.1 are the seven salient characteristics of maximum intellectual, creative, productive, physical, emotional, ethical, and spiritual development conceptualized by these writers. These characteristics address the immediate needs and the major developmental tasks of all adolescents, particularly those with gifted potential.

Defining Underachievement
Among Students with Gifted Potential

For the purposes of helping the gifted achieve their maximum intellectual, productive, creative, emotional, and ethical potential, the three following factors should be emphasized in defining gifted underachievement:

1. Achievement among gifted students must be defined as the developing of *all* the four aspects of giftedness depicted in Figure 10.1.
2. Underachievement among gifted students must be defined as underachievement in *any* of the four areas necessary for the manifestation of giftedness.
3. Underachievement in any of the four areas of gifted potential is significant.

Since one of the primary psychological tasks of adolescence is development of self-concept and socialization, emotional, ethical, and social development should take precedence over academic achievement.

There are three major advantages to using this conceptualization of underachievement among the gifted. First, this approach provides a

Table 10.1 Survey of Salient Characteristics of Maximum Human Potential

AREA OF POTENTIAL DEVELOPMENT	Dabrowski (1967)	Frankl (1980)	Fromm (1951)	Govinda (1974)	Jung (1963, 1964)	Kohlberg (1981,1983)	Kohut (1970)	Krathwohl (1964)	Lao Tzu (1972)	Maslow (1964,1970)	Miller (1981)	Mookerjee (1982)	Muktananda (1978)	Richert (1986)	Roeper (1982)	Sartre (1967)	Torrance (1979)
INTELLECTUAL (critical thinking)	●	●		●	●	●			●	●		●	●	●	●	●	●
CREATIVE	●	●		●	●		●	●	●	●	●	●	●	●	●		●
PRODUCTIVE					●				●	●		●	●	●	●		●
PHYSICAL, SENSUAL	●			●	●				●	●		●	●	●	●		●
EMOTIONAL	●	●	●	●	●	●	●	●	●	●	●	●	●	●	●	●	●
Self-initiated productivity; intrinsic motivation	●	●	●	●	●	●	●	●	●	●	●	●	●	●	●	●	●
Self-concept accepts limitations, values strengths	●	●	●	●	●				●	●	●	●	●	●	●		●
Self-esteem independent of external judgment	●					●			●	●	●	●	●	●	●		●
Capacity for intimacy and commitment	●	●	●	●	●	●			●	●	●	●	●	●	●		●
Sense of potency/independence from external constraints (internal locus of control)	●	●		●	●	●	●		●	●	●	●	●	●	●	●	●
Risk taking to develop self or help others	●	●	●	●	●				●	●		●	●	●	●	●	●
Capacity for compassion, empathy	●	●	●	●	●			●	●	●	●	●	●	●	●		
ETHICAL	●	●	●	●		●		●	●	●	●	●	●	●	●		
Nonjudgmental, authentic relations with others	●	●	●	●	●	●	●		●	●	●	●	●	●	●	●	●
Values transcend societal norms	●	●		●		●			●	●	●		●	●	●	●	●
Acceptance of consequences of actions	●	●	●	●	●	●			●	●		●	●	●	●		
Actions based on universal ethical or transpersonal (spiritual) principles	●	●	●	●	●	●			●	●		●	●	●	●	●	●
SPIRITUAL	●	●		●	●	●			●	●		●	●	●			●

philosophical foundation that is in the best interests of both students and society. Underachievement must be defined in terms of students' intellectual, ethical, and emotional needs as opposed to evaluation criteria related primarily to academic performance.

Second, the goals and possible errors of identification that may foster underachievement are clarified. Since most identification procedures in the United States rely primarily on measures of academic performance, one of the most crucial problems of gifted underachievers is that they tend *not* to be identified or served in gifted programs and they may never learn what their potential is. The reported 30%–70% underrepresentation of minorities in gifted programs nationally makes it certain that many economically, culturally, or socially disadvantaged students who most need special programs are excluded and may therefore not develop their full potential (Richert, 1987, 1991; Richert et al., 1982). The recommendations in this chapter optimistically assume that equitable identification procedures have been used to identify the gifted, including academic underachievers of all economic and ethnic backgrounds (Richert, 1987, 1991). The goal of identification is to discover students with exceptional ability or potential in any of the four areas depicted in Figure 10.1 since they may *need* learning or experiences that an appropriate curriculum can offer to evoke potential in all four areas. When I use the term *gifted student*, I mean *students with gifted potential*.

Third, this conceptualization can also help in determining curriculum objectives for the gifted. The goal of gifted programs—for both academic achievers and academic underachievers—should be to develop potential in all four areas in Figure 10.1, and the traits listed in Table 10.1, as opposed just to raising test scores or producing teacher-pleasers who get good grades.

PATTERNS OF UNDERACHIEVEMENT AMONG THE GIFTED

Psychologist Abraham Maslow (1970) found very few people who had realized their full intellectual and emotional potential. The psychoanalytical theory of Heinz Kohut (1970) suggests that a significant factor preventing self-actualization may be the lack of "mirroring." Kohut insists that in order to develop their full potential, all children need to have others reflect their best and nonjudgmentally accept their worst. This echoes the views of the gifted poet William Blake, who two hundred years ago blamed "mind-forg'd manacles" as the prime cause of the loss of joy, energy, and creativity.

"Mind-forg'd manacles," the acceptance of externally imposed emotional or intellectual expectations, limit everyone's potential. Children, as well as their parents, are pressured to conform to what their parents, teachers, employers, neighbors, spouses, or other children expect of them. For two reasons the gifted, unfortunately, bear a heavier burden. First, the more exceptional the child, the more likely that the expectations will be inaccurate or unfair. Second, because of the prevalent myths concerning the nature of the gifted (e.g., they will always make it on their own; they are excellent students; they are agreeable and charming), formal identification in school may only serve to reinforce distorted self-concepts.

Kohut (1970) and Miller (1981) argue that expectations mold self-concept and influence use of latent cognitive, emotional, and ethical abilities. As Figure 10.2 illustrates, everyone has the choice to accept, reject, transcend, or withdraw from others' expectations, but each of these responses also exacts a distinctive price, either short or long range. None is easy, yet some are more conducive to survival and fulfillment of giftedness. The gifted pay a higher social and personal price than average people. When the gifted blindly conform to external expectations, they lose a great deal of themselves. If they deny their uniqueness, their values, and their needs, the cost is self-alienation and loss of emotional and creative energy. They have a much greater potential to lose than others, if they withdraw from expectations. However, if they overtly reject group norms, their rebellion may be so extreme as to invoke severe penalties.

The gifted—even more than the rest of society—are continually assaulted by the expectations, or mind-forg'd manacles others try to impose on them. Miller's poignant book, *Prisoners of Childhood* (1981), depicts the drama of gifted children imprisoned by their parents' narcissistic ambitions. *Money* magazine had a very powerful article and cover picture showing an adolescent impaled with arrows, representing the pressures to meet the expectations and needs of his parents' self-esteem, the desires of schools to demonstrate "successful" academic programs, and the ambitions of colleges to appear to be the most competitive (Schurenberg, 1989).

There are different patterns of underachievement among males and females (Kerr, 1985; Shaw & McCuen, 1960). While gifted boys seem to start their academic underachievement early, underachievement among gifted girls becomes more prevalent in adolescence. Twice as many males as females underachieve academically in school, but over an individual's lifetime, females as a group are the greater underachievers. Some of these gender differences will be discussed in the description of patterns of response to expectations.

Figure 10.2 Patterns of Achievement and Underachievement in Response to Expectations in Relation to Potential

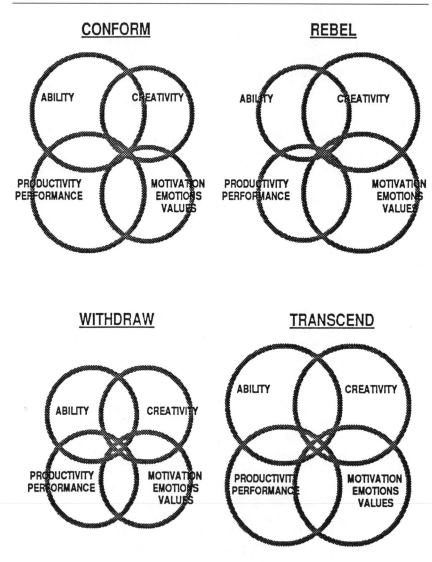

146

From my clinical experience with gifted children and adults, including underachievers, I have observed that in response to externally imposed values, they seem to develop one of four survival strategies: accepting others' expectations (conformity); withdrawal from others' expectations; rejecting the expectations of others (rebellion); or transcending others' expectations (independence). From my observations I have developed a model in which each of these strategies is suggestive of a distinctive personality style or tendency, and each fosters or hinders the development of certain aspects of self-concept, social relations, and the emotional impact of experiences. In different contexts with different degrees of demands, the same student may react differently. The more rigid the expectations, the more extreme a student's response is likely to be. Table 10.2 depicts the four possible responses to externally imposed expectations.

Conformity—The Closet Gifted Child

The very existence of norms demonstrates that for the sake of survival, most people—including the gifted—take the path of least resistance and accept what others require of them. Many gifted children *do* accept, conform, and perform. First they learn to please their parents and teachers, then their employers, spouses, and friends. The gifted child's excellent grades, intense competitiveness, and need to excel may be motivated not by confidence, but by insecurity. The unhealthy pattern of narcissism analyzed by Kohut (1970) can make children become dependent on continual external reinforcement of their worth by grades, test scores, parental praise, and friends' admiration. As adults, they can become ambitious workaholics who are never satisfied by their achievements, but continually crave another recognition of their worth: a credential, promotion, raise, publicity, or award. This is hardly surprising since our society encourages people—males in particular—to value themselves according to how many of these external narcissistic status symbols they acquire. Personal relationships of narcissists can also be based solely on expediency (Kohut, 1970; Miller, 1981).

For females in our society, pleasing others—whether teachers, parents, or friends—can become far more important than other measures of achievement. The pressures for both males and females to conform are great. The unquestioning acceptance of conventional academic standards is counseled by many parents and advisors because it offers the most immediate rewards and ostensibly the surest route to success (or yuppiedom) as defined by our culture. Conforming to social expectations is based on denial of individual values, a reluctance to accept mistakes, repression of creativity and independence, and a fear of being

Table 10.2 Patterns of Response to Expectations

Aspects of Potential	Accept		Reject	Transcend
	Conformity	*Withdrawal*	*Rebellion*	*Maximizing*
Ability Achievement Productivity	Successes satisfy others Extrinsically motivated	Safe mediocrity/ Evades pressure to perform	Failure/Rejects external expectations	Satisfies own values Intrinsically motivated
Values	Based on norms Externally dependent	Evades external judgment	Reacts against	Independent
Creativity	Repressed Fear of failure	Repressed/ Refuses to take risks	Divergent Negative	Creative Risk taker
Self-Esteem	Insecure/Dependent on others' perceptions External locus of control	Follower/Avoids competition External locus of control	Dependent/Internalizes negative external judgment External locus of control	Independent Self-accepting Internal locus of control
Social Relations	Roles that lead to rewards/Pleases others	Follower/Avoids competition	Loner or gang leader Isolated or domineering	Withdraws or takes leadership May have few friends
Emotional Impact of Experiences Vulnerability	Reinforces dependence on external rewards and approval for self-esteem	Reinforces feeling of self-dissatisfaction and fear of judgment	Punishment Betrayal Rejection	Potency: Asserts control over own life Compassion

©1990 E. Susanne Richert

unmasked or rejected. If the traits in Table 10.1 are considered, conformity is a distinctive kind of emotional and ethical underachievement, for which the term "closet" gifted seems most appropriate.

Without the development of creativity, a child can be successful—but not gifted. Yet even more serious than the repression of creativity is the emotional dependence that, in the long run, makes these children insecure and inordinately susceptible to external criticism (Kohut, 1970; Miller, 1981). Some closet gifted children—and adults—can be so devastated by what seems to be the exposure of their true worthlessness, such as getting their first C's or even B's, that they can become self-destructive.

Withdrawal from Competition

Other children accept external standards but—unlike the closet gifted—feel they cannot meet them and withdraw from competition before they can be defeated or rejected. Withdrawn gifted children fear success because it can heighten the pressure to perform. Therefore, they hedge their bets psychologically by avoiding both failure and success. They become so adept at underachievement that they perform and achieve like "average" children and are often not even identified for classes for the gifted. By consistently delivering less of themselves—both personally and academically—these children lower others' expectations so there are fewer public emotional risks.

Some boys respond in this way to external values, especially if they have an older sibling, male or female, who is very successful in school. Withdrawal, however, is probably more typically a feminine response. For females, success in terms of academic, professional, or financial achievement, which males can rely on for self-esteem, can endanger personal relationships. So if girls win in one arena they may lose in another. The value of females and males is still judged differently. Many women fear or avoid professional success because their self-esteem is based on how well they please males in general. Some females still dare not risk the approval of males who are emblems of their value, so they may settle for "safe" mediocrity. This path is the most debilitating and limiting "mind-forg'd manacle."

Rebellion

Some gifted children—frequently those whose thinking is most divergent—respond by totally rejecting any external expectation. They choose to rebel against rules or restrictions they find confining. However, the vociferous assertions of rebels are indications of dependence rather than independence. Unlike revolutionaries who object to the status quo because they want to establish a superior order, rebels are only reacting against rules or norms. Adults can mistake aggressive protests of teenagers against cleaning rooms, completing homework, or arriving at meals on time as arrogance or self-confidence rather than an insecure ploy to reject others before they are themselves rejected as inadequate.

In counseling sessions, teenage rebels in a half-way house and a youth shelter have revealed to me that while they reject rules, they still believe in the judgments others impose on them. They accept the "mind-forg'd manacles" that label them as "bad" students or children. Since they feel rejected and betrayed, they use their divergent thinking abilities to undermine authority figures and risk the punishment or failure that might result.

In school, if various expressions of creativity—wild ideas, day-dreaming, tolerance of disorder, lateness, sloppiness—are not accepted or are punished, creative children can feel rejected and respond by rebellion. To some exceptionally creative children, being a rebel can become a lifestyle with many more risks than rewards. For other children, this stance will emerge only in very rigid, restrictive situations or in adolescence as they strive to release their uniqueness.

While closet gifted children strive for acceptance by revealing no less than their best and hiding their weaknesses, rebels use the opposite tactic. Presenting their anger, impatience, sloppiness, and selfishness, they calculate that if their worst is accepted, then they are indeed loved unconditionally. They may well be right. However, since few parents or teachers are blessed with infinite patience, it is hardly surprising that this approach is usually counterproductive.

Maximizing Potential

If the gifted are to develop their maximum emotional and ethical, as well as intellectual, potential, the healthiest and most constructive response—according to the sources shown in Table 10.1—is to transcend group expectations and work toward an independent self-concept and values. This approach leads to resilience when one is confronted with the inevitable conflicts with norms and externally imposed limitations. Self-esteem liberated from external approval unleashes potential creativity and energy and allows achievement to be motivated by personal interests and values as opposed to the need for grades, approval, prestige, or money as proof of self-worth.

"Maximizing" behavior may look like that of other personality types. Students may appear to agree or disagree with rules, but the critical issue is *why* they have made that choice. For example, on a typical school evening, four exceptional children may have to prepare for four tests. The closet gifted child calculates that by spending one hour on each subject, she can pull in four A's. The withdrawn child feels overwhelmed by the task but decides that quick token reviews in all the subjects will suffice to avoid abysmal failure. The rebel argues that four tests are too many anyway, so he risks failure by deciding to spend the evening watching a science fiction movie. The child who is on the road toward self-actualization reasons that by continuing to work on the science project he cares about, he will be preparing for both the science and math tests, but won't have time to review for the English and social studies tests. He also acknowledges that he may perform very well in the first two subjects and less well in the last two. It is only for the latter response to expectations that content, purpose, or intrinsic value of a task is an issue. The other children are merely reacting to expectations.

One of the key indicators of a person who has maximized her potential is the ability to make choices based on personal commitment and to accept the consequences of those decisions (refer to Table 10.1). It is essential for gifted children who have the potential for original contributions to be willing to take two types of risks: incurring the disapproval of others and the risk of failure. Seward, Jefferson, Mahler, van Gogh, and Joyce had to endure the censure of political and artistic critics. Edison failed more than 120 times before he found the right filament for the incandescent light bulb that has become a symbol for original invention. In our schools and institutions failure is an epithet, and mistakes are irrevocably recorded in grades or test scores. The cost of developing creativity can therefore be very high, and the gifted must become strong enough to pay.

APPROACH TO OVERCOMING UNDERACHIEVEMENT

Review of Research

The review of the research on programs for gifted underachievers is not very helpful, particularly in light of the definitions proposed in this chapter. However, the following generalizations about fostering achievement among gifted adolescents may be made:

1. Early intervention is important to prevent increasing gaps between potential and achievement (Shaw & McCuen, 1960).
2. Long-term programs are necessary for changes in achievement (Dowdall & Colangelo, 1982; Gallagher, 1979; Raph, Goldberg, & Passow, 1966).

3. Family members need to be involved in interventions (Dowdall & Colangelo, 1982; Rimm, 1986; Shaw & McCuen, 1960; Whitmore, 1980).
4. Counseling programs without curricular changes are unlikely to boost achievement (Broedel, Olsen, & Proff, 1958).
5. While many writers argue for homogeneous grouping of gifted students to maximize achievement, it is clear that without modifications in curriculum, grouping alone will not make a significant difference (Goldberg, 1959).
6. Strategies of grouping underachievers together may aggravate rather than alleviate the problem (Perkins, 1969). Grouping achievers and underachievers together is more likely to be beneficial for emotional and academic development (implicit in Richert, 1982a, 1982b).
7. Different strategies are required for different forms of underachievement (Richert, 1982a, 1982b; Rimm, 1986; Whitmore, 1980).
8. Equitable identification of gifted potential is necessary to find underachievers, particularly among the economically disadvantaged and various minority groups (Richert, 1982a, 1987, 1991).
9. The first goal of education should be to foster physical survival. Adolescents with gifted potential are under even greater emotional stress than other students (Richert, 1982a, 1982b; Webb, Meckstroth, & Tolan, 1982). While conflicting data exist, the highly gifted and high achievers may well be at even greater risk (Sargent, 1984; Seiden, 1966). Meeting the emotional needs of the gifted should be the first concern of all counseling programs and a primary goal of curriculum for the gifted.
10. The inclusion of emotional and ethical, perhaps even spiritual, development as objectives for gifted underachievers is necessary not only for these children to achieve their potential, but for the protection of society. It is instructive to remember that because of his remorse about inventing dynamite, Nobel created the prizes bearing his name to inspire the gifted to use their abilities for peaceful rather than destructive purposes.
11. Finally, unless programs for the gifted have goals and evaluation criteria that include creativity and maximum emotional and ethical development, the curriculum itself may foster forms of gifted underachievement.

Strategies for Maximizing Potential

I have developed a heuristic model that not only includes the 11 requisites for an effective approach to overcoming underachievement, but also incorporates the views of many of the sources listed in Table 10.1.[2] While quantitative data have not yet been gathered for this model, informal responses over a decade (1980-1990) from many groups of parents, counselors, and teachers who deal with gifted adolescents suggest that all three groups are able to identify the different patterns of achievement and that the recommended strategies are specific enough to be practical.

Whatever a child's socially recognized achievements, unless emotional potential is realized, including the understanding and acceptance of self and others, even the gifted will in some ways be underachievers. The approach to developing unachieved potential is to create situations that will counteract inappropriate expectations; make children resilient to external judgments; and evoke children's maximum potential (including special abilities, productivity, creativity, emotions, and values). Six strategies that educators, counselors, parents, and advocates of the gifted can use are depicted in Table 10.3. The effectiveness of specific strategies will vary according to a child's distinctive personality pattern: closet (conforms), withdrawn (avoids competition), rebellious (rejects any rules), or maximizing (determines own values).

Strengthening Self-Concept. A positive or healthy self-concept distinguishes the best and the weakest parts of the self while also accepting the imperfect condition of being human. To strengthen self-concept, nonjudgmental classroom and home environments should be created. Home and classroom rules should reflect the highest level of emotional and ethical development and incorporate the universal injunction, "Thou shalt not judge," in order to provide the experience of "mirroring" that Kohut (1970) argues is a prerequisite for a healthy self-concept. No one— whether child or adult—should be allowed to make judgmental statements, which can be as emotionally destructive as physical abuse. It is the ethical responsibility of authority figures to prevent such emotional abuse.

For the closet or withdrawn gifted child, hidden faults and errors ought to be revealed and accepted, so that eventual exposure is not feared (further discussed below). Patience will be required to regain the trust of rebels so that they are willing to expose their interests. Rebels' strengths and interests, academic and other, should be legitimized by being incorporated into assignments.

---

2. Some other writers have developed effective materials and approaches that include some aspects of emotional potential discussed here (Betts, 1985; Delisle, 1986; Galbraith, 1983, 1987; McCutcheon, 1985; Webb, Meckstroth, & Tolan, 1982).

Table 10.3 Strategies for Achieving Maximum Potential

Personality Patterns GOALS	Closet	Withdrawn	Rebel	Maximizing
Strengthen Self-Concept	Evoke weakness / Accept limits / Avoid judgments	Reinforce strengths / Accept limits / Avoid judgments	Reinforce strengths / Legitimize interests / Avoid judgments	Accept independence / Provide safety / Avoid judgments
Help Cope with Failure/Success	Inoculate against failure	Generate success / Inoculate against failure	Generate success by incorporating interests	Allow freedom to choose criteria/ Assist in calculating costs
Help Unleash Creativity	Encourage divergence / Push risk taking	Value divergence / Have patience with anxiety	Value divergence / Have patience with imperfect products	Accept divergence / Find audience for products
Teach Planning	Avoid making decisions for/ Force choices / Involve in goal setting	Generate choices/ Avoid making decisions for / Have patience with low motivation	Avoid giving orders / Generate choices / Have patience with mistrust	Generate new options / Accept goals / Offer resources
Teach Evaluation	Liberate from external evaluation/ Reward risk taking more than product excellence / Develop self-evaluation skills	Liberate from external evaluation/ Reward both excellence and risk taking / Develop self-evaluation skills	Liberate from external evaluation/ Reward task-commitment more than excellence / Develop self-evaluation skills	Value producer above product / Reinforce self- evaluation / Generate criteria for self-evaluation
Provide Role Models	Match with R&M gifted / Be model for W & R / Exhibit self-acceptance	Match with R&M gifted children and adults / Exhibit self-acceptance	Match with C & M children and adults / Exhibit self-acceptance	Match with M adults / Be model for C,W,R / Exhibit self-acceptance

©1990 E. Susanne Richert

Children working toward maximizing their potential also need their teachers and parents to be nonjudgmental mirrors who reflect and accept their worst as well as their best. I have previously developed a "self-concept" curriculum for all students, which consists of a series of questions appropriate for small group class discussions, counseling sessions, or a personal journal (Richert, 1985). In addition, James Alvino and I (1989) have written a text on gifted adolescents, with sections specifically for boys and for girls, which is designed to develop various aspects of maximum potential.

Helping Cope with Failure and Success and Encouraging Creativity. Some strategies can help adolescents cope with failure and success, while evoking their creativity. For closet gifted children, success is earned at the exorbitant cost of repression of creativity and the fear of failure. They need protection against both the inevitable judgments that can devastate them and the rewards that can inhibit their creativity. Closet and withdrawn gifted children should be encouraged to embark on new tasks while taking risks to be creative. This can be fostered if adults set an arbitrary limitation; tell them not to repeat a safe, successful achievement; require them to find an alternative; or help them to brainstorm other options. The new task may be a different responsibility for a family trip (planning the itinerary rather than packing the car) or another way of approaching a school assignment (composing a song or poem rather than writing a report on a reading assignment). The risk may be the first independent clothing purchase or the first attempt at negotiating an alternative homework assignment with a teacher. Just a slight dose of mistakes or failure can inoculate them against the greatest danger closet gifted students can face—someone's inevitable judgment that their work is not good enough.

Rebels and withdrawn gifted children share the need to overcome the stigma of failure. Too often these children are unfairly accused of being unmotivated, irresponsible, or lacking task-commitment. To generate success, strengths need to be evoked. Rebels should be given the freedom to work in an area of interest to them. Underachievement can be overcome by a sensitive teacher who incorporates a required skill into a topic that interests a child. For example, a boy who refuses to memorize the multiplication tables will learn them if he needs them in order to use international exchange rates to assess the value of his coin collection in various currencies. A girl who is impatient with spelling will ask for help if the teacher suggests that if her story met spelling standards, it might be suitable for publication in a classroom magazine.

Rebels with divergent views that are very often rejected need encouragement to bring one of their ideas to fruition. They may be asked to select one idea among several options, or they may be required to finish an assignment by a mutually agreed upon deadline. Teachers may offer rebellious students options such as making up questions instead of answering those at the end of the chapter; recording notes on a tape recorder rather than writing them on index cards; taking photos of animals for a project rather than drawing them by hand; composing a song or poem in response to reading rather than a repetitive book report; or creating a spelling list from personal writing or reading rather than using one from a book. Elsewhere I have listed many other alternative student interest-based assignments for reading, language arts, and English that can help students fulfill curricular requirements (Richert, 1978).

Parents could agree to allow children the following creative alternatives: mowing the lawn in a zigzag rather than rectangular pattern, baking cookies in a frying pan, using old pipes as a sculpture in the perennial garden, or setting their own bedtime for a week. Once the task is finished, the rebel needs recognition both for completing the project and for trusting the teacher or parent not to judge him unfairly. A rebellious child should be helped to negotiate alternative tasks at school or at home. For instance, a parent might suggest that instead of saying, "No, I won't do the dishes," the children could offer an alternative such as, "I'd rather set the table and make the salad." This helps break the pattern of failure, judgment, rejection, and rebellion.

Approaches required by both closet and rebel gifted children are needed by the child who tends to withdraw. Both weaknesses and strengths need to be evoked and confronted without the evaluations the child so fears. Children who tend to withdraw from competition and fear external evaluation may be asked to list two activities they do best at home and two at school and two activities they do not do well at home or at school. To help them overcome evasion, the children should be asked to commit themselves to carrying out one activity from each category. Upon completion, the teacher or parents can discuss how they feel after completing each task. This will help them to accept both their strengths and limitations. It will also help for the adult to admit his or her own strengths and weaknesses. Knowing that their teachers and parents have such anxieties, yet manage to cope, will greatly reduce children's fear of being required to do too much. It is important to accept their anxieties as real, yet encourage them to act in spite of the anxieties.

Adolescents with anxieties need adults to accept their anxieties as real, but also to encourage them to act in spite of their trepidations. All risk-taking children should be able to enjoy the psychological safety of knowing that their risk taking is a factor in their evaluation. Whatever the quality of their performance or product, they should feel they cannot fail if they take a major risk. The best response to the first wobbly geodesic dome built by the girl who previously got A's is not the dishonest judgment that it's good. Rather, the teacher should admit that while her building skills are not great, risking imperfection shows strength.

Teaching Planning. It is essential to avoid making decisions for adolescents because it either fosters dependence (among closet and withdrawn children) or rebellion (among rebels), or inhibits independence (among maximizing students). Children must be given choices and required to make decisions while setting their own goals. Discipline and motivation must be shifted from dependence on teachers or parents to internal feelings and values as the prime basis for action. Within the parameters of school and family responsibilities and mutually accepted standards, children should choose among alternatives. The parent's or teacher's role should be not to direct, but instead to generate options. The adult should guide discussions of the consequences of each alternative while carefully avoiding either offering implicit preferences or making explicit recommendations. It is particularly important for exceptional children, who must eventually function independently while developing their unique abilities, to be involved in goal setting, as well as in changing plans and goals as needed.

Generating options avoids reinforcement of counterproductive responses to expectations. Closet gifted children are prevented from merely conforming because they are required to choose for themselves. Rebels are given nothing to rebel against. The pressure to perform is reduced for withdrawn children, yet they too must apply their abilities by choosing. Children aiming for development of maximum potential can risk independence without penalty.

Teaching Self-Evaluation. The closet gifted child—more than any other—gets trapped into valuing himself according to his grades, but there never seems to be enough adulation. These children crave approval as if it were an addiction. Kohut (1970) points out that pathological narcissism—the insatiable craving for approval—results from parents failing to accept nonjudgmentally both positive traits and limitations of children. Miller (1981) explicitly states that neurotic parents of gifted children, whose own self-esteem is dependent on external demonstrations of worth, can often be narcissistic in exploiting their children's accomplishments. These parents, like the parents of the boy who commits suicide in the 1989 film *Dead Poets' Society*, feel self-esteem only to the degree their children earn the visible rewards of success: spectacular grades, impressive test scores, and/or public acclaim such as awards.

Children who continually bend their ideas to please others need the help of parents, counselors, peers, and an appropriate curriculum to overcome dependence on others for self-esteem. All children, most particularly the closet gifted child and the withdrawn child, need to learn self-evaluation skills based on the following four principles:

1. *Children must learn to distinguish between themselves and their schoolwork.* Language is important! A child may get A's in math, but she should not be called an "A student." Productivity may be encouraged in a gifted program, but children should not be called "producers," since it identifies them with their work rather than their intrinsic value.

2. *The most important purpose of evaluation is to help students assess their personal progress, not how they compare with each other.* Evaluation should not be based on comparing students. The essential question self-evaluation should address is, "What can I do now that I couldn't do before?" Gifted programs should help students answer that question, but parents and counselors can also assist in liberating children from unproductive competition. Report cards can be occasions for discussing not whether the grades are good enough, but, "What have you learned in math?" or "Have you progressed in writing?" Personal emotional growth must be stressed. Product perfection, so prized by closet gifted children, should have less emphasis than originality. Withdrawn children and rebels should recognize that the value of their progress in task-commitment is more important than their imperfect products. Children should be encouraged to evaluate the strengths and weaknesses of their own work so they can determine directions for improvement.

3. *Creativity, originality, and risk taking ought to be major evaluation criteria.*

4. *Children need to be aware of the criteria for evaluation in different fields.* While children should not be compared, products and performance are compared in the real world, and therefore children need this information in order to decide how they will respond to external demands.

Providing Role Models. Gifted programs that segregate academically achieving students from creative or underachieving students foster unhealthy competition. Overemphasis on competition reinforces students' insecurity and dependence on grades, represses their creativity, and denies them risk-taking, creative role models, such as rebels or students attempting to maximize their potential.

Gifted children with all four patterns of response to expectations have complementary strengths and weaknesses. They should be grouped together so they can serve as effective peer role models for each other. Rebels can learn from closet gifted children that completing a task does not necessarily require the sale of their souls. Withdrawn and closet gifted children can learn from rebels that being creative, risking failure, and making mistakes does not lead to irrevocable rejection. Everyone can learn from children taking risks to develop their maximum potential that independence can bring strength—but also has its price.

The following suggestions are offered for meeting the different needs of gifted males and females: help them find self-actualizing, same-sex mentors; encourage the development of authentic friendships (as opposed to just "romantic" relationships) with members of the opposite sex; and foster relationships with same- and opposite-sex parents (Alvino & Richert, 1989).

The single most awesome influence educators and parents have are as role models. Since statistically Maslow's (1970) research indicates that very few people in our culture are likely to be self-actualizing, there may be an almost inevitable conflict in adult teachers, counselors, and parents attempting to be effective role models for adolescents or even tolerating adolescents who are moving toward independence. Yet it is not necessary to be a perfect human being, or even to be self-actualizing, in order to be a useful role model for gifted students. There are two approaches that can be used by advocates of the gifted. First, since it is helpful for adolescents to understand the obstacles to self-actualization in our society, role models should be willing to reveal their own struggles. It is not easy to resist conforming or seeking approval when adults' insecurities are continually reinforced by constant evaluations and judgments of supervisors, colleagues, family, and sometimes even friends.

Second, and more important, adults, whether educators or parents, ought to work on what they hope adolescents will achieve, by using the strategies for themselves that are listed here for children. Until the adults from whom the gifted initially acquire their self-concepts can become nonnarcissistic, nonjudgmental, accepting, risk-taking, empowering, and capable of operating on the highest ethical levels, the gifted will have a very costly struggle to develop their unique potential in the face of strong external pressures to conform. Until more members of our society, particularly parents and educators, unlock their "mind-forg'd manacles" in order to develop their own emotional and ethical potential, the social dynamics of being gifted will continue to be very burdensome.

REFERENCES

Alvino, J., & Richert, E. S. (1989). *Gifted boys/Gifted girls.* Unpublished manuscript.

Betts, G. T. (1985). *Autonomous learner model for the gifted and talented.* Greeley, CO: Alps.

Blake, W. (1968). London. In M. H. Abrams (Series Ed.), *The Norton anthology of English literature* (p. 259). New York: Norton. (Original work published 1794).

Broedel, J., Olsen, M., & Proff, F. (1958). *The effects of group counseling on gifted underachievers.* Paper presented at the meeting of the American Psychological Association, September 1958.

Dabrowski, K. (1967). *Personality-shaping through positive disintegration.* Boston: Little, Brown.

Delisle, J. R. (1986). Death with honors: Suicide among gifted adolescents. *Journal of Counseling and Development, 64,* 558–560.

Dowdall, C., & Colangelo, N. (1982). Underachieving gifted students: Review and implications. *Gifted Child Quarterly, 26,* 179–184.

Frankl, V. (1980). *Man's search for meaning.* New York: Pocket Books.

Fromm, E. (1951). *The art of loving.* London: Routledge and Kegan Paul.

Galbraith, J. (1983). *The gifted kids survival guide (for ages 11–18).* Minneapolis: Free Spirit.

Galbraith, J. (1987). *The gifted kids survival guide II (for ages 11–18).* Minneapolis: Free Spirit.

Gallagher, J. J. (1979). Issues in education for the gifted. In A. H. Passow (Ed.), *The gifted and the talented: Their education and development.* Chicago: University of Chicago Press.

Gardner, H. (1983). *Frames of mind.* New York: Basic Books.

Goldberg, M. (1959). A three year program at DeWitt Clinton High School to help bright underachievers. *High Points, 4,* 3–35.

Govinda, L. A. (1974). *Foundations of Tibetan mysticism.* New York: Samuel Weiser.

Gowan, J. C. (1957). Dynamics of the underachievement of gifted children. *Exceptional Children, 24,* 98–101, 122.

Hollingworth, L. S. (1926). Gifted children. New York: Macmillan.

Hoyt, D. P. (1965). *The relationship between college grades and adult achievement: A review of the literature* (ACT Research Report No. 7). Iowa City: American College Testing Program.

Jung, K. G. (1963). *Modern man in search of a soul.* New York: Harcourt, Brace & World.

Jung, K. G. (1964). *Man and his symbols.* Garden City, NY: Doubleday.

Kerr, B. (1985). *Smart girls, gifted women.* Columbus: Ohio Psychology Publishing.

Kohlberg, L. (1981). *The philosophy of moral development: Essays in moral development.* New York: Harper & Row.

Kohlberg, L. (1983). *The psychology of moral development.* New York: Harper & Row.

Kohut, H. (1970). *The analysis of the self: A systematic approach in the psychoanalytical treatment of narcissistic personality disorders.* Independence, MO: International University Press.

Krathwohl, D. R., Bloom, B. S., & Masia, B. B. (1964). *Taxonomy of educational objectives: Handbook II. The affective domain.* New York: David McKay.

Lao Tzu. (1972). *Tao te ching.* New York: Vintage Books.

Maslow, A. (1964). *Religion, values and peak experiences.* Columbus: Ohio University Press.

Maslow, A. (1970). *Motivation and personality.* New York: Harper & Row.

McCutcheon, R. (1985). *Get off my brain: A survival guide for lazy students.* Minneapolis: Free Spirit.

Miller, A. (1981). *Prisoners of childhood: How narcissistic parents form and deform the emotional lives of their gifted children.* New York: Basic Books.

Mookerjee, A. (1982). *Kundalini yoga: The arousal of the inner energy.* New York: Destiny Books.

Muktananda, S. (1978). *Play of consciousness.* Oakland, CA: S.Y.D.A. Foundation.

National Commission on Excellence in Education. (1984). *A nation at risk: The imperative for educational reform.* Washington, DC: U.S. Government Printing Office.

Perkins, H. V. (1969). *Human development and learning.* Belmont, CA: Wadsworth.

Raph, J. B., Goldberg, M. L., & Passow, A. H. (1966). *Bright underachievers.* New York: Teachers College Press.

Renzulli, J. S. (1978). What makes giftedness: Reexamining a definition. *Phi Delta Kappan, 60,* 180–184.

Richert, E. S. (Ed.). (1978). *Holistic language arts and literature for the gifted.* Sewell, NJ: Educational Information and Resource Center.

Richert, E. S. (1982a, September). Personality patterns of gifted children. *Gifted Children Monthly,* pp. 1–3, 20.

Richert, E. S. (1982b, October). Strategies for self-fulfillment of the gifted. *Gifted Children Monthly,* pp. 1–3, 20.

Richert, E. S. (1985). Identification of gifted children in the United States: The need for pluralistic assessment. *Roeper Review, 8,* 68–72.

Richert, E. S. (1986). Toward the Tao of giftedness. *Roeper Review, 8,* 197–204.

Richert, E. S. (1987). Rampant problems and promising practices in identification of disadvantaged gifted students. *Gifted Child Quarterly, 31,* 149–154.

Richert, E. S. (1991). Rampant problems and promising practices in the identification of gifted students. In N. Colangelo & G. Davis (Eds.), *The handbook of gifted education.* Boston: Allyn & Bacon.

Richert, E. S., Alvino, J., & McDonnel, R. (1982). *The national report on identification: Assessment and recommendations for comprehensive identification of gifted and talented youth.* Sewell, NJ: Educational Information and Resource Center, for U.S. Department of Education.

Rimm, S. (1986). *Underachievement syndrome: Causes and cures.* Watertown, WI: Apple.

Roeper, A. M. (1982). How the gifted cope with their emotions. *Roeper Review, 1,* 21–24.

Sargent, M. (1984). Adolescent suicide: Studies reported. *Child and Adolescent Psychotherapy, 1*(2), 49–50.

Sartre, J. P. (1967). *Essays in existentialism.* Secaucus, NJ: Citadel Press.

Schurenberg, E. (1989, May). The agony of college admissions. *Money,* pp. 142–156.

Seiden, R. (1966). Campus tragedy: A study of student suicide. *Journal of Abnormal Psychology, 13,* 242–245.

Shaw, M. C., & McCuen, J. T. (1960). The onset of academic underachievement in bright children. *Journal of Educational Psychology, 51,* 103–108.

Sternberg, R. (1985). *Beyond I.Q.* Cambridge: Cambridge University Press.

Tannenbaum, A. J. (1983). *Gifted children: Psychological and educational perspectives.* New York: Macmillan.

Taylor, C. W., Albo, D., Holland, J., & Brandt, G. (1985). Attributes of excellence in various professions: Their relevance to the selection of gifted/talented persons. *Gifted Child Quarterly, 29,* 29–34.

Terman, L. M., & Oden, M. H. (1947). *The gifted child grows up.* Stanford, CA: Stanford University Press.

Torrance, E. P. (1964). *Education and the creative potential.* Minneapolis: University of Minnesota Press.

Torrance, E. P. (1972). Career patterns and peak creative achievement of creative high school students 12 years later. *Gifted Child Quarterly, 16,* 75–88.

Torrance, E. P. (1979). *The search for satori and creativity.* Buffalo, NY: Creative Education Foundation.

Webb, J. T., Meckstroth, E. A., & Tolan, S. S. (1982). *Guiding the gifted child.* Columbus: Ohio Psychology Publishing.

Whitmore, J. R. (1980). *Giftedness conflict and underachievement.* Old Tappan, NJ: Allyn & Bacon.

CHAPTER 11

The Paradoxical Needs of the Disabled Gifted

Marlene Bireley

Terman and his colleagues (Terman, 1925) established the primary vision of giftedness as that of intellectual, emotional, and physical superiority. The current *zeitgeist* compel us to expand that definition to include gifted persons with characteristics that contradict the Terman ideal. One paradoxical group is that which we choose to call the dually labelled or the disabled gifted. This chapter explores the unique identification, programming, and counseling needs of this interesting subpopulation of the gifted community.

IDENTIFYING THE DUALLY LABELLED

Learning Disability

The most prevalent disabled gifted population may be the learning disabled. This group certainly has received the most attention (e.g., Fox, Brody, & Tobin, 1983; Whitmore, 1980). The description of this condition has evolved throughout the last 50 years. To paraphrase one popular definition, that of the National Joint Committee on Learning Disabilities, the group identified as learning disabled have a presumed central nervous system dysfunction that is manifested by significant difficulties in listening, speaking, reading, writing, reasoning, or mathematical abilities. Additionally, problems in self-regulatory behaviors, social perception, and social interaction may exist ("NJCLD LD definition," 1989).

Another subgroup often found in the LD gifted population are those with Attention Deficit Disorder with Hyperactivity (ADD-H) or, as it was recently relabelled, Attention-Deficit Hyperactive Disorder (ADHD) (American Psychiatric Association, 1987). ADHD may or may not be combined with the central nervous system dysfunctions described above. Those who have this condition may be served as learning disabled because of their inability to demonstrate achievement, particularly in large group settings such as the regular classroom. While the effects of ADHD usually can be controlled through a structured classroom environment, supported in more difficult cases by stimulant and, less frequently, anti-depressant medications (Lerner, 1985), the societal concerns about medication for children sometimes persuade parents to avoid the latter type of treatment (Divoky, 1989). Consequently, many children spend years trying to maintain their attention with limited assistance, even though the part of the brain that controls attention, the reticular activating system, is inefficient or inadequate for that purpose (Hooper & Boyd, 1986). Giftedness in this group can be overlooked because the scattered behavior of the uncontrolled ADHD child often results in incomplete assignments when sustained periods of written work are required.

Psychometric identification of the LD or ADHD gifted child may occur when the individual is referred for special education placement. The three-factor interpretation of the Wechsler Intelligence Scale for Children–Revised (the WISC-R), described by Kaufman (1979), has enhanced the use of this scale as a useful tool in identifying this population. Kaufman has refined the previous practice of comparing discrepancies in the Verbal and Performance sections of this test, by distinguishing a third factor, Freedom from Distractibility (the Arithmetic, Digit Span, and Coding Subtests), from two others that he labels Verbal Comprehension and Perceptual Organization (these consist of the Verbal and Performance Scales minus the Distractibility subtests). Since the Freedom from Distractibility triad usually is depressed in ADHD children, finding high scores in the other two factors may indicate a potential for high achievement if distractibility can be controlled. Group intelligence tests do not have similar identification capabilities (and ADHD children are poor workers in group settings). Any children who appear to have "flashes of brilliance" but are poor achievers in their daily work should be given an individual intelligence test and, if needed, an individual test of achievement regardless of their functioning on group tests.

Emotional and Behavioral Disorders

Adolescents with emotional disturbance or behavior disorders may manifest these problems by withdrawing or by acting out aggressive actions. The former youngsters tend to be considered emotionally disturbed, while the latter will more likely be labelled behavior disordered. While giftedness in this population has not been studied sufficiently, it is known that the gifted are not immune to these disorders. Other chapters in this book discuss some of the specific emotional problems of the gifted. If those concerns extend over a long time, exist to a marked degree, and begin to interfere with the educational performance of the individual, the label of serious emotional disturbance may be attached to that person. The definition in the rules and regulations governing the implementation of PL 94–142 (Education for All Handicapped Children Act) includes those requirements and further states that additional symptoms may be the inability to maintain satisfactory relationships with peers and teachers, inappropriate types of feelings or behaviors in normal circumstances, a general pervasive mood of unhappiness or depression, or a tendency to develop physical symptoms or fears associated with personal or school problems (U.S. Department of Health, Education, and Welfare, 1977).

Unlike the lifelong limitations of physically based exceptionalities, emotional disturbances may be improved so that the individual can return to normal functioning. Recognizing the intelligence of such a person, using the intellect in the treatment plan, and encouraging a return to the status of achiever would appear to be worthwhile goals for this population. Unless the individual is incapable of being tested, intelligence test scores, even when widely scattered, should give indications of ability in much the same way as described above. Additional techniques such as projective techniques and tests of creativity may lend further insight into specific needs and talents.

For the handicapped teenager whose problems are not so severe as to be labelled as emotional disturbance, the adolescent years may present major adjustment problems. Looking or feeling different is a critical issue in adolescence. Several authors cite the deleterious effect that a disabling condition may have on an adolescent particularly as social acceptance and sexuality take on increasing importance (Blackman, 1987; Kopp, 1973; Lerner, 1985; Murphy & Newlon, 1987; Tuttle, 1984).

One must conclude that the disabled adolescent is very much a person at emotional risk. Whether high intelligence assists or magnifies this problem could be debated. We do have the biographical and autobiographical accounts of bright individuals who have conquered adversity, supporting the contention that the coping mechanisms of the more highly intelligent are helpful. However, it could be anticipated that the higher goals of the disabled gifted person, if thwarted, could result in more frustration and a greater sense of loss. It is unlikely that those who have not found the support to fulfill their aspirations have chronicled this failure.

Low Incidence Disabilities

The conditions of visual, hearing, and physical impairment and other health conditions are referred to as low incidence disabilities. The rarity of most of these conditions magnifies the difficulty of identifying the giftedness of a child whose abilities may be hidden by the disability. Since many of these conditions are related to neurological impairment, professionals who teach or counsel the low incidence population may gear their programming and thinking to a multiply handicapped, below average population. When a gifted child emerges, teachers and support personnel may have little experience in challenging such an intellect. Pairing the need to accommodate the physical impairment with the need to enrich the intellect is a particularly difficult task, and the latter may be minimally addressed in a typical special education setting. This enhances the need to identify and provide special program options for such a student.

The Hearing Impaired. According to Desch (1987), hearing impairment can be described by decibel loss, by age of onset, or by etiology (cause). Decibel loss categories range from Level I (26–53 decibels loss) to Level IV (90 decibels or greater loss). Age of onset categories include prelingual (by age 2 or 3), prevocational (by 18 or 19), and late adult onset. The first category, the only one that has significance for this discussion, has an incidence of about 1 in 1,000 children.

Hearing impairment has a strong genetic link. It is estimated that 40%–60% of the deaf come from families with deafness. Other significant causes of hearing impairment include the ingestion of toxic compounds, maternal rubella, cytomegalovirus (CMV), high risk pregnancies or deliveries, and middle ear infections in the first 2 years of life. Since a number of these conditions may lead to significant neurological impairment, it can be hypothesized that those with genetic deafness or impairment resulting from middle ear infections are the most likely candidates for unimpaired intelligence. Educators should pay particular attention to these etiological groups when considering potential candidates for gifted screening.

The Visually Impaired. Visual impairment is a relatively rare childhood condition. The figure of 0.1% is most often cited for prevalence in the school population (Hardman, Drew, & Egan, 1987). It is estimated that half of the incidence of blindness in children is genetically linked. Other major causes are infectious agents; perinatal (at birth) conditions such as retrolental fibroplasia (RLF), which results from overrich oxygen being given to premature newborns (now confined to fewer than 500 cases a year); maternal infections such as gonorrhea; and postnatal causes such as untreated strabismus or amblyopia (Desch, 1987). Since the genetically blind and the postnatal group would be less likely to have neurological impairment, they should be the focus of the most stringent screening for high intelligence.

Physical and Other Health Impairments. This category of disability contains a long list of relatively rare conditions that may afflict children. Some are so debilitating and/or fatal at such a young age that the identification of a gifted adolescent with such a condition would seem to be an unlikely occurrence. Other conditions, however, are connected with near normal lifespans in spite of continuing needs to manage the inconveniences associated with the disability. Many of these children may typically have normal intellectual capacities even though their frequent health problems may interrupt normal schooling and deter normal achievement.

One of the most prevalent of the physical impairments is cerebral palsy. Multiple problems exist in this population. Blackman (1987) estimated that 50%-67% are in the retarded range, 12.5% have visual problems, and 35%-45% have epilepsy; concomitant factors such as dental disease, feeding problems, language impairment, and social/emotional stress are common. One can scarcely imagine the frustration of the person of high intellect whose abilities are masked by some combination of the above physical disabilities. While speech problems may be a major deterrent to identification, the advent of augmentative communication devices, described later, have allowed many individuals with cerebral palsy to communicate and aspire to goals considered impossible a very few years ago.

Bleck and Nagel (1982) identified the following physical/health conditions as significant ones that have the potential for both normal intellect and a lifespan reaching into the adult years: asthma, childhood cancer, cystic fibrosis, juvenile diabetes mellitus, heart disease, hemophilia, osteogenesis imperfecta (brittle bones), juvenile rheumatoid arthritis, scoliosis (lateral curvature of the spine), spina bifida or myelomeningocele (incomplete closure of the spine), short stature, and sickle cell anemia. The reader is referred Bleck and Nagel (1982) or a similar resource for a description of the particular characteristics of each of these conditions. The major problems for children or adolescents, regardless of the specific physical disability, are that the condition itself can become the focus of their life; the inconveniences associated with the condition; the attitudes of parents, peers, and others toward the chronically ill or disabled; and the lack of a sequential, consistent educational experience. Any of these problems might deter the identification and programming of the gifted child in this situation.

MOTIVATION IN THE DISABLED GIFTED

Regardless of the type of specific disability, the ultimate success of a disabled gifted adolescent may depend as much on the will to succeed as the demands of the disability. Part of the paradox of the dually labelled person is that studies of various aspects of motivation divulge different patterns in the disabled and the gifted in the areas of locus of control, field dependence/independence, and achievement motivation. Another concept, learned helplessness, has been applied to disabled populations, but, to the best of my knowledge, not to the gifted.

The concept of locus of control was described by Tetenbaum and Houtz (1978) as attribution of control over oneself as being more internally (self) controlled or externally (environmentally) controlled. Witkin and his associates (Witkin, Moore, Goodenough, & Cox, 1977) described field dependent individuals as those who are better at social learning material, prefer physical closeness, are drawn to people, and are interested in what others say and do; while field independent people have a more impersonal orientation (social autonomy), like to impose structure on stimulus materials, cluster concepts in tight groups, and organize materials. In other words, field dependent individuals are somewhat controlled by what people may think, while field independent individuals tend to control their environment. Achievement motivation is the concept that the drive to succeed is relatively stable, that the strength of the expectancy is based on the belief that success will follow effort, and that the attractiveness of success provides the incentive value for further success (Atkinson, 1964).

Finally, learned helplessness is a condition in which individuals attribute failures to circumstances that they perceive as uncontrollable and beyond their ability to overcome (Licht & Dweck, 1984). This phenomenon was first noted in laboratory dogs who did not try to escape shock after a period of inescapable shock (Seligman & Maier, 1967). Similar behavior was later observed in certain children in a variety of settings (e.g., Diener & Dweck, 1980; Dweck & Reppucci, 1973; Licht & Dweck, 1984). Dweck and her associates noted that helpless children were more likely to spontaneously attribute their failures to uncontrollable, external factors, while mastery children viewed their success as attributable to their own abilities and well within their own control. In special education, learned helplessness has become most associated with the condition that accompanies a disability when parents and other adults refuse to allow the disabled child to grow in independent behavior with increasing age and maturity. Those who have "learned helplessness" feel generally noncompetitive, inadequate in their responses to others, and anxious often resulting in aggressive or withdrawing behavior (Sabatino, Miller, & Schmidt, 1981). This behavior is in stark contrast to the persistence and task commitment which characterizes gifted students, as that term is conceptualized by Renzulli (1978).

In each instance (locus of control, field dependence/independence, achievement motivation, or learned helplessness) in which gifted or disabled populations have been studied, the gifted tend to emulate the more independent adult pattern at an earlier age than their peers (e.g., internal control, field independence, and expectation of success), while the disabled tend to prolong the more dependent patterns (e.g., Quigley & Kretschmer, 1982, studying a deaf population; Witkin, Birnbaum, Lomanaco, Lehr, & Herman, 1968, studying congenitally blind children). Each of these concepts hold additional meaning for the dually labelled person. In those cases where treatment of the individual is as a disabled person to the neglect of the intellectual ability, the individual is likely to assume the "handicapped" or immature pattern. In contrast, one must assume that, given the proper environment, the "gifted" pattern could emerge. This is but another framework that underscores the importance of the development of a self-concept of ability and possibility in the disabled gifted.

EDUCATING THE DUALLY LABELLED

Education of the dually labelled student presents particular problems. Those compensatory skills which will link the student to a knowledge base or will allow communication (e.g., braille, augmentative communication aids, taped texts) must be made available in a setting where the student can gain expertise in their use. At the same time, it can be anticipated that prolonged attendance in special education programs that stress the acquisition of special compensatory skills and basic academic skill acquisition over advanced content will widen the knowledge gap and decrease the probability of success in high school and postsecondary settings. The concept of "least restrictive alternative" mandates consideration of placement in a regular classroom as quickly and as fully as possible for the individual. For success in this endeavor, several skills need to be acquired by the integrating student. It is, in my opinion, imperative that the affective/social skills be given equal weight with the cognitive ones if "mainstreaming" is to be successful. Whitmore and Maker (1985) discussed in some detail a previous study by Maker and others (Maker, Redden, Tonelson, & Howell, 1978), which explored the experiences of successful scientists with disabilities. Those scientists attributed their success to the development of skills in seven areas. Those areas would make an excellent basis for a curriculum designed to integrate the intelligent disabled person into secondary and higher education. They included acquiring specific learning strategies to enhance ability, working harder in both academics and social contacts, being persistent in spite of obstacles, using mechanical aids, using other people for role models and counselors, developing a will to succeed, and developing a personality that reflects a good self-image and risk-taking ability.

Students who have begun to develop a sense of self and an ability to apply specific strategies in each of these areas would have an excellent chance of survival and success in a regular setting. But what about participation in a gifted program? In only a few instances have programs been developed to serve the dually labelled. Some of these are described later. A disabled gifted student is more likely to be integrated into an existing gifted program. At the secondary level, these programs are likely to be advanced placement, mentorships, job shadowing, independent study, special seminars, or leadership training (Cox, Daniel, & Boston, 1985). Students with adequate skills for integration into regular classes would appear to have little additional difficulty in such programs. Limitations would most likely be the attitudes of others, the development of an adequate knowledge background prior to high school, and the ability to maintain the "speed" of an advanced class. With proper planning, each of these probable obstacles could be overcome, but success might be contingent on early identification of the student and specific planning for this goal during the elementary years.

Technological Aids and Support Services

Technological advances and other support services have expanded opportunities for all physically and sensorially handicapped persons since the advent of the computer age and the legal recognition of the rights of the disabled. Close-captioning, total communication (a combination of oral and sign language), and greater availability of interpreters have assisted in the integration of the deaf population. Augmentative communication devices that allow those with physically based language impairment to speak, type, or point out messages on computers or communication boards have given opportunities to those who previously had no voice. Several adjuncts to large type books, braille, and taped textbooks, such as the optacon scanner (which translates printed material into tactile messages) and the Kurzweil Reading machine (which uses printed material to produce synthetic speech), have allowed the visually impaired wider access to printed information (Hardman, Drew, & Egan, 1987). New techniques are emerging each year. Teachers of the gifted and regular educators will need to maintain close communication with specialists to learn how to manage the student who uses some combination of these supportive services. The availability of such services increases the likelihood of the identification and integration of the disabled into regular or gifted education classrooms.

Specific Programs for the Dually Labelled

Meeting the needs of the dually labelled in programs for their specific abilities/disabilities is rare, but some models now exist. One program for elementary learning disabled gifted children has been described by Baldwin and Gargiulo (1983). This program stressed the remediation of weaknesses while developing problem-solving strategies to build strengths, specific activities to enhance self-worth based on classroom meetings, value clarification, creative problem-solving exercises, behavior modification programs, and a planned, sequential reintegration into the regular classroom and gifted resource room. The amalgamation of two opposing systems (the highly structured, task analytic approach of special education and the holistic, enriching approach of gifted education) seemed to account for the success of this program.

Somewhat in contrast, Whitmore (1980) developed a program for highly gifted underachievers in which she chose to forego the typical structured approach of special education in favor of encouraging student participation in decision making, higher level and creative thinking, and motivational activities. Multiple objective and observational data indicated improvement in all targeted areas.

Hackney (1986) conducted a 6-week summer program for 15 visually impaired students, grades 6–11, at the Texas School for the Blind. The curriculum included critical thinking and problem solving, advanced mathematics, creative writing, a mentorship in a career field of the student's choice, creative dramatics, outdoor risk taking, independent living, and counseling. It is interesting to note that unnamed critics were skeptical about the differences between Hackney's population and other blind students and that charges of "elitism" were made about the program.

In another approach, hearing impaired high school students were exposed to the Instrumental Enrichment Program (IE) developed by Reuven Feuerstein (1980). This highly sequenced pencil and paper program consists of over 500 pages of exercises designed to improve spatial relations, ability to use abstract analogies, problem solving, direction reading, and planning and sequencing. This group had higher achievement than a control group in several academic and problem-solving areas. Teacher and self-reports indicated better work habits and behavior patterns (Jonas & Martin, 1985). Given the known achievement deficits of the deaf, it is interesting to contemplate the effect that early training in IE might have on the achievement levels of bright deaf children (e.g., Trybus and Karchmer, 1977, reporting on 6,871 subjects, found that at age 20 the median reading level for the deaf was 4.5 and that only 10% read at or above eighth-grade level).

Preparing for Adulthood

With or without a disability, the goals of finding one's life work and establishing oneself as an independent adult are critical to maintaining one's sense of self-worth. While the bright disabled adolescent is making career decisions, it is important that educators assume that postsecondary education is a possibility and that the secondary curriculum include the development of college coping skills as well as career exploration and independent living training.

Various authors have suggested that the specific skills that should be included in pre-adult preparation for college include the development of skill in the use of technological aids (Corn, 1986), selection of a college that will address the particular needs of the disabled and allow meaningful integration (Reineke & Lyth, 1973), training in the use of support services offered by the college (Bireley, Landers, Vernooy, & Schlaerth, 1986; Mangrum & Strichart, 1984), and high school experiences that reflect the types of requirements students will face in college (Mangrum & Strichart, 1984).

Whether or not the young adult wishes to attend college, balancing independence and necessary dependency are needed to establish oneself in a career or the community. Some may need personal care attendants, readers, or travelling companions. Others may need adapted and accessible living quarters. Training in finding and keeping such necessary services in place should be included in secondary special education programs.

Finally, the gradual movement from parental and educator dependency to that of one in charge of one's own life may be the most critically needed skill of all. Only the most unfeeling of observers could fail to understand the ease with which the parents of a disabled child can fall into a pattern of overprotectiveness, which, in turn, can produce learned helplessness. Many special educators, in their roles as student advocates, take on similar behaviors. Given the importance of adult independence, professionals need to consider their own behavior toward the adolescent with a disability and should seriously consider the importance of assisting parents in the difficult task of "letting go." Certainly, the points stressed throughout this discussion—the need to develop self-esteem and persistence, the acceptance of one's ability while realistically appraising and managing one's disability, the need for career guidance and gradual movement toward independence—are legitimate areas for counseling support for all members of the family of the disabled adolescent.

SUMMARY

In conclusion, the words of Whitmore and Maker (1985) seem most appropriate: "It appears that there are no positive effects but only negative ones of specific disabilities on the individual's self-concept and self-esteem" (p. 220). Counteracting these negative effects and encouraging the gifts they may hide constitute a major challenge for special and gifted educators alike. It is a challenge that will be met only if both groups expand their awareness of the needs of the dually labelled population and are willing to develop cooperative, innovative programs for this unique and deserving group.

REFERENCES

American Psychiatric Association. (1987). *Diagnostic and statistical manual of mental disorders* (3rd ed., revised). Washington, DC: Author.

Atkinson, J. (1964). *An introduction to motivation.* New York: Van Nostrand.

Baldwin, L. J., & Gargiulo, D. A. (1983). A model program for elementary-age learning-disabled/gifted youngsters. In L. H. Fox, L. Brody, & D. Tobin (Eds.), *Learning-disabled/gifted children: Identification and programming* (pp. 207–222). Baltimore: University Park Press.

Bireley, M. K., Landers, M. F., Vernooy, J. F., & Schlaerth, P. (1986). The Wright State University Program for learning disabled students: Implications of the first decade. *Journal of Reading, Writing, and Learning Disabilities, 2,* 349–357.

Blackman, J. (1987). Disorders of motor development. In M. Wolraich (Ed.), *The practical assessment and management of children with disorders of development and learning* (pp. 164–193). Chicago: Year Book Medical Publishers.

Bleck, E., & Nagel, D. (1982). *Physically handicapped children: A medical atlas for teachers* (2nd ed.). New York: Grune & Stratton.

Corn, A. (1986). Gifted students who have a visual handicap: Can we meet their educational needs? *Education of the Visually Handicapped, 18*(2), 71–84.

Cox, J., Daniel, N., & Boston, B. (1985). *Educating able learners: Programs and promising practices.* Austin: University of Texas Press.

Desch, L. (1987). Disorders of sensation: Hearing and visual impairment. In M. Wolraich (Ed.), *The practical assessment and management of children with disorders of development and learning* (pp. 413–444). Chicago: Year Book Medical Publishers.

Diener, C., & Dweck, C. (1980). An analysis of learned helplessness II: The processing of success. *Journal of Personality and Social Psychology, 39*, 940–952.

Divoky, D. (1989). Ritalin: Education's fix-it drug? *Phi Delta Kappan, 76*, 599–605.

Dweck, C., & Reppucci, N. (1973). Learned helplessness and reinforcement responsibility in children. *Journal of Personality and Social Psychology, 25*, 109–116.

Feuerstein, R. (1980). *Instrumental enrichment.* Baltimore: University Park Press.

Fox, L. H., Brody, L., & Tobin, D. (1983). *Learning-disabled/gifted children: Identification and programming.* Baltimore: University Park Press.

Hackney, P. W. (1986). Education of the visually handicapped-gifted: A program description. *Education of the Visually Handicapped, 18*(2), 85–95.

Hardman, M., Drew, C., & Egan, M. W. (1987). *Human exceptionality* (2nd ed.). Boston: Allyn & Bacon.

Hooper, S. R., & Boyd, T. A. (1986). Neurodevelopmental learning disorders. In J. E. Obrzut & G. W. Hynd (Eds.), *Child neuropsychology: Clinical practice* (Vol. 2, pp. 15–58). Orlando, FL: Academic Press.

Jonas, B. S., & Martin, D. (1985). Cognitive improvement of hearing impaired students through instruction in Instrumental Enrichment. In D. Martin (Ed.), *Cognition, education, and deafness* (pp. 172–175). Washington, DC: Gallaudet University Press.

Kaufman, A. S. (1979). *Intelligent testing with the WISC-R.* New York: Wiley.

Kopp, H. G. (1973). Adolescence: Adjustment or rebellion? In W. H. Northcutt (Ed.), *The hearing impaired child in the regular classroom: Preschool, elementary, and secondary years* (pp. 209–211). Washington, DC: Alexander Graham Bell Association for the Deaf.

Lerner, J. (1985). *Learning disabilities: Theories, diagnosis, and teaching strategies* (4th ed.). Boston: Houghton Mifflin.

Licht, B., & Dweck, C. (1984). Determinants of academic achievement: The interaction of children's achievement orientations with skill area. *Developmental Psychology, 20*, 628–636.

Maker, C. J., Redden, M. R., Tonelson, S., & Howell, R. M. (1978). *The self-perceptions of successful handicapped scientists.* Albuquerque: University of New Mexico, Department of Special Education.

Mangrum, C. T., & Strichart, S. S. (1984). *College and the learning disabled student.* Orlando, FL: Grune & Stratton.

Murphy, J., & Newlon, B. (1987). Loneliness and the mainstreamed hearing impaired college student. *American Annals of the Deaf, 132*, 21–25.

NJCLD LD definition adopted. (1989). *NASP Communique, 17*(7), 1.

Quigley, S. P., & Kretschmer, R. E. (1982). *The education of deaf children: Issues, theory, and practice.* Baltimore: University Park Press.

Reineke, J., & Lyth, W. (1973). College—changes, challenges, and rewards. In W. H. Northcutt (Ed.), *The hearing impaired child in the regular classroom: Preschool, elementary, and secondary years* (pp. 231–236). Washington, DC: Alexander Graham Bell Association for the Deaf.

Renzulli, J. (1978). What makes giftedness? Reexamining a definition. *Phi Delta Kappan, 60,* 180–184.

Sabatino, D., Miller, T., & Schmidt, C. (1981). *Learning disabilities: Systemizing teaching and service delivery.* Rockville, MD: Aspen.

Seligman, M., & Maier, S. (1967). Failure to escape traumatic shock. *Journal of Experimental Psychology, 74,* 1–9.

Terman, L. M. (1925). *Genetic studies of genius: Vol. 1. Mental and physical traits of a thousand gifted children.* Stanford: Stanford University Press.

Tetenbaum, H., & Houtz, J. (1978). The role of affective traits in the creativity and problem-solving performance of gifted urban children. *Psychology in the Schools, 15,* 27–31.

Trybus, R., & Karchmer, M. (1977). School achievement scores of hearing impaired children: National data on achievement status and growth patterns. *American Annals of the Deaf Directory of Programs and Services, 122,* 62–69.

Tuttle, D. W. (1984). *Self-esteem and adjusting with blindness: The process of responding to life's demands.* Springfield, IL: Charles C Thomas.

U.S. Department of Health, Education, and Welfare (1977, August 23). Education of Handicapped Children (implementation of Part B of the Education of the Handicapped Act). *Federal Register, 42*(163), p. 42478.

Whitmore, J. R. (1980). *Giftedness, conflict, and underachievement.* Boston: Allyn & Bacon.

Whitmore, J. R., & Maker, C. J. (1985). *Intellectual giftedness in disabled persons.* Rockville, MD: Aspen.

Witkin, H. A., Birnbaum, J., Lomanaco, S., Lehr, S., & Herman, J. (1968). Cognitive patterning in congenitally totally blind children. *Child Development, 39,* 767–786.

Witkin, H. A., Moore, C. A., Goodenough, D. R., & Cox, P. W. (1977). Field-dependent and field-independent cognitive styles and their educational implications. *Review of Educational Research, 47,* 1–64.

CHAPTER 12

University and Community–Based Programs for the Gifted Adolescent

Raymond H. Swassing
George R. Fichter

Educational options for the gifted and talented have increased dramatically during the 1980s. The increase has been in both number and diversity. The number of such programs continue to grow annually. The variety continues to give ample evidence of the creative solutions being implemented to meet the learning needs of children whose educational requirements exceed the traditional notions of education. Public and private sectors have linked with elementary and secondary schools. Colleges and universities have become involved in efforts to enrich and challenge the nation's most able learners and performers. The efforts to provide enriching and challenging experiences have led program planners away from the traditional restrictions of the clock, the calendar, and the school building.

The purpose of this chapter is to examine some of the ways in which educational options are being devised by organizations not commonly identified with elementary and secondary education. The options examined include governor's schools, summer programs, mentorships, and specialized content programs. Since Chapter 8 addressed primarily the arts, the emphasis of this chapter will be on programs in other content areas.

Efforts to provide experiences for gifted children within the community have a long history. It is almost traditional to "trot out" the Greeks and Romans when discussing the history of gifted education. We will break with tradition. Yet, particularly in the arts and in literature, opportunities outside the educational system have a long history (Kitano & Kirby, 1986). Many musicians and artists have been "students" of the masters (see, for example, Bloom, 1985, on the development of talent). In the twentieth century, organized community efforts in the arts appear to have been around the longest (Hobbs, 1951). Hobbs (1951) identified an art museum program in Worcester, Massachusetts, that had been running for about 35 years. Worcester also provided a year-long program in drama and music. In 1951, Lawrence, Kansas, was providing summer art for about 200 children in grades K–12, and had been doing so for about 30 years. Hobbs (1951) also identified poetry writing in Dallas, Texas, and a long-standing library program in New York City. In the sciences, however, programs organized outside the traditional school framework have a much shorter history.

GOVERNOR'S SCHOOLS

History

The origin of the idea of formal governor's schools for the gifted can be traced to 1963, when the Governor's School of North Carolina began as a summer residential school for exceptionally talented secondary-school youngsters. Novelist John Ehle, a special assistant to Governor Terry Sanford, is generally credited with proposing and developing the idea. Support for the first school came primarily from the Carnegie Corporation of New York, with other business and foundation support from within the state. The school brought 400 senior students, selected by competition in academic areas, and by audition in the fine and performing arts, to a central university setting for a seven-week program. Tuition was free and no grades were given. Faculties were drawn from secondary schools and colleges in North Carolina. Curriculum was based on work by Virgil Ward (1961), and included aptitude development, general intellectual development, and personal development. Curriculum for summer schools for the gifted is discussed in depth elsewhere in this chapter.

Growth

The success of the North Carolina school prompted other states to explore and initiate similar events. It was recognized by State Departments of Education that the gifted high school student had not always been afforded the several alternative educational approaches available, because of overriding priorities in the total educational program. By 1981, eight governor's schools had been established, seven of them in sunbelt states. The schools ranged in length from 4 to 6 weeks and served from 140 to 800 students each summer. The number of campuses or school locations varied from one (4 states) to nine sites (Florida). Grade levels served included sixth through twelfth, with grades 11 and 12 the targets in 6 states. Only two of the states charged nominal fees. Curriculum included science in six centers and multidisciplinary courses in six; all eight schools offered experiences in the arts (Karnes & Pearce, 1981).

Current Status

By 1989, 28 states were conducting governor's schools. Several of the states have initiated links with secondary schools, employing faculty and developing curriculum relevant to advanced classes in the states' secondary schools. Most continue to be tuition free and expand in numbers of students served each year. Many focus on developing leadership, assisting personal and social development, refining critical and creative thinking skills, and encouraging lifelong learning. Each creates its own unique community enabling gifted students from varied backgrounds and localities to exchange ideas and explore potentials. A major goal of each school is to permit the students to learn about new technologies, interact with nationally recognized experts, and share new experiences with other students. Several states are also putting a major focus on "process-oriented" arts experiences. These programs include the visual arts, music, creative writing, dance, film and video, and theatre. Both California and Pennsylvania have noteworthy governor's schools for the arts.

There are several elements common to all the schools. First and foremost, the faculty are selected from many areas—research organizations, communities, the arts, colleges, and high schools—wherever the highest quality instruction can be found. Usually, there is no cost for instruction. Most of the programs are residential, or have residential facilities available to all participants. The content is designed to supplement, not supplant, the standard educational curriculum. There are considerable "after hours" opportunities for academic growth through tutors and study groups. The need for socialization is not ignored; all schools address socialization through both organized and leisure-time schedules.

Ohio's Martin W. Essex School for the Gifted (Wolf, Swassing, & Fichter, 1984) is a one-week summer program for students about to enter their senior year in high school. This program, started in 1976, is supported by state funds and sponsored by the Ohio Department of Education. The 60 participants are selected by a panel of experts representing a cross-section of Ohio in demographics, occupations, and interest in gifted education. The theme, "Investing in Futures," is designed to provoke the participants into thinking about their roles and responsibilities for the future and the future of their planet.

The Ohio Governor's Schools, initiated in 1986 in response to calls to expand the Essex School, are supported by legislative action that directs that each of the 13 state-supported universities plan and hold a 3-week educational program for 250 sophomore and junior students at each site. Further legislation in 1989 directed that three private universities and/or colleges be included, for a total of 16 sites each year.

Projections

In 1987, the first conference for Directors of Governor's Schools for the Gifted was hosted by the Kentucky Department of Education. Those in attendance found that there were many common goals among the 28 programs. Providing learning that challenges and changes students' lives was the top priority. Fostering intellectual debates and encouraging students toward social and civic responsibility are growing concerns among the directors. Long-range plans include expansion in numbers of students, grade levels included, and numbers of sites. A concern in most states is continued and increased financing by both the state and contributing educational institution. The consensus, however, indicates that state legislatures are viewing governor's schools for the gifted as wise expenditures of tax dollars and an investment in the future of the participating state and the nation.

UNIVERSITY AND COLLEGE PROGRAMS

The Study for Mathematically Precocious Youth (SMPY) (Stanley, 1977) was initiated at Johns Hopkins University in 1971, with the support of a grant from the Spencer Foundation. The purpose of the project was to identify seventh- and eighth-grade students who were "precocious" in mathematics and to facilitate their further mathematical reasoning. The students were identified during the seventh and eighth grades using the mathematical portion of the College Entrance Examination Board's Scholastic Aptitude Test (SAT-M), a test of mathematical reasoning for above average eleventh and twelfth graders.

The search was initiated to find students who scored at or above 600 by age 13 (in the 89th percentile of male high school seniors) (Keating, 1974). Once identified, the students were accelerated through high school and college level mathematics as rapidly as each student could progress. The project was not a curriculum project or a mathematics revision process. It made use of the good existing courses available. Many students enrolled for summer programs; others were concurrently enrolled in both high school and college mathematics classes. Students enrolled in college early, some with enough college credits to matriculate as sophomores.

Since its start in 1971, SMPY has grown to a nationwide program with "searches" conducted in five regions. Search programs are located at the Center for Academic Precocity (CAP), Arizona State University; the Center for Talented Youth (CTY), Johns Hopkins University; the Rocky Mountain Talent Search, University of Denver; the Talent Identification Program, Duke University; and the Midwest Talent Search (MTS), Northwestern University. The original intention of SMPY was to identify and nurture talent. Since then the several programs have instituted research components in conjunction with their searches. The emphasis is still on talent identification and development, but the recognized need for a research base in talent growth has given impetus to programs of longitudinal and basic research. The extent of the database, encompassing the five centers, offers a remarkably large and clearly defined population for major studies.

As an example of the size of the search programs, in 1987–88, MTS received applications from more than 25,000 students. Over three-quarters of the applicants followed through to completion of the SAT. The program does not stop with testing. The Center for Talent Development (CTD), the programming office of MTS, offers summer programs for students in such areas as math, computer science, Latin, writing nonfiction, and futuristics. The SAT score requirements range from 430–500 math, 430–500 verbal, or a combined score of 900 (*Talent Development*, 1989).

MENTORSHIP PROGRAMS

Definition

Mentorship is one of the oldest instructional models we know. The notion of individual instruction goes back to Socrates, who was mentor to Plato; Aristotle, to Alexander the Great; Saul, to David. The name has been revived in recent years to describe individual direction and role modeling outside the classroom and outside the home. It names a mode of education particularly effective for able students whose needs are difficult to meet in the regular curriculum of our schools.

The goal of a mentorship is usually some combination of practical experience, career education, and cooperation between the school and an outside agency (Cox & Daniel, 1983). Boston (1976) suggested that a mentorship presumes a commitment on the part of the student and the mentor as its goal in the shaping of the student's life outlook.

The terms *mentor, intern, apprentice,* and *assistant* often overlap and are used casually by many people. The relationship labelled mentorship is not confined to specific tasks, projects, or situations, but spills over into other areas of the lives of both persons. Mentorships are significant in the education of gifted and talented students because they create opportunities for learner access to professional expertise in the community, offer real-life experiences by providing an experientially based framework for enriching the curriculum, and present traditional and nontraditional role models of competence in the pursuit of a commitment to excellence.

In general, any school district, university, and community can cooperate in the development of a mentorship program. The focus should be directed toward matching a specific interest of a student in the classroom with a community resource. Mentorships may be divided into two major types: career development and skill enhancement. Career-development mentorships focus on career explorations of interest to the student. Examples include science, business, engineering, hospital work, personnel management in industry, or work with a psychologist or social worker in the mental health field. Skill-enhancement mentorships emphasize one or more skills considered important to the learner. Examples include working with a legislator for leadership training or a chemist in industry to enhance research skills, or in a strategic planning office to develop problem-solving abilities.

Mentorships can be organized on an individual basis linking the student to a community resource program. They may be an enrichment component of a regular course, a part of a school-wide community/ career program, a community agency-based education program, or a computer-assisted global information network integrated into any learning experience.

In developing the mentorship program, it is necessary to select students who have the intensity of interest and commitment to explore learning beyond the classroom. The university and community resource people selected must have an expressed interest in pursuing such a relationship.

An orientation program should be developed to define roles: students as co-learners, teacher as facilitator, and mentor as networker. Communication and research skills should be developed, including data collection, analysis, and presentation. Self-directed learning skills—decision making, problem solving, critical thinking, effective communication, and self-evaluation—are integral to the mentorship process.

Both the university and community-based mentors must know that mentorships are negotiated learning experiences that require commitment and compatibility from all participants. It takes time to develop learning partnerships, and it must be stressed that the mentors' interests and expertise supplement rather than replace the teacher and curriculum.

Nash, Borman, and Colson (1980) developed a career education model in the 1970s for gifted and talented students. They noted the special need that able students have for career education. Such students frequently possess multiple abilities and therefore may face more complicated career and educational decisions than other students making the transition from secondary to higher education. The authors suggested that seniors be released from school to participate in a guidance lab, a mentorship trip phase, and finally an internship. The goal during the mentorship phase was twofold: (1) The student would develop a close relationship with an adult whom the student could see as guide and role model, and (2) the student would gain a sense of both the lifestyle associated with the profession or occupation and the educational course leading to it.

A more recent study of mentorships and their benefits was conducted in Minnesota (Beck, 1989). The students were juniors and seniors in high school who excelled in the areas of ability, motivation, and creativity and had identified a specific area of interest to pursue through a mentorship. They were matched with mentors from the university and community to learn about educational and career options. The participants felt that career development was the area most affected by the mentorship. It gave them the opportunity to examine lifestyles and characteristics of professionals, see how persons within a profession interact with each other, and make contacts leading to employment interviews. Without the mentor relationships, the students would not have had this guidance and direction. It is of some interest to note that the female students felt more strongly than the males that the mentorship helped them look at ways to integrate career and family.

Many states have integrated mentorships into curricula for the gifted. Ohio's *Rule for School Foundation Units for Gifted Children* (Ohio Department of Education, 1984), for example, has mentorships built into the standards for state-supported programming. The mentorship must be monitored by a certified person from the school district, who assists in student selection, curriculum preparation, scheduling, and evaluation. This program is included as an educational option and allows the student to earn school credit for study outside the school.

The literature on *monitoring* evaluation of mentorship programs has revealed that many educators have recommended that mentorships be an integral part of gifted programs, and that these programs provide excellent learner benefits. A recurring problem appears to be that many mentorships remain unfocused as to how the learning interaction between expert and student should occur (Ellingson, Haeger, & Feldhusen, 1986; Moseley & Todd, 1983; Runions, 1980).

Current and Needed Research

Mentorships, governor's schools, and the variety of programs identified here purport to stress some, if not all, of the following: development of personal and social skills, critical and creative thinking, leadership, career development and leadership, inquiry, and lifelong learning. Debate about ethics, human values, responsible decision making occur frequently in most of the program models. A question that comes readily to mind is whether the programs do what they are said to do. There is a clear consensus that they do what is claimed for them (Stewart, 1987). Do they do so better than other options? Evaluation is an ongoing effort if the work is to be maintained by each program's consumer groups. In other areas of research, do students have better understanding of themselves as a result of attending such programs? Is self-concept better for students who have had the experiences than for those who did not? Kolloff & Moore (1989) found that self-concepts were positively affected by summer programs. The evaluation of programs by the participants immediately following the programs generally indicates the highly positive nature of the experiences for the students. Their outlook on learning "seems to have changed," and the responses are "overwhelmingly positive" (Stewart, 1987, p. 14). Much remains to be done to understand the effects of such programs. Will the knowledge and abilities acquired in academic achievement, career directions, fields of investigation for the participants, personal growth, and interpersonal skills generalize to other situations?

Work in knowledge engineering suggests many fruitful lines of investigation. Ongoing research now being conducted cooperatively by the Delaware (Ohio) City Schools and the Ohio State University is attempting to provide a more systematic framework, language, and method of problem solving between student and mentor prior to field activities. The researchers are initiating knowledge engineering methodologies that employ a set of principles and procedures for a learner to interact with a specific domain expert in a highly focused manner in the areas of science and mathematics. Any opportunity to gain insight into the learning and cognitive processes of the gifted is a welcome addition to the research literature.

Serious work remains to be done on the development of leadership among gifted adolescents and young adults. Understanding of gifted children's social-emotional needs and the techniques necessary to support them in crises are also proper fields for investigation. Summer programs offer opportunities for such studies (a well-developed research program can take place without detriment to students' participation in the program). The questions are far greater than the number of answers.

SUMMARY

The past decade has seen considerable growth in alternative and summer programs. Colleges and universities, public and independent schools, private agencies and individuals are offering special experiences. That there are many choices is positive. It also means that choices became more complex.

Boyle (1987), when considering this issue, identified some key questions about summer options, which can be directed to any other option as well:

- What is the purpose of the program and how does that purpose meet special needs?
- Does the program have a good reputation among participants and consumer groups; is the reputation sound among those who seek advanced students?
- How are faculty identified, recruited, and trained?
- What are the participant selection criteria?
- How is the program evaluated and how are the results shared with consumer groups?
- Is the program residential; what are the costs and are scholarships available?

Many of the educational options considered in this chapter are exciting and of great service. In directing gifted children, these programs offer experiences unavailable in any other way. The options are great; the potential outcomes are even greater.

REFERENCES

Beck, L. (1989). Mentorships: Benefits and effects on career development. *Gifted Child Quarterly*, 33(1), 22–28.

Bloom, B. S. (Ed.). (1985). *Developing talent in young people*. New York: Ballantine.

Boston, B. (1976). *Sorcerer's apprentice*. Reston, VA: CEC/ERIC.

Boyle, J. (1987). Finding the "right" summer program. *Gifted Children Monthly*, 8, 8.

Cox, J., & Daniel, N. (1983, September/October). The role of the mentor. *G/C/T*, pp. 54–55.

Ellingson, M. K., Haeger, W. W., & Feldhusen, J. F. (1986). The Purdue mentor program. *G/C/T*, ,pp. 2–5.

Hobbs, N. (1951). Community recognition of the gifted. In P. Witty (Ed.), *The Gifted Child* (pp. 163–184). Boston: D. C. Heath.

Karnes, F. A., & Pearce, N. (1981, May/June). Governor's honors programs: A viable alternative for the gifted and talented. *G/C/T*, pp. 8–11.

Keating, D. P. (1974). The study of mathematically precocious youth. In J. C. Stanley, D. P. Keating, & L. H. Fox (Eds.), *Mathematical talent: Discovery, description, and development* (pp. 23–46). Baltimore: Johns Hopkins University Press.

Kitano, M. K., & Kirby, D. F. (1986). *Gifted education: A comprehensive view*. Boston: Little, Brown.

Kolloff, P. B., & Moore, A. D. (1989). Effects of summer programs on the self-concepts of gifted children. *Journal for the Education of the Gifted*, pp. 268–276.

Moseley, V. A., & Todd, E. W. (1983). Mentorships for gifted students (Report No. 141). Cleveland, OH: Cleveland Public Schools.

Nash, W. R., Borman, C., & Colson, S. (1980). Career education model for gifted and talented students: A senior high school model. *Exceptional Children*, 46, 404–405.

Ohio Department of Education (1984). *Rule for school foundation units for gifted children*. Columbus: Ohio Department of Education.

Runions, T. (1980). The mentor academy program: Educating the gifted and talented for the 80's. *Gifted Child Quarterly*, 24, 152–157.

Stanley, J. C. (1977). The rationale of the study of mathematically precocious youth (SMPY) during its first five years of promoting educational acceleration. In J. C. Stanley, W. C. George, & C. H. Solano (Eds.), *The gifted and creative: A fifty-year perspective* (pp. 75–112). Baltimore: Johns Hopkins University Press.

Stewart, E. (1987). Governor's schools build for tomorrow. *Gifted Children Monthly*, 8, 14–15.

Talent Development. (1989). A publication of the Midwest Talent Search. Evanston, IL: Center for Talent Development.

Ward, V. S. (1961). *Educating the gifted: An axiomatic approach*. Columbus, OH: Merrill.

Wolf, J. S., Swassing, R. H., & Fichter, G. R. (1984). Anatomy of a school. *Roeper Review*, 6, 228–229.

PART III

LIFESTYLE AND CAREER ISSUES

Gifted adolescents become gifted adults. Among the major tasks of adolescence are decisions regarding the type of career, the relative emphasis of family and career (especially for young women), and the values that the young person will carry into adulthood. We now realize that the old adage, "You can be anything you want to be," is neither useful nor necessarily true. A second, often neglected, piece of advice which should be given to gifted adolescents is, "But there are many things you can do that will not make you happy."

For this part of the book, we have chosen three topics that are pertinent to choosing appropriate adult lifestyles. These topics are learning styles (Chapter 13), careers (Chapter 14), and moral and spiritual development (Chapter 15). Although the issues associated with career selection by the gifted adolescent and the particular problems faced by each gender have been discussed elsewhere, they are important enough to be summarized and repeated here. In contrast, the sizable bodies of literature that exist regarding learning styles and moral and spiritual development rarely have addressed the needs of gifted persons as separate, specific topics.

We believe that looking at learning styles provides a useful way for gifted adolescents to clarify many of their doubts about career choice, as well as serving as a basis for understanding themselves and those around them. Of equal importance, in our opinion, is the need to provide opportunities for gifted adolescents to develop skills in clarifying those values on which they will base their adult decisions. Providing safe, nonjudgmental places in which the exploration of moral and spiritual choices can take place, supporting adolescents during those predictable phases in which they will seemingly reject the values of those around them, and discussing the real and needed application of positive values in the workplace are but a few of the tasks that can be shared by educators, counselors, and parents.

CHAPTER 13

Learning Styles: One Way to Help Gifted Adolescents Understand and Choose Lifestyles

Marlene Bireley

In both average and gifted populations, variations in learning style and personality types occur. Gifted persons, however, are likely to cluster in certain style/type patterns that differ from those of the average population. I believe that, up to now, these known patterns have been underrated and underused as a method for helping gifted persons of all ages. By describing the available learning style/personality type instruments available and the research that supports their usefulness, I am hopeful that others will share my enthusiasm for this way of looking at and working with gifted adolescents.

ASSESSING LEARNING STYLES
AND PERSONALITY TYPES

Rita Dunn (1983) defined learning style as "the way individuals concentrate on, absorb, and retain new or difficult information or skills" (p. 496). Personality type (the label preferred by some authors) has a similar connotation. Myers (1962) described Jungian type theory, upon which the type indicators described below are based, as the notion that "much apparently random variation in human behavior is actually quite orderly and consistent, being due to certain basic differences in the way people prefer to use perception and judgment" (p. 1). While many of the traits associated with style/type differences can be observed by the knowledgeable onlooker, a variety of instruments exist to assess individual patterns. It is suggested that one of these instruments be considered as the basis for counseling the gifted adolescent.

Several factors will determine which of the style/type instruments one might choose. Many provide similar information. Accessibility, time needed for administration, cost of protocols, and availability of needed training can become important variables, as can one's own background (teacher or psychologist). The following instruments illustrate the wide variety now available from which an appropriate selection can be made:

- The Learning Style Inventory (Dunn, Dunn, & Price, 1979) consists of 135 items grouped into 24 subscales. The major elements tapped are environmental (sound, light, temperature, and formal vs. informal design of space); emotional (motivation, persistence, responsibility, and structure vs. options); sociological (thinking and working with peers, by oneself, in pairs, in teams, with adults, or varied); physical (by perceptual strength—auditory, visual, or tactile/kinesthetic, with or without food/drink intake, by time of day, and by degree of mobility allowed); and, finally, by psychological style (analytical vs. global or holistic, by hemispheric preference, and impulsive vs. reflective). As the list indicates, these dimensions reflect a combination of internal characteristics and external, environmental conditions. It is hypothesized that maximum potential can best be attained by teaching children and adolescents the combination of conditions that optimize learning or by providing options for those conditions in the classroom.

Rita Dunn (1983) summarized the strengths of this instrument as its wide range (it can be used from first grade through adults), its usefulness in assisting students to identify their own styles, its potential for matching teachers' and students' styles toward the goal of higher achievement, and its ability to describe subpopulations such as the gifted and handicapped. In Dunn's review of studies completed on gifted populations (from grades 4–12), recurring characteristics included independence, persistence, self-motivation, internal control, nonconformity, and perceptual strength. The relative ease with which one can be trained on this instrument and the ease with which it can be administered are characteristics that have made it one of the most popular in educational research.

- The Learning Style Profile (Keefe & Monk, 1986) bears much resemblance to the Learning Style Inventory of Dunn, Dunn, and Price (1979); in fact, Rita Dunn was a member of the task force that developed it. It consists of 108 multiple choice items that were normed on sixth through twelfth graders. It contains 23 independent scales clustered in four areas (cognitive skills, perceptual responses, study preferences, and instructional preferences). The manual states that "it provides the basis for a more personalized approach to student advisement and placement, to instructional strategy, and to the evaluation of learning" (p. 1). For those secondary teachers who wish to provide such a supportive atmosphere in their classrooms, this instrument should be considered.

• The Learning Styles Inventory (Renzulli & Smith, 1978) is more narrowly focused than the other instruments reviewed; its sole purpose is to determine student preferences for different instructional techniques. The 66-item questionnaire covers nine different strategies: projects, drill and recitation, peer teaching, discussion, teaching games, independent study, programmed instruction, lecture, and simulation. In a factor analysis study of the instrument, Howell and Wikoff (1984) found that lecture and teaching games merged with other factors, and a new category, library research, emerged. These authors contend that their categories form a better version of the instrument. As one might expect, gifted students have been found to favor such techniques as independent study, discussion, teaching games, and peer teaching, while disliking drill, recitations, and lectures (Ricca, 1984; Stewart, 1981).

• The Learning Style Inventory (Kolb, 1976) consists of nine sets of four descriptors of human behavior (e.g., receptive, relevant, analytical, and impartial). The respondent ranks the four descriptors from "least like" to "most like" oneself. Those responses are translated into four different learning modes: concrete experience (CE), reflective observation (RO), abstract conceptualization (AC), and active experimentation (AE). Kolb interprets these modes or orientations as "being involved in experiences and dealing with immediate human situations in a personal way" (CE); "understanding the meaning of ideas and situations by carefully observing and impartially describing them" (RO); "using logic, ideas, and concepts" (AC), and "actively influencing people and changing situations" (AE) (Kolb, Rubin, & McIntyre, 1984, p. 34). The learning modes are then plotted on intersecting axes, and the strength of the resulting quadrants is determined. The characteristics of those who fall in each quadrant are summarized by the following labels: diverger (brainstormer, good imagination), assimilator (model maker, integrator), converger (decision maker, practical application), and accommodator (risk taker, action-oriented). The reader is referred to *Organizational Psychology* (Kolb, Rubin, & McIntyre, 1984) for a complete description of the theory and application of this inventory and several self-evaluation exercises that can be used by high school, college, or adult groups.

• The Gregorc Style Delineator (Gregorc, 1982b) is a schema somewhat like Kolb's, but Anthony Gregorc identified four learning styles based on preferential differences within the areas of perception and ordering. Abstractness and concreteness are manifestations of perceptual

abilities through which one grasps information. Sequence and random-
ness are differing types of ordering abilities that are used to "arrange,
systematize, reference and dispose of information" (Gregorc, 1982a,
p. 5). (In Gregorc's Energic Model of Styles he identified additional
inductive/deductive processing and separative/associative relationship
dimensions, but prefers to introduce the latter categories only to those
who are well grounded in the initial concepts [Gregorc, 1985].)

Individuals complete the delineator by ranking 10 groups of four
words each from "most like" to "least like" oneself. The scoring system
used to determine the four types utilizes a two-axis, four-quadrant system
similar to that used by Kolb. The resultant types related to quadrant
strength are labelled abstract sequential (intellectual, logical, data-based,
nonemotional); abstract random (metaphysical, subjective, relationship-
oriented); concrete sequential (practical, sensory, reality-oriented, and
ordered); and concrete random (intuitive, impulsive, and change-
oriented). The accompanying manual provides a practical description of
each of the style groups.

Advantages of the Gregorc instrument are that it can be self-adminis-
tered and scored quickly and is supported by good interpretive information. One disadvantage in a school setting is that, as an adult instrument,
its use would be limited to older students. However, it would appear that
gifted high school students would have little difficulty understanding the
test items.

• The Herrmann Brain Dominance Instrument (Herrmann, 1981)
taps a number of areas of functioning (handedness, best/worst subjects,
work elements, descriptive adjectives, hobbies, energy level, motion
sickness, introversion/extraversion, and personal-preference statements).
Similar to some of the other instruments, responses are plotted on a four-
quadrant, two-axis chart. The four resulting types include cerebral left
(logical, analyzer, mathematical, technical, problem solver); cerebral
right (creative, synthesizer, artistic, holistic, conceptualizer); limbic left
(controlled, conservative, planner, organizer, administrator); and limbic
right (interpersonal, emotional, musical, spiritual, talker) (Herrmann,
1981). Herrmann's work is interesting in that he has used current brain
research as a basis for the items in his inventory. While accessibility to this
instrument can be a problem (training and distribution are controlled by
the author), a recent publication (Herrmann, 1988) provides an excellent
guide to Herrmann's work and should result in wider distribution of this
model. A major portion of that book provides guidelines for developing
personal creativity and choosing careers based on one's style.

• The Myers-Briggs Type Inventory (MBTI) (Briggs & Myers, 1977)
consists of 126 or 166 (Forms G or F) forced choice items that tap 16

different types. The concepts and language level of the MBTI limit its use below seventh grade level for gifted students and below high school for the general population. The dimensions assessed by the instrument are based on the work of the psychologist Karl Jung (see Campbell, 1971, for a detailed discussion of Jungian theory) and consist of attitudes toward the inner/outer world (introversion [I] vs. extraversion [E]), ways of perceiving (sensing [S] vs. intuition [N]), ways of decision making (thinking [T] vs. feeling [F]), and a lifestyle dimension (judging [J] vs. perceiving [P]). The lifestyle dimensions were not Jungian types, but were added by the authors of the MBTI. According to our research (Hoehn & Bireley, 1988), the most typical gifted type is INFP (introversion, intuition, feeling, perception). An INFP individual prefers to process information by thinking by him- or herself; is future- rather than present-oriented; uses subjective, people-oriented decision-making processes; and prefers a spontaneous, flexible lifestyle, rather than one that is planned and orderly. Other types can be described by using similar, appropriate descriptors.

• The Learning Preference Inventory (LPI) (Silver and Hanson, 1978) consists of 35 sets of four responses that are rated by the child from "most like" to "least like" oneself. Scoring yields types in introversion/ extraversion, sensing/intuiting, and thinking/feeling, but omits the judging/perceiving functions. A strength of this instrument is the manual (Silver & Hanson, 1980), which suggests many ways for providing an optimal environment for children of each type. While it is more useful for younger children, it can be used with early adolescents. I would recommend it to those who want to assess type at an early age in a schema that is compatible with Jungian philosophy. By starting with the LPI or the Murphy-Meisgeier Type Indicator for Children, which is described next, one can develop long-range data on children who cannot be assessed by the Myers-Briggs Type Indicator until junior high school.

• The Murphy-Meisgeier Type Indicator for Children (MMTIC) (Meisgeier & Murphy, 1987a) consists of 70 forced choice items that can be administered to children grades 2–8. Unlike the Learning Preference Inventory (Silver & Hanson, 1978), which omits the judging/perceiving functions, all dimensions of the MBTI are reported on this inventory, making the MMTIC an attractive choice for the elementary grades. The manual (Meisgeier & Murphy, 1987b) provides an informative history of type, but has fewer teaching suggestions than does the manual that accompanies the LPI. Combining childhood information from the LPI or MMTIC with that of the MBTI for the adolescent or adult, can form the basis for lifelong classroom, personal, and career counseling and decision making.

USING LEARNING STYLE RESEARCH

Classroom Implications

Those who favor a learning style approach have found many specific classroom applications for their work. One of the most noteworthy is Bernice McCarthy (1980), who developed the 4Mat system of teaching based on the work of David Kolb (1976). McCarthy recognized classroom reality by acknowleding that no one teacher can accommodate the styles of all students simultaneously. Instead, she developed an eight-step teaching sequence that addressed Kolb's (1976) four quadrants and, additionally, right and left hemispheric functioning. In 4Mat, the lesson is introduced through an experiential activity that is designed to integrate the new material with previous experience (the affective, personal application needs of Kolb's diverger type are best served by this phase). Facts and concepts are then presented (the lecture phase) to expand on the introduction and address the assimilator's "watching" needs. The third phase consists of hands-on practice and application, which best suit the converger. Finally, analyzing the concept and applying it in new, more complex situations matches the strength of the accommodator group. While persons in each style group are most comfortable and like best those activities aimed at their group, they are able to function quite well with the two adjacent styles. It is only when the activities of the opposite styles (i.e., diverger-converger and assimilator-accommodator) are in progress, that lack of interest or difficulty may arise. It is McCarthy's contention that accommodating all of the people three-quarters of the time is preferable to teaching primarily in and to one's own style and neglecting the needs of the other three quadrant types.

Both Myers and McCaulley (1985) reporting on the MBTI (Briggs & Myers, 1977) and Silver and Hanson (1980) in interpreting their own instrument, the LPI (Silver & Hanson, 1978), have suggested that optimum classroom learning can take place when teachers and students are aware of their own types and when classroom options are developed for each. Teachers can accommodate type variations in the classroom by providing opportunities for different working conditions and a variety of assignments or reporting methods. Comparing introverts and extraverts, the former would tend to choose individual projects and working alone, while the latter would prefer group-oriented tasks and discussions. Sensors prefer practical, hands-on activities, while intuiters want imaginative, open-ended, more complex challenges. Thinkers are attracted by routine, logic, theories, and structure, while feelers need people-oriented, interactive projects. Finally, judgers need structure, routine, and self-control, while perceivers prefer spontaneity and many activities progressing at once.

Functioning With and Against Type

In addition to providing varying classroom opportunities, two other questions arise when dealing with the gifted. First, to what extent should children be required to function against type? Second, if teachers and students are very different in style, is it possible that children are labelled as uncooperative and unrealistic if they rebel when consistently confronted with "against type" activities and assignments?

The former question concerned us (Hoehn & Bireley, 1988) after our research revealed that the predominant type for gifted children is NF (intuitive, feeling). Given the ST practical, precise nature of the basic skills curriculum and the percentage of teachers who are sensors (nearly half of elementary and about 42% of high school instructors, according to Myers & McCaulley, 1985), it is little wonder that a frequent complaint about gifted students is that they resist completing basic skills assignments. Indeed, in my experience, releasing some students from regular classes for attendance in gifted pullout programs causes dissension because regular class teachers perceive these children as "lazy," resistive nonworkers, who could not possibly be "gifted." In the gifted classroom, these same children often become highly creative dynamos. From a learning style framework, the better match of the typical gifted child's style preferences and the more open-ended, individualized curriculum of the pullout program are understandable explanations for the difference. Nevertheless, around 80% of the typical gifted child's school time and much of adult life consists of against type (that is, routine) action. Gifted children need to be counselled about this phenomenon and the necessity for all of us to learn tolerance for "boring" activities. On the other hand, denying such a child access to the gifted program on the basis of nonproductivity in the regular class should be considered carefully and applied in only the most extreme cases.

Secondary students appear to be less at risk for the scenario described above. Through a wider selection of courses and extracurricular activities, most style differences can be accommodated, given reasonably good teaching. However, if experiences in elementary school have been negative, attitudes toward education and learning may continue to have implications during the high school years. Turned-off underachievers may not develop the academic record and knowledge base needed to pursue later career choices without remediation. Others may continue to struggle against the system and go unrecognized as gifted throughout their secondary school years.

Social and Emotional Implications

While style theory can easily deteriorate into "pop" psychology or daily horoscope simplicity, the clues that one can gain about oneself and others are of great help in interpreting varying reactions to life events. The two basic pathological reactions to stress—aggression and withdrawal—are predictable extensions of extraversion and introversion, respectively. The former group is more likely to break societal rules, but the latter will more likely turn the pain inward and resort to depression, perfectionism, eating disorders, and suicide. These topics are covered in this book as those most associated with the gifted population. It should come as no surprise, then, to find that while the general population is about 75% extraverted, the reverse is true of gifted persons (Myers & McCaulley, 1985). Introverted gifted persons can, predictably, become their own worst enemies. Similarly, the sensing predominance of the general population (75%) contrasts with a similarly high percentage of gifted intuiters. This practical, "now" orientation of the sensers vs. the possibility, future orientation of the intuiters can provide the basis for a productive team effort or can be a significantly divisive force. The gifted student who feels different or who can find few people who "understand what I'm talking about" may be reflecting frustration associated with the rarity of intuitive peers.

In regard to the thinking/feeling dimension on the MBTI, gifted males at the secondary level followed the gender pattern preference of thinking over feeling, while females followed the typical reverse pattern. Both groups clearly preferred feeling at the elementary level, as did an average group studied by Silver and Hanson (1980) (all groups were in the 60%–70% range). The adolescent movement toward the more logical, objective style of the thinker (apparent in both males and females, but to a greater degree in males) may reflect a movement from the egocentrism of the younger child, an adaptation of societal gender expectations, a response to curricular demands, or a maturation of the ability to think more objectively and logically (Hoehn & Bireley, 1988).

Finally, Myers and McCaulley (1985) reported a very slight preference for judging over perceiving (about 55%–60%) in the general population, but a consistent skewing (about two-thirds) toward perceiving in gifted junior high students, National Merit finalists, and creative men and women. Since high perceivers tend to be drawn into many activities without the need to reach closure, they need to guard against the "overload" that may result when one tries to pursue more interests than time will allow. Perceivers may prefer creative opportunities rather than those that require structure and detail (e.g., creative writing over scientific experimentation), while the reverse may be true of the more structured

J's. Forced participation or lower achievement in against type classes or activities may result in frustration, resistance, or emotional distress. Becoming aware of personal feelings under different conditions increases in importance when career options are explored.

Career Choice Implications

Kolb, Rubin, and McIntyre (1984), Myers and McCaulley (1985), and Herrmann (1988) all focused much of their attention toward the matching of learning style and career choice. Kolb, Rubin, and McIntyre (1984) related their converger type to the physical sciences; divergers to counselors, organization development specialists, and personnel managers; assimilators to research and management personnel; and accommodators to marketing and sales persons.

Similarly, Herrmann (1988) grouped entrepreneurs, playwrights, artists, and trainers as cerebral rights; nurses, musicians, social workers, and teachers as limbic rights; planners, bureaucrats, administrators, and bookkeepers as limbic lefts; and lawyers, engineers, bankers, and doctors as cerebral lefts.

Myers and McCaulley (1985) have compiled research on thousands of individuals who have taken the MBTI. This compilation revealed that all 16 types exist in each profession, but that anticipated stereotypes are prevalent, as indicated in the following examples:

- Marketing personnel, insurance agents, and sales clerks are among the most extraverted, while librarians, chemists, and electrical engineers are the most introverted;
- Factory workers, police, and farmers are high sensers, while social scientists and creative entertainers are high intuiters;
- Sales managers, research analysts, computer systems analysts, and auditors are high thinkers, while clergy, teachers, and receptionists are highest in feeling;
- Engineers, vocational teachers, and managers show the highest preferences for the orderly life of the judger, while carpenters, performing artists, and journalists are among the most represented spontaneous perceivers.

Similar breakdowns occur for the 16 specific types. These known relationships between type and career can be most useful to students who are involved in the decision-making process.

Looking at those values that seem to cluster with each type is another way to assist the adolescent. Kolb, Rubin, and McIntyre (1984) have suggested that the pertinent goals one should attend to when doing life planning include career satisfaction, status and respect, personal relationships, leisure satisfactions, learning and education, spiritual growth and religion, and material rewards and possessions. Each person should place a high, medium, or low value on each area, consider the cross-impact of stressing one area over another, and, eventually, aim toward a *life plan* in which career is but one element. Once this process has been completed and used to supplement information based on a learning style instrument, mentorships or job shadowing in preferred or unexplored areas can be selected to provide experience in a range of type options. This would be most critical when a student has decided on an against type career. A careful study of all of these variables is important for a student whose postsecondary education may entail many years of study and a sizable monetary commitment.

WHEN TEACHERS, PARENTS, AND STUDENTS DISAGREE

The adversarial relationship that can develop between educators and gifted students can be brought into a better perspective when viewed from learning style theory. Ideally, through the study of learning style, teachers and students can learn to better understand and tolerate differences. When teachers and students cannot resolve their differences, others may need to become involved. Mediators in such relationships may point out stylistic differences and negotiate mutually acceptable compromises (e.g., students will do and turn in homework that they consider redundant and unnecessary, and teachers will allow a variety of ways to report on required reading). When either students or teachers are intractable (and I fear it may more likely be the latter), the mediator or counselor may wish to teach the more flexible persons the skills needed to tolerate the rigidity of others.

Teachers may be temporary annoyances in the scheme of life, but families are forever. Critical issues may arise when the styles of a mother and father are in opposition, and a child is caught in the middle (e.g., father as disciplinarian and mother as comforter is a traditional gender enactment of the thinking/feeling differences between the sexes). Most research indicates that learning style opposites attract because we admire in others those qualities that we lack. However, once the match is made, living with style opposites requires a level of tolerance and compromise not ordinarily anticipated in our living happily ever after fantasies. This in-house "battle of the sexes" may be positive in that some children learn at an early age to tolerate the differences in each parent and generalize them to the world at large. Other children can be caught in an emotionally deterimental middle, if parents rigidly oppose each other. Explaining style differences may be an ideal method for assisting families in such a situation, because of the nonpathological connotation of stylistic variation.

Another deterimental circumstance may result when the child emerges as a very different type from what the family values (e.g., the artist son of a military officer, or the child who needs high structure but must live in a spontaneous, disorganized household). The databank of the MBTI (available in Myers & McCaulley, 1985) can provide useful information for an adolescent with different type parents, particularly if there is pressure from the parents to pursue a certain career or lifestyle. That databank indicates that every profession or professional organization needs people of every type. Counselors can note that a surgeon's child who may not possess the dexterity or the patience (sensing, judging characteristics) for that specialty may become a superb, highly intuitive diagnostician or psychiatrist (professionals who tend to be intuitive perceivers) (Myers & McCaulley, 1985). While we would hope that all gifted adolescents would be free to choose the career and life best suited to their own emerging styles and value systems, reality and "purse strings" sometimes dictate otherwise. Looking for variations within the family theme may provide a compromise choice for all concerned.

SUMMARY

In summary, the range of application of learning style and personality type information is wide and meaningful. I believe that an understanding of personal style is one of the most accessible and critical variables that can be shared with gifted adolescents during their quest for self-understanding.

REFERENCES

Briggs, K. C.,& Myers, I. B. (1977). *Myers-Briggs Type Indicator*. Palo Alto, CA: Consulting Psychologists Press.

Campbell, J. (Ed.). (1971). *The portable Jung*. New York: Penguin.

Dunn, R. (1983). Learning style and its relation to exceptionality at both ends of the spectrum. *Exceptional Children, 49*, 496–506.

Dunn, R., Dunn, K., & Price, G. (1979). *Learning Style Inventory*. Lawrence, KS: Price Systems.

Gregorc, A. (1982a). *An adult's guide to style.* Columbia, CT: Author.

Gregorc, A. (1982b). *Gregorc Style Delineator: A self-assessment instrument for adults.* Columbia, CT: Author.

Gregorc, A. (1985). *Inside styles: Beyond the basics.* Columbia, CT: Author.

Herrmann, N. (1981). *Herrmann Brain Dominance Instrument.* Lake Lure, NC: Applied Creative Services.

Herrmann, N. (1988). *The creative brain.* Lake Lure, NC: Brain Books.

Hoehn, L., & Bireley, M. K. (1988). Mental processing preferences of gifted children. *Illinois Council for the Gifted Journal, 7,* 28–31.

Howell, H., & Wikoff, R. (1984). A factor analysis of the Renzulli and Smith Learning Style Inventory with gifted children. *Roeper Review, 7,* 119–123.

Keefe, J. W., & Monk, J. S. (1986). *Learning Style Profile.* Reston, VA: National Association of Secondary School Principals.

Kolb, D. A. (1976). *Learning Style Inventory.* Boston: McBer.

Kolb, D. A., Rubin, I. M., & McIntyre, J. M. (1984). *Organizational psychology: An experiential approach to organizational behavior* (4th ed.). Englewood Cliffs, NJ: Prentice-Hall.

McCarthy, B. (1980). *The 4Mat System.* Arlington Heights, IL: EXCEL.

Meisgeier, C., & Murphy, E. (1987a). *The Murphy-Meisgeier Type Indicator for Children.* Palo Alto, CA: Consulting Psychologists Press.

Meisgeier, C., & Murphy, E. (1987b). *Murphy-Meisgeier Type Indicator for Children manual.* Palo Alto, CA: Consulting Psychologists Press.

Myers, I. (1962). *Manual: The Myers-Briggs Type Indicator.* Palo Alto, CA: Consulting Psychologists Press.

Myers, I. B., & McCaulley, M. H. (1985). *Manual: A guide to the development and use of the Myers-Briggs Type Indicator.* Palo Alto, CA: Consulting Psychologists Press.

Renzulli, J. S., & Smith, L. H. (1978). *Learning Styles Inventory: A measure of student preference for instructional techniques.* Mansfield Center, CT: Creative Learning Press.

Ricca, J. (1984). Learning styles and preferred instructional strategies of gifted students. *Gifted Child Quarterly, 28,* 121–126.

Silver, H. F., & Hanson, J. R. (1978). *Learning Preference Inventory.* Moorestown, NJ: Institute for Cognitive and Behavioral Studies.

Silver, H. F., & Hanson, J. R. (1980). *User's manual: The TLC Learning Preference Inventory.* Moorestown, NJ: Institute for Cognitive and Behavioral Studies.

Stewart, E. D. (1981). Learning styles among gifted/talented students: Instructional technique preferences. *Exceptional Children, 48,* 134–138.

CHAPTER 14

Career Choices for Gifted Adolescents: Overcoming Stereotypes

Constance L. Hollinger

For many gifted and talented adolescents, choosing a career is a highly complex, challenging, and frequently anxiety-producing task. Multiple gifts and talents, ambiguity regarding future careers, expectations for the "realization of one's potential," and recognition of the degree of commitment of time and financial resources have all been cited as issues compounding the career-development tasks confronting the gifted. Though these issues are indeed major, none has quite the pervasive, insidious impact of the human phenomenon of stereotyping. Through subtle and blatant, implicit and explicit messages that permeate our culture, stereotypes deny individual uniqueness and restrict career, as well as life, choices. Stereotypes of the gifted, sex-role stereotypes, and occupational stereotypes independently and interactively foreclose options and limit freedom of career choice, particularly for gifted women. The impact of such stereotypes is seen in differential representation of men and women in junior high programs for the gifted, in math and science course taking, in accelerated programs for the gifted, and ultimately in high status careers, particularly those in math and the sciences. Such differential representation is particularly striking in light of the documented decline of sex differences in even those few ability areas where differences had been documented (Jacklin, 1989).

While this chapter focuses primarily on the gifted female adolescent, stereotypes have a negative impact on the male adolescent as well, perhaps less so with respect to career choice and achievement but possibly more so with respect to his realization of potential in other life roles. Whether male or female, gifted adolescents must confront and overcome any of a number of stereotypes if they are to realize their unique potential. In order for them to do so, the nature and function of stereotypes must be recognized and understood.

THE NATURE OF STEREOTYPES

The Stereotyping Process

The ability to form concepts is central to human functioning. Concepts are essential for effective and efficient interaction and communication. They enable us to organize our experience of reality and reduce an overwhelmingly complex array of sensory information to manageable proportions. Stereotypes serve similar functions. A "person" represents an extremely complex stimulus. Social stereotypes enable us to reduce such complexity on the basis of a few physical cues, such as sex, race, and attire, or a few labels, such as "rabbi," "physician," or "liberal." In reviewing stereotypes and the stereotyping process, Frieze and her colleagues (1978) concluded that "the propensity to categorize and to stereotype is indeed a powerful phenomena [sic]. Perhaps it is even one of the basic processes of our cognitive development" (p. 128). Therefore, it is easy to understand why stereotypes are so resistant to change and difficult to overcome.

Unfortunately, stereotypes are as detrimental as they are functional. In rigidly assigning common traits or characteristics to all members of a group, stereotypes obscure within-group differences, deny the uniqueness of individuals, and reflect societal bias and prejudices more than reality. Behaving in accordance with its stereotypical perceptions, society positively reinforces behaviors consistent with stereotypical expectations, punishes behaviors that deviate from the "norm," and, in effect, creates a self-fulfilling prophecy (Lerner, 1986). For the individual recipient of society's stereotyped messages, two options are available. At best, the individual recognizes the inaccuracies of stereotypically assigned traits and experiences anger and frustration with societal prejudices. At worst, the assigned traits are internalized, regardless of accuracy, into the individual's self-belief system and form the basis for internal barriers to the realization of potential.

Effect on the Gifted Adolescent

While many must cope with stereotypes related to race, religion, handicapping conditions, and socioeconomic status, all gifted adolescents are confronted by the stereotypes associated with giftedness, sex roles, and occupations. Despite decades of data to the contrary, the predominantly negative stereotype of the gifted individual persists. The mere assignment of the label *gifted* sets up a broad range of expectations among teachers, parents, and peers. Such stereotyped perceptions of, and the concomitant expectations for, the gifted have a negative impact on adolescents when expectations to "realize one's potential" directly conflict with their need to "fit in with" and "be just like" their peers, or with their desire to pursue vocational or unconventional career options.

However, the most powerful stereotype, particularly with respect to career choice, is the sex-role stereotype, those "widely held conceptions about the sexes that attribute certain sets of characteristics uniquely to one sex . . . [and] exaggerate or distort the actual degree of difference between the sexes" (Cook, 1985, p. 3). There is a clear societal consensus as to what characteristics are "feminine" and what characteristics are "masculine." The majority of these characteristics can be categorized into either an instrumental–expressive (Parsons & Bales, 1953) or an agentic–communal (Bakan, 1966) dichotomy. Instrumental or agentic attributes, such as "confident," "logical," "independent," and other characteristics essential for academic and career achievement, are stereotypically assigned to men. Expressive or communal attributes, such as "sensitive to others," "kind," "cooperative," and other characteristics central to social or interpersonal "achievements" (see Eccles, 1985), are stereotypically assigned to women. Sex-role stereotypes further specify that these attributes are polar opposites. Being instrumental not only means being "masculine" but also means *not* being "feminine."

The adolescent's career exploration is further limited by the fact that disciplines and careers are also gender stereotyped. The majority of high status careers, particularly those in business, math, and the sciences, are stereotyped as masculine, while lower status careers, especially those of a clerical, service, or helping nature, are stereotyped as feminine (Eccles & Hoffman, 1984; Gottfredson, 1981). This stereotyping of occupations, seen among children as early as 2 to 3 years of age, increases from preschool through the elementary school years. By adolescence, career exploration tends to be limited to those careers congruent with the adolescent's gender identity.

For the gifted male adolescent, the masculine stereotype and concomitant instrumental attributes are congruent with and conducive to academic and career achievement. Society's sex-role stereotypical expectation is that he will realize his potential and prove successful in some challenging, high status, and/or high paying career. Unfortunately, these expectations may also exacerbate the press to succeed, contributing to burnout or "Type A" personality development, and restrict his career and life choices. While research on the effects of stereotyping on gifted males is all but nonexistent, the strong, negative social reactions to men who deviate from sex-role appropriate behavior are well documented. A gifted young man is far from being free to choose to become a nurse, a kindergarten teacher, or a househusband.

Gifted women, in contrast, face a major conflict between femininity and achievement. Neither instrumental attributes central to achievement nor challenging career options are feminine, according to societal stereotypes. This "dilemma of the gifted woman" (Noble, 1987)—a three-way interaction of conflicting role expectations—accounts for the "disappearance" of many gifted women (Reis, 1987; Schwartz, 1980). The conflict emerges in adolescence, when biological changes, social pressures, and a need to conform lead the female adolescent to question whether she is "feminine enough" to fit in with her peer group and to be attractive to male peers. Concurrently, achievement-related pressures increase as she works toward gaining acceptance to the "right" college or university and ultimately selecting a career direction, typically from among multiple options. Given the magnitude of these developmental tasks, the additional stress generated by conflicting role expectations can be overwhelming. By abandoning achievement, avoiding math and science, opting out of gifted programs, and eliminating "masculine" career options, many gifted female adolescents reduce the complexity and escape the stress of conflicting role expectations. It is for these gifted female adolescents that assistance in overcoming stereotypes is imperative.

COMBATTING THE EFFECTS OF STEREOTYPES

Efforts to overcome stereotypes should focus primarily on society and the significant others who directly and indirectly teach the cultural stereotypes to children. Attention should be directed toward all who create, condone, or remain unaware of stereotypical portrayals in the media, in advertising, and in textbooks, programs, and curricula. Stereotypes reside within the culture, not innately within the individual. The virtual absence of programs designed to alter the stereotypes themselves and to educate the social agents who perpetuate them testifies to the need for externally focused efforts. Directing interventions solely toward gifted women perpetuates the game of "catch-up" in which the onus of responsibility continues to rest with the victim rather than the source. Unfortunately, cultural restructuring requires time, during which generations of those "victimized" by stereotypes would fail to realize their potential. In the interim, efforts directed toward gifted young women must be continued.

Many would argue that adolescence is "too late" for effective intervention. However, because of the unique characteristics of this developmental period, adolescence affords an excellent opportunity for intervention. With increasing cognitive maturity, the adolescent is capable of dealing with abstractions and making more subtle and refined differentiations. Concurrent with this increased cognitive sophistication is an increased flexibility with respect to sex-role stereotypes (Kohlberg, 1966). In fact, Ullian (1976) suggests that if androgynous attitudes are to develop at all, they will during adolescence, a crucial developmental period in which exposure to discrepant role models can produce alteration of sex-role stereotypical schemata (Rebecca, Hefner, & Oleshansky, 1976). Finally, for the gifted young woman, the salience and stresses of conflicting role expectations may actually enhance her readiness and receptivity for intervention. While early intervention is preferable, the fatalistic view that adolescence is "too late" is simply unwarranted.

Facilitating the career development of gifted young women is a highly complex task. A comprehensive intervention model would be multidimensional, beginning with a basic, comprehensive career education program elaborated and modified to address the unique needs of the gifted in general and gifted young women in particular. Second, intervention needs to be multimodal, including such diverse components as information labs and community-based mentorships. Intervention efforts need to be individualized or diagnostic/prescriptive in nature in order to avoid creating new stereotypes while in the process of overcoming the current ones. Not all gifted women fear success, avoid advanced mathematics, and choose nursing over neurosurgery, although many do. Finally, the search for a panacea needs to be abandoned!

Program Components and Intervention Strategies

The relatively new and sparse literature on the career development of women reveals a variety of approaches to the problem of overcoming stereotypes. While longitudinal research and program evaluation are needed to identify the most effective intervention models, the following components have been used successfully in a number of programs.

Academic Advising. Combatting the effects of stereotyping must begin well before actual career choices are made, if a full range of options is to remain available. Academic advising plays a critical role in preventing premature foreclosure of options, as occurs when the gifted female adolescent opts out of advanced math and science coursework in high school. In doing so, she discovers only later that she has inadvertently foreclosed her options for admission to the many universities, colleges, and majors that require substantial math and science high school backgrounds. Advisors must do more than merely inform the adolescent about the importance of math and science. Given predominant social values, interests, and career goals, female adolescents frequently perceive math and science as having minimal task value and as requiring extraordinary effort. Comprehensive academic advising must therefore include exploration of values, future goals, self-perceptions of ability, and the relevance of math and science. As Higham and Navarre (1984) have noted, many young gifted women are surprised to learn of the centrality of math and science to the helping professions. In general, advising is needed that will move gifted adolescents away from dichotomous, either/or thinking, enabling them to see the art in mathematics and science as well as the math and science required by the arts.

Instructional Strategies and Classroom Climate. The consistently documented gender differences in classroom interaction are congruent with sex-role stereotypes. Males dominate the classrooms, science labs, and computer labs, and receive attention and encouragement from teachers for doing so. Female students typically assume passive observer or secretarial roles. They not only are rewarded for such passivity but may also be punished for assertive behavior that violates the stereotypical norm. Unfortunately for gifted young women, passivity directly contradicts the sound pedagogical admonition of learning by doing, and precludes the active involvement and self-assertion essential to the learning process.

To break the stereotype-perpetuating cycle, "girl-friendly" classes are suggested, especially in the traditionally male areas of math and science. Such classes should be taught by female instructors, consist entirely or predominantly of female students, provide hands-on and leadership experiences, emphasize real-life and career applications, provide opportunities for success in the absence of real or perceived social sanctions, and be characterized by cooperation rather than competition (Casserly, 1980). The attitudes and behaviors of the teacher toward women and their achievements, rather than the sex of the teacher, may ultimately prove to be the key ingredients in creating a psychologically safe learning environment for gifted young women.

Psychological Education. Psychological education provides the information essential for understanding human behavior in general, and stereotyping in particular. Whether integrated into the existing curriculum or presented as a separate unit or course, the content should include stereotyping functions and processes, the barriers created by sex-role socialization, the historical and cultural origins of gender stereotypes, and true sex and gender variations in human behavior. In the process, students should be challenged to examine "unasked" questions and to seek new perspectives (e.g., Why do women choose nursing? Why don't men become kindergarten teachers? What expressive attributes should a computer scientist possess?). Finally, students should be encouraged to read the biographies of eminent women as well as books that address specifically female issues (such as Braiker, 1986; Kerr, 1985).

Self-exploration. For Super (1963, 1980), career choice represents the expression of one's self-concept, with individuals rejecting occupations incongruent with their self-view in favor of those that maximize the opportunity for self-expression. Gifted young women need not only to identify their specific self-beliefs but also to evaluate critically the origins and validity of those beliefs, if they are to overcome stereotypical thinking. They should also be encouraged to explore those beliefs that are not part of their self-concept, but that have been excluded, according to gender schema theory (Bem, 1981), because they were incongruent with the gender schema. Having critically evaluated those self-beliefs that are and are not part of her self-concept, the gifted female adolescent can move forward to greater refinement and differentiation of her self-belief system.

Recognizing the context specificity of attributes (e.g., the "aggressive" tennis player who is also the "gentle and loving" parent) and the questionable validity of assigning any attribute or ability to one sex or the other, is critical to the refinement and differentiation of the self-belief system. Both gifted young men and women need to recognize that possessing both instrumental and expressive qualities not only enhances the range of one's potential responses to situations but also corresponds with higher self-esteem, greater occupational confidence, less traditional career interests, and, ultimately, greater life satisfaction (Hollinger & Fleming, 1988). Such psychological androgyny is central to the realization of one's potential, provided it is not imposed as a new social straight-jacket but is introduced as a concept that can be tailored to be congruent with one's nature.

Young women need particular assistance in evaluating their perceptions of their abilities. They tend to underestimate their strengths and focus on their weaknesses, even to the point of comparing their own areas of weakness with others for whom those areas are individual strengths. Such inaccurate evaluations frequently lead to avoidance of career options in which, on the basis of objective data, they could compete quite successfully. The *Career Data Books* (Flanagan, Tiedeman, Willis, & McLaughlin, 1973) provide one tool for gaining a more objective perspective of one's abilities in relation to various career options. Following re-evaluation of abilities, gifted young women need to examine their abilities collectively in a profile rather than in isolation. Mathematically talented female adolescents with math/science career aspirations have been found to differ from their more traditionally oriented counterparts not in their self-perceptions of math ability but in lower self-evaluations of artistic ability (Hollinger, 1985). For some, their career goal seems to be a choice by default.

Finally, self-exploration in relationship to achievement is essential since internal psychological barriers frequently prevent gifted young women from fully realizing their potential. Fear of perceived negative consequences of success, discomfort in competitive situations, low self-esteem, and lack of assertiveness are but a few such barriers. Interventions designed to overcome those barriers may include specific skill training (e.g., assertiveness training). However, a greater need is for each young woman to formulate a specific, personal definition of success and achievement; determine the personal benefits and costs perceived to be related to the definition; and examine associated conflicts and dilemmas that exist or may arise. Assistance may be needed to move from either/or (marriage or career) and if/then ("If I get an A in AP physics, then no one will date me") thinking to more integrative and creative problem solving.

Career Exploration. Existing career education programs for the gifted need revision if they are to combat stereotypical decision making. Many career assessment instruments are sex-biased and need to be used cautiously. Occupational realities need to be addressed directly if stereotyped perceptions of occupations are to be overcome. While Perry Mason may portray the occupational image of a lawyer, law library research is closer to a lawyer's reality. Accurate sex-ratio representations of occupations need to be presented, examined, and thoroughly discussed. Finally and most critically, careers must be explored as but one facet of life (Astin, 1985; Farmer, 1985; Tittle, 1983). Compared to men, women's career patterns are quite complex. Gifted young women need to be introduced to options such as flex time and job sharing as well as to the consequences of the "Superwoman Syndrome" (Noble, 1989).

Skill Development. Four career-development skills appear particularly salient for gifted young women: lifework planning skills, decision-making skills (particularly as related to dual-career relationships), negotiation skills, and compromising strategies. Compromising, in particular, needs to be addressed since, for gifted women, compromise frequently means lowering aspirations or, at best, choosing traditionally feminine specialties (biology rather than physics, pediatrics rather than surgery) as concessions to sex-role stereotyping rather than as personal preferences.

Role Models. Exposure in print or in person to role models who contradict stereotypes is critical. The cognitive dissonance set up by seeing Sally Ride perform as an astronaut assists in modifying the belief that only men can be astronauts. Unfortunately, a critical mass of female role models is needed or the "exception to the rule" may be regarded as deviant. Freud attributed the significant contributions of his daughter, Anna, to psychoanalytic theory to her "unresolved masculinity complex" (Young-Bruehl, 1988). Length of time of exposure must be examined as well. Brooks, Holahan, and Galligan (1985) were unsuccessful in significantly increasing women's choice of nontraditional careers after a 5-week exposure to them. While some specifics for success are unknown, the need for role models is apparent. Having successful women share their experiences with vocational and lifestyle choices, the realities of multiple life roles, and the challenges of internal and external barriers appears to be essential and most effective, provided that both role models and students are prepared in advance for the experience.

Mentors. The role of mentors has been addressed in Chapter 12. In our context, the opportunity for this one-to-one relationship can be particularly helpful. While true mentorship relationships cannot be "assigned," opportunities for significant interaction can be provided. In optimal experiences, the pair is matched in style and personality, have time for frequent and unhurried interactions, and are prepared in advance for their roles (Edlind & Haensly, 1985). For gifted young women, it is particularly important that the initial power imbalance inherent in mentorships move toward equity, or the mentorship will serve to perpetuate the stereotype of women as dependent and powerless and may actually become counterproductive. Despite disagreement in the literature, it appears that either women or men can serve successfully as mentors to young gifted women, provided they possess appropriate behaviors and attitudes. In reality, female mentors are simply not available in all areas.

Support Groups. Same-sex peer support groups appear to be a key factor in enabling gifted female adolescents to overcome the effects of stereotypes (Casserly, 1980). For many adolescents, peers are more effective than adults in counteracting the feeling of social isolation and "lone deviancy." It is insufficient, if not unethical, to encourage young women to be assertive, pursue achievement, and aspire to nontraditional careers, without providing support for coping with the negative responses that may be elicited from others.

Representative Programs

Over the past 20 years, numerous programs for combatting the effects of stereotyping have been designed and implemented using some of the strategies described above. "Girl-friendly" mathematics and science programs have been described by Rand and Gibb (1989), Brody and Fox (1980), and MacDonald (1980). Psychological education and self-exploration have been the focus of Guttentag and Bray (1976), O'Neil (1980), and Bell (1989). Bell's program, Project REACH, is of note because of its emphasis on externalization. The goal of enabling gifted young women to realize that the "fault" does not reside within themselves but rather within society is a unique and critical one.

Kerr's (1986) work, the Career Awareness Model for Girls (Tobin & Fox, 1980), and our own Project CHOICE (Fleming & Hollinger, 1979) focused on career development, self-exploration, psychological education, skill development, and role models or mentors. Project CHOICE is unique in its diagnostic/prescriptive approach that recognized individual differences with respect to talents and abilities, presence or absence of internal or external barriers, as well as stage of career development and nature of career aspiration.

Two programs that relied almost exclusively on role models or mentors were described by Nash, Borman, and Colson (1980) and Shamanoff (1985). The former used university faculty as role models and developed community-based internship programs in career areas of student interest. The latter, entitled the Women Mentor Project, offered an early intervention approach by providing mentors for gifted girls in grades 4–12.

While the above programs focus on young women, some are wholly or partially designed to assist parents, teachers, and counselors to examine their own stereotypical beliefs and expectations. EQUALS (Kreinberg, 1978) focused on the behaviors of teachers of mathematics. Both Action Science (Rand & Gibb, 1989) and Project CHOICE involved parents, teachers, and counselors in some of the training experiences.

The need for broadened programmatic efforts is made clear by research findings on the attitudes of gifted young men who, for the most part, hold very traditional views of women and their careers. Kerr's (1986) work with gifted adolescent males in lifework planning groups is one of the rare programs that facilitate young men's exploration of such issues as androgyny, dual-career marriages, and the integration of career and family. By failing to assist gifted young men, we not only allow them to remain trapped within their own stereotypical constraints, but also contribute to future conflict between the sexes and their expectations for each other.

EVALUATING THE EFFECTIVENESS
OF INTERVENTION EFFORTS

While most projects have chosen to commit funds to program implementation rather than evaluation, several conclusions can be drawn regarding the immediate impact of intervention:

- The programs have been well received by the participants, their parents, and counselors.
- They seem to achieve most of their stated goals on a short-term basis.
- Mentorships are related to creative indices in adulthood, although men may view the experience more positively than do women.
- The multiple strategy approach has made it difficult to discern the most effective interventions.
- Long-term evaluations produce mixed results.

There is clearly a need for further research and evaluation to provide the following:

- Longitudinal studies
- Sharper definition of "successful" (Can a program that enables just one gifted adolescent to transcend the barriers of stereotyping be labelled "unsuccessful"?)
- Closer match between participant and strategy (an ineffective technique for a group may be highly effective for certain individuals)
- Refinement of the statistical/research methodology used to evaluate the complicated designs of most projects
- More precise definition of the constructs of "success," "achievement," and "realization of potential"

As Janis and Mann (1977) contend, "There is no dependable way of objectively evaluating the success of a decision" (p. 11). We can only evaluate the quality of the processes used in making a career choice and the degree to which that choice is free of stereotypical constraints.

SUMMARY

I have described a number of intervention strategies and programs that have made successful inroads into the problem of overcoming stereotypes. Reis and Callahan (1989) rightfully caution that celebration may be premature. We must also take care to avoid the development of new stereotypes such as androgyny and superwoman, which, while they might replace traditional concepts, would be no less constraining if they were to become the cultural norm. Above all, we need to realize that stereotyping is a human characteristic that, in some manifestations, will always be with us.

REFERENCES

Astin, H. S. (1985). The meaning of work in women's lives: A sociopsychological model of career choice and work behavior. *Counseling Psychology, 12*(4), 117–126.

Bakan, D. (1966). *The duality of human existence.* Chicago: Rand-McNally.

Bell, L. A. (1989). Something's wrong here and it's not me: Challenging the dilemmas that block girls' success. *Journal for the Education of the Gifted, 12*(2), 118–130.

Bem, S. L. (1981). Gender schema theory: A cognitive account of sex typing. *Psychological Review, 88*, 354–364.

Braiker, H. B. (1986). *The Type E woman.* New York: Nal Penguin.

Brody, L., & Fox, L. H. (1980). An accelerated intervention program for mathematically gifted girls. In L. H. Fox, L. Brody, & D. Tobin (Eds.), *Women and the mathematical mystique* (pp. 164–178). Baltimore: Johns Hopkins University Press.

Brooks, L., Holahan, W., & Galligan, J. (1985). The effects of a nontraditional role-modeling intervention on sex-typing of occupational preferences in career salience in adolescent females. *Journal of Vocational Behavior, 26*, 264–276.

Casserly, P. (1980). An assessment of factors affecting female participation in advanced placement programs in mathematics, chemistry and physics. In L. H. Fox, L. Brody, & D. Tobin (Eds.), *Women and the mathematical mystique* (pp. 138–163). Baltimore: Johns Hopkins University Press.

Cook, E. P. (1985). *Psychological androgyny.* New York: Pergamon.

Eccles, J. S. (1985). Why doesn't Jane run? Sex differences in educational and occupational patterns. In F. D. Horowitz & M. O'Brien (Eds.), *The gifted and talented: Developmental perspectives* (pp. 251–295). Washington, DC: American Psychological Association.

Eccles, J., & Hoffman, L. W. (1984). Sex roles, socialization and occupational behavior. In H. W. Stevenson & A. E. Siegel (Eds.), *Research in child development and social policy* (Vol. 1, pp. 367–420). Chicago: University of Chicago Press.

Edlind, E. P., & Haensly, P. A. (1985). Gifts of mentorships. *Gifted Child Quarterly, 29*(2), 55–60.

Farmer, H. S. (1985). Model of career and achievement motivation for women and men. *Journal of Counseling Psychology, 32,* 363–390.

Flanagan, J. C., Tiedeman, D. V., Willis, M. B., & McLaughlin, D. H. (1973). *The career data books: Results from Project Talent's five-year, follow-up study.* Palo Alto, CA: American Institutes for Research.

Fleming, E. S., & Hollinger, C. L. (1979). *Project CHOICE: Creating her options in career exploration.* Boston: Educational Development Corporation.

Frieze, I. H., Parsons, J. E., Johnson, P. B., Ruble, D. N., & Zellman, G. L. (1978). *Women and sex roles: A social psychological perspective.* New York: Norton.

Gottfredson, L. S. (1981). Circumscription and compromise: A developmental theory of occupational aspirations. *Journal of Counseling Psychology, 28*(6), 545–579.

Guttentag, M., & Bray, H. (1976). *Undoing sex stereotypes.* New York: McGraw-Hill.

Higham, S., & Navarre, J. (1984). Gifted adolescent females require differential treatment. *Journal for the Education of the Gifted, 8*(1), 43–58.

Hollinger, C. L. (1985). Self perceptions of ability of mathematically talented female adolescents. *Psychology of Women Quarterly, 9*(3), 323–336.

Hollinger, C. L., & Fleming, E. S. (1988). Gifted and talented young women: Antecedents and correlates of life satisfaction. *Gifted Child Quarterly, 32*(2), 254–259.

Jacklin, C. N. (1989). Female and male: Issues of gender. *American Psychologist, 44*(2), 127–133.

Janis, I. L., & Mann, L. (1977). *Decision making.* New York: Free Press.

Kerr, B. (1985). *Smart girls, gifted women.* Columbus: Ohio Psychology Publishing.

Kerr, B. A. (1986). Career counseling for the gifted: Assessments and interventions. *Journal of Counseling and Development, 64,* 602–604.

Kohlberg, L. (1966). A cognitive-developmental analysis of children's sex role concepts and attitudes. In E. E. Maccoby (Ed.), *The development of sex differences* (pp. 82–173). Stanford, CA: Stanford University Press.

Kreinberg, N. (1978). EQUALS in math. *Independent School, 37*(4), 47–49.

Lerner, R. M. (1986). *Concepts and theories of human development* (2nd ed.). New York: Random House.

MacDonald, C. T. (1980). An experiment in mathematics education. In L. H. Fox, L. Brody, & D. Tobin (Eds.), *Women and the mathematical mystique* (pp. 115–137). Baltimore: Johns Hopkins University Press.

Nash, W. R., Borman, C., & Colson, S. (1980). Career education for gifted and talented students: A senior high school model. *Exceptional Children, 46*(5), 404–405.

Noble, K. D. (1987). The dilemma of the gifted woman. *Psychology of Women Quarterly, 11,* 367–378.

Noble, K. D. (1989). Living out the promise of high potential: Perceptions of 100 gifted women. *Advanced Development Journal, 1,* 57–75.

O'Neil, J. M. (1980). Research on a workshop to reduce the effects of sexism and sex role socialization on women's career planning. *Journal of Counseling Psychology, 27*, 355–363.

Parsons, T., & Bales, R. F. (1953). *Family, socialization and interaction process.* Glencoe, IL: Free Press.

Rand, D., & Gibb, L. H. (1989). A model program for gifted girls in science. *Journal for the Education of the Gifted, 12*(2), 142–155.

Rebecca, M., Hefner, R., & Oleshansky, B. (1976). A model of sex-role transcendence. *Journal of Social Issues, 32*, 197–206.

Reis, S. M. (1987). We can't change what we don't recognize: Understanding the special needs of gifted females. *Gifted Child Quarterly, 31*(2), 83–89.

Reis, S. M., & Callahan, C. M. (1989). Gifted females: They've come a long way— or have they? *Journal for the Education of the Gifted, 12*(2), 99–117.

Schwartz, L. L. (1980). Advocacy for the neglected gifted: Females. *Gifted Child Quarterly, 24*(3), 113–117.

Shamanoff, G. A. (1985). The Women Mentor Project. *Roeper Review, 7*(3), 163– 165.

Super, D. E. (1963). Self concepts in vocational development. In D. E. Super, R. Starishevsky, N. Matlin, & J. P. Jordaan (Eds.), *Career development: Self concept theory* (Research Monograph No. 4, pp. 1–16). New York: College Entrance Examination Board.

Super, D. E. (1980). Life span, life space approach to career development. *Journal of Vocational Behavior, 16*, 282–298.

Tittle, C. K. (1983). Studies of the effects of career interest inventories: Expanding outcome criteria to include women's experiences. *Journal of Vocational Behavior, 22*, 148–158.

Tobin, D., & Fox, L. H. (1980). Career interests and career education: A key to change. In L. H. Fox, L. Brody, & D. Tobin (Eds.), *Women and the mathematical mystique* (pp. 171–191). Baltimore: Johns Hopkins University Press.

Ullian, D. Z. (1976). The development of conceptions of masculinity and femininity. In B. Lloyd & J. Archer (Eds.), *Exploring sex differences* (pp. 25–47). London: Academic Press.

Young-Bruehl, E. (1988). *Anna Freud: A biography.* New York: Summit.

CHAPTER 15

Moral and Spiritual Development of the Gifted Adolescent

Karen B. Tye
Marlene Bireley

Adolph Hitler and Charles Manson were gifted leaders. Today's insider traders, industrial/military spies, and computer invaders and "virus" spreaders are described in the media as talented, intelligent persons. Most, before their downfall, were admired for their respective abilities. In the face of these historical and modern negative examples, it seems important to discuss those processes whereby gifted adolescents are guided to use their gifts for the good of humankind. Yet, this has been a most difficult chapter to research and write. While a sizable body of research on the cognitive and affective needs of the gifted is available, voiced interest in the moral and spiritual development of this group has been sparse. However, it does exist.

Tannenbaum (1972) believed that gifted children perceive a need for a closer link between the intellect and the conscience. He stressed a need for redefining the goals of education to include such a link through an educational emphasis on the human consequences of knowledge. Similarly, Vare (1979) called for a confluent model of moral education based on gifted children's unique cognitive and affective needs that would respect human autonomy.

Tan-Willman and Gutteridge (1981) noted that rational/scientific thinking alone has not been successful in solving worldwide problems. They concluded that "another dimension of human experience which is most urgently needed to be developed hand and hand with the power to create is . . . the power to search for the right behavior or the good in a person's relationship with his/her fellow creatures in the universe" (p. 149). They further suggested that creativity without morality is a potentially destructive force, while morality without creativity can lead to rigidity and anachronism.

DEVELOPING MORALITY AND SPIRITUALITY

Wellman (1988) defined ethics as that branch of philosophy dealing with general and theoretical issues. It is the study of what makes an act right or wrong and can be the basis for intelligent moral choices. Morality is the application of ethics to a specific and practical problem. Is abortion right or wrong? Is genetic engineering of humans desirable? Can civil disobedience arise from a moral imperative? These are important modern moral dilemmas.

Spirituality connects the individual to the supernatural. It may take the form of a specific religious belief or a more general search for what is beyond human ability to understand. Conn (1986) included philosophical and psychological, as well as religious, understandings in her definition. She pointed out that philosophers talk about human spirituality as "our capacity for self-transcendence, a capacity demonstrated in our ability to know the truth, to relate to others lovingly, and to commit ourselves freely to persons and ideals" (p. 3). Psychologists, by contrast, describe "that aspect of personal essence that gives a person power, energy, and motive force" (p. 3). Finally, religious persons prefer "the actualization of human self-transcendence by whatever is acknowledged as the ultimate or the Holy, that is, by whatever is considered religious" (p. 3). At root, spirituality is a search for meaning and purpose.

Whether the approach is more general and philosophical or one that pursues a narrow theological perspective, the search for a framework for deciding one's personal definitions of good and evil is a very important aspect of the adult lifestyle one will choose.

Moral Development

Most of the research that has linked the gifted to moral decision making has been carried out in the framework of Lawrence Kohlberg's (1972) stages of moral judgment. He defined these stages as

1. An orientation to punishment and reward, and to physical and material power
2. A hedonistic orientation in which the beginnings of reciprocity or exchange of favors exists
3. A "good boy/good girl" stage in which morality is tied to winning the approval of those in one's immediate group
4. An orientation to a fixed order in which rigid adherence to existing laws and authorities is maintained

5. An orientation to social-contract obligations, democracy, and equality
6. A morality of individual principles of conscience in which the highest value is placed on equality, dignity, and human life

Kohlberg (1972) considered the first two stages as "premoral" and typical of young children and delinquents, the middle two stages as typifying the "conventional" morality of the majority of the adult population, and the latter two as "principled" stages. It was his contention that about 20%–25% of the adult population reach the last two stages, but that only 5%–10% attain Stage 6.

Kohlberg (1972) defined moral development as a rational, cognitive-developmental process, rather than a spiritual-religious one. He perceived the major factor in this process as social experience that allows the individual to take on multiple roles and encounter multiple perspectives. In fact, he concluded from his research that the home, peer group, school, and larger society were instrumental factors in encouraging moral development, but that "religious affiliation and attendance are unrelated to moral development" (p. 16).

The measurement of moral reasoning is the purpose of the Defining Issues Test (DIT) (Rest, 1974). This test presents six moral dilemmas based on Kohlberg's stages and relates the results to principled (Stages 5 and 6) and unprincipled (Stages 1 through 4) considerations. Tan-Willman and Gutteridge (1981) administered both the DIT and the Torrance Test of Creative Thinking, Form A (Torrance, 1966) to 115 gifted adolescents (55 females and 60 males) who were 16 or 17 years old. The female subjects performed better on both tests, with the relative importance attributed to principled considerations (Stages 5 and 6) reaching .01 significance. Most typically, the gifted adolescents responded at conventional levels (Stages 3 and 4), but with higher scores than average adolescents. The authors concluded that, while this group compared favorably with average adolescents, they were "underdeveloped" given their intellectual, creative, and socioeconomic advantage.

In another study, Lawrence (1987) compared 23 college philosophy students, 23 upper middle class (but not necessarily gifted) high school students, and 16 male graduates from an extremely conservative fundamentalist seminary. The adolescents ranked lower than the philosophy students, but higher than the seminary group, in principled vs. unprincipled responses. The latter group had difficulty dealing with moral concepts except as religious exercises, going so far as to refuse to answer some items that they could not infuse with religious meaning. This would seem to support Kohlberg's differentiation between moral and religious development.

In a review of studies using the DIT, Rest, Davison, and Robbins (1978) concluded that about one-third of junior and senior high students reach the principled stages; one-half of college and seminary students do so; and about two-thirds of those who receive doctorates in philosophy and political science do so. The authors further concluded that there is a large cognitive component in moral reasoning, but that it is distinctively different from the verbal IQ, Piagetian formal operations, or logical development in general. Their research indicated that moral education of several months duration could raise DIT scores, but that short-term interventions were not successful.

In another approach to modern moral dilemmas, Clark and Hankins (1985) posed 25 philosophical questions to 152 pairs of elementary children, ages 6–10, who were matched except that one was average and the other intellectually gifted. Typical questions included "What do you think is the worst thing that could happen to the world in real life?" and "Who do you think is the best person in the world, living or dead?" Gifted children more often cited concern about war, more often listened to or read national and world news, had a better knowledge of other countries, and were less likely to perceive God as the best and the Devil as the worst person. The authors concluded (as had George & Gallagher, 1978, and Torrance, 1983, before them) that gifted children tended to be more pessimistic about the future than their average peers, and suggested group interaction, participation in future problem solving, and values clarification as intervention strategies.

Spiritual Development

Unlike moral development, literature describing the relationship of spirituality and the gifted is nonexistent. No direct reference to this topic was found in a review of a number of articles and texts on giftedness (Buescher, 1985; Clark, 1988; Davis & Rimm, 1989; Freeman, 1985; Hogan, 1980; Leroux, 1986; Miller & Silverman, 1987). While the topic is discussed in general adolescent texts, the authors spend relatively little time on it (Conger, 1977; McKinney, Fitzgerald, & Strommen, 1982; Nielsen, 1987). Only in religious education literature (e.g., Davis, 1986; Moore, 1988) can discussions of spirituality be found, and these tend to focus on ways to help young people find meaning and purpose through the particular doctrinal stance of the authors.

One major research project that studies the concerns of intellectually undifferentiated adolescents with the meaning and purpose of life is that of Strommen (1988). His current database includes the input of 20,000 young people who are church affiliated (a group that comprises two-thirds of the total population of American youth, ages 14–18). Strommen talked to these adolescents about their values, beliefs, opinions, and concerns. He grouped their responses into "cries" or preoccupations with certain needs and values that characterize and, at times, dominate the lives of young people. There were five such cries:

1. The cry of self-hatred, expressing adolescents' feelings of loneliness and their need for self-esteem
2. The cry of the psychological orphan, expressing the adolescent experience of family conflict and the need for love
3. The cry of protest, which gave voice to the young people's sense of outrage at social conditions and their interest in the welfare of others
4. The cry of prejudice, which revealed an adolescent selfishness and a focus on personal advantage
5. The cry of faith, which expressed the desire for a meaningful life

This latter cry was one of the most dominant and can be translated into our contention that adolescents are searching for meaning and purpose in life. If adolescents want and need to "discover an overall sense of their place in the universe" and "seek for trustworthy answers in which meaning might be found and around which life's goals might be staked" (Davis, 1986, p. 259), where does that search seem to take them?

THE SEARCH FOR MEANING

Organized Religion

While logic would lead us to believe that some gifted adolescents will be seeking meaning and purpose in organized religion, we can only turn to the body of research that focuses on adolescent involvement in general. As noted, Strommen (1988) concluded that two-thirds of our young people identified with a specific church body. Gallup poll surveys conducted between 1977 and 1983 (*Religion in America*, 1984) identified a similar 7 in 10 as church members.

There were other findings in the Gallup report, however, that would lead us to question how serious this adolescent involvement in organized religion is and how much young people really turn to the organized church for answers. While the latest surveys indicated a "rising tide of interest in religion and spiritual matters" (*Religion in America*, 1984, p. 64), there was also evidence that many young people remained "turned off" by organized religion. Only a quarter of the adolescents surveyed expressed a high degree of confidence in organized religion, a figure much lower than for the adult population. An overwhelming majority believed that a person could be a good Christian or Jew without going to church or synagogue. The report concludes that "many young people including regular attenders of churches and synagogues as well as nonattenders, are not finding the spiritual dimensions they seek in their traditional religious upbringing" (*Religion in America*, 1984, p. 66).

Community Service

Community service is another arena to which gifted adolescents might turn to find meaning and purpose for their lives. Seeking to find meaning through helping others seems a logical process for gifted adolescents who have a strong idealism and commitment to justice and fair play (Davis & Rimm, 1989). Again turning to the general literature, some information on the effects of volunteering on adolescent social development does exist (Hamilton & Fenzel, 1987; Hedin & Eisikovits, 1982; *Youth Volunteers in Action*, 1986). These studies suggest that participation in community service has positive effects on adolescents' "pro-social attitudes, upon their developing sense of themselves, and upon the knowledge and skills they exercise in their voluntary activities" (Hamilton & Fenzel, 1987, p. 20). Community service encourages adolescents to become genuinely interested in and concerned for the welfare of their communities, it releases their creative energies and develops their sense of idealism, it broadens their activities and associations, and it helps them realize responsibility and develop internal standards of judgment (Hedin & Eisikovits, 1982). These benefits make community service a real and attractive source for the development of meaning and purpose in the life of the adolescent.

Nontraditional Religious Groups

Nielsen (1987) states that "data show that adolescents are more likely than adults to be members of nontraditional religious groups" (p. 604). Parker (1985) contends that "it is evident that many people today, particularly adolescents and college students, are attracted to cults at least for short periods of time" (p. 50). While this attraction may be perceived by most as a negative or dark side of the search for spirituality, it should not be ignored.

Andron (1983) has suggested that cults may hold a particular attraction for gifted adolescents. Part of the reason can be found in the nature of adolescence itself. This is the critical time when young people formulate a system of beliefs that will guide them through the remainder of their lives (Hauser, 1981). Cults provide complete and definitive answers to such questions as "Who am I?" and "What am I doing here?" The support and acceptance of cult members may provide a sense of belonging for a gifted teenager who feels isolated from peers. Other characteristics of the gifted adolescent—such as idealism, a keen sense of justice, a low tolerance for ambiguity, a natural sense of curiosity, an attraction to the mysterious, the willingness to take risks, and the need for emotional support (Andron, 1983; Buescher, 1985; Davis & Rimm, 1989; Dean, 1982)—may attract an individual to a nontraditional approach. While we in no way wish to "cry wolf" in regard to the gifted and cults, we do find it interesting that the discussion by Andron (1983) is the only one we found that specifically links the gifted adolescent population to religious affiliation of any type. It is certainly a topic for contemplation and further study.

THE ROLE OF TEACHERS, COUNSELORS, AND PARENTS

While we lack research on gifted adolescents' moral, ethical, and spiritual development, this group has an obvious interest in these topics. What, then, should be the role of those who teach, counsel, or parent them?

Facilitating Moral Development

In the course of writing this chapter, Bireley posed this question to a graduate class in gifted education: "Why, with all our concern about the affective well-being of gifted persons, the need to develop tomorrow's leaders, and our emphasis on risk taking, have educators not tackled this important subject?" The responses were immediate and telling. As public school educators, these graduate students continue to feel a very strong community sentiment toward the separation of church and state, the home as the purveyor of values and religion, and the need for objectivity in presenting specific values. On the other hand, students pressure teachers to share their personal viewpoints in discussions where the students are asked to express their opinions. Given these constraints and pitfalls, these topics are more likely to be skirted than faced in the typical classroom. Yet, by daily example, teachers actively and passively play a very important role in the adolescent search for meaning and purpose.

While educators must take care not to violate the responsibilities of parents, a number of areas exist in which teachers can explore the greater issues of life within the context of gifted education. Ward (1961) proposed that curriculum for the gifted should explore concepts integrating several branches of knowledge. He suggested Adler's (1952) *The Great Ideas: A Syntopicon of Great Books of the Western World* as a source for identifying these themes and concepts. The list of *Syntopicon* topics provided by Feldhusen (1988) includes change, desire, eternity, evolution, fate, good and evil, honor, immortality, life and death, metaphysics, reasoning, religion, sin, theology, truth, virtue and vice, and wisdom, to name only some. These topics are certainly conducive to the development of moral, ethical, and spiritual values.

Maker (1982) devotes a chapter in *Teaching Models in the Education of the Gifted* to Kohlberg. In that chapter, she describes Kohlberg's approach as a response to indoctrination and contends that "the school's and the teacher's responsibility is not to indoctrinate children as to what values they should hold, but to assist them in following a process whereby they think seriously about what values they hold and what values they should hold" (p. 137). She advocates the processes suggested by Raths, Harmin, and Simon (1966), which consist of choosing from alternatives, prizing and affirming oneself and one's beliefs, and acting upon those choices. Maker (1982) suggests that while Kohlberg did not specifically address the gifted, the more rapid development of abstract thought and the earlier interest in humanitarian issues in gifted students make it probable that, with proper experience, the gifted are more often capable of the attainment of a high level of moral development. She believes that the discussion of moral dilemmas would be "interesting and helpful to gifted students" (p. 147) and combines the suggestions of Kohlberg with Hilda Taba's *Resolution of Conflict Strategy* (Institute for Staff Development, 1971) to provide a multistep outline for the study of dilemmas. Those steps include

1. Presenting the dilemma
2. Listing the facts of the situation
3. Exploring the perspectives of the different characters
4. Identifying the two or three major alternatives of the protagonist
5. Exploring the consequences of the identified alternatives
6. Identifying a tentative position
7. Dividing the class into small groups for discussion

8. Having the whole class discuss conclusions and reasons
9. Re-evaluating original student positions

Foster and Silverman (1988) believe that the ideal place for moral education in the gifted curriculum is in the area of leadership education. They contend that "leadership education must be conjoined with moral education in order to educate future leaders toward moral choices they will eventually face as they address local, state, or national issues" (p. 367). In addition to the study of moral dilemmas, they advocate studying the historical development of philosophies and societies, examining moral and ethical issues as presented in the modern media, simulations or role-plays, values clarification, and community service as ways to provide moral and ethical development in an educational context.

Guiding Meaning-Making

One guideline for those who bear the responsibility of assisting the gifted adolescent may be the work of Kegan (1980, 1982), a constructive-developmental psychologist, who believes that the activity of meaning-making constitutes what it means to be human. To be a person (a self), we must make meaning or sense out of our life and experiences. Our ongoing growth and development as human beings are rooted in this ability to make ever greater distinctions between our selves and the world. This process involves an ongoing tension between differentiation and integration, between independence and inclusion. Mature growth also involves being able to relate, to include, to be a part of something else. In fact, we need the other in order to know what we are not. The search for meaning-making, according to Kegan, takes place in "holding environments." These refer to those people and institutions that constitute the "world" of the person at any given stage of development. For gifted adolescents, that world comprises not only family, school, and peers, but an expanding sense of society as a whole.

The task of this holding environment in assisting adolescents in meaning-making is threefold. First of all, it needs to "hold on" to adolescents by providing confirmation of and support for their unique identity; by giving them unconditional love and acceptance; by letting them know they belong and are a part of the family, the school, the church or synagogue, and even wider social circles; and by being there for them no matter what.

The second task is "letting go"—challenging adolescents to be aware of other ways of viewing themselves, contradicting what seem to be false and inappropriate images, providing alternative ways of looking at things and indicating that not everyone sees things the same way, and encouraging change.

The final task is that of "staying put," being a safe haven to which the person can return, providing continuity by remaining in place even as the adolescent changes, accepting rejection but not rejecting in return, and being available for reintegration and inclusion in the life of the young person in new ways when the appropriate time comes.

Performing these tasks calls for skills at balancing what can be contradictory functions, but such balancing is necessary if we are to assist the growth process. The search for meaning and purpose will be facilitated by the right combination of unconditional acceptance and the appropriate kinds of challenges to existing belief systems. The balancing is not always easy. Parents of young adults have found that holding on is the easiest of the tasks to perform. Part of this is due to the reality that holding on is often in parents' own vested interest. Since Kegan (1980, 1982) believes that meaning-making continues throughout life, those who are called upon to be a "holding environment" for adolescents can find themselves in the midst of their own life changes. In such a situation, change in others may be threatening and cause parents to hold on even tighter.

In addition to our own resistance to change, we can sometimes be resistant to adding more conflict to the lives of those gifted adolescents about whom we care. When we have witnessed the pain some gifted young people already feel because of their struggles to find acceptance from peers who do not understand them, we are reticent to add to their conflict. Miller and Silverman (1987) point out that too often guidance of gifted youth is geared toward adjustment, setting realistic standards, and avoiding conflict. It is important that we see conflict as a natural part of the gifted adolescent's growth and maturity.

Perhaps the most important thing we can do for gifted adolescents in their search for their own moral, ethical, and spiritual standards is to stay put and avoid the temptation to provide them with answers. Our task as educators, counselors, and parents is not to "give" meaning or to do their search for them. To do so can take on the character of indoctrination. However, we cannot abandon them in their search. Their own discomfort with ambiguity and the internal conflicts that are part of the adolescent quest for identity make them vulnerable to groups that will provide them with answers. What we need to do is voice with clarity our own meaning, talk about our own beliefs and values and how we have come to them. We need to live out those beliefs and values in our own lives, with integrity and consistency. Beyond that, our task is to be a "holding environment" for our gifted youth, to hold on where necessary, to let go when needed, and to "be there" with consistency.

SUMMARY

Important aspects of the lifestyle chosen by gifted adults are the moral, ethical, and spiritual values that they have developed during their childhood and adolescence. The traditional separation of church and state, and the uncertain home/school division of responsibility for the development of these values seem to have led to relatively little research on these topics as they relate to the gifted individual. What does exist strongly suggests that it is imperative for educators, as well as parents, to develop ways to assist gifted youth in their request for meaning-making, if we are to develop leaders whose abilities include the application of moral and humane values to the dilemmas of modern humankind.

REFERENCES

Adler, M. (1952). *The great ideas: A syntopicon of great books of the western world*. Chicago: Encyclopedia Britannica.

Andron, S. (1983). Our gifted teens and the cults. *G/C/T, 6,* 32–33.

Buescher, T. M. (1985). A framework for understanding the social and emotional development of gifted and talented adolescents. *Roeper Review, 8,* 10–15.

Clark, B. (1988). *Growing up gifted* (3rd ed.). Columbus, OH: Merrill.

Clark, W., & Hankins, N. (1985). Giftedness and conflict. *Roeper Review, 8,* 50–53.

Conger, J. (1977). *Adolescence and youth: Psychological development in a changing world* (2nd ed.). New York: Harper & Row.

Conn, J. (Ed.). (1986). *Women's spirituality.* New York: Paulist Press.

Davis, G. A., & Rimm, S. (1989). *Education of the gifted and talented* (2nd ed.). Englewood Cliffs, NJ: Prentice-Hall.

Davis, G. L. (1986). Spiritual direction: A model for adolescent catechesis. *Religious Education, 81,* 267–278.

Dean, R. (1982). Youth: Moonies' target population. *Adolescence, 17,* 567–574.

Feldhusen, J. (1988). Developing units of instruction. In J. VanTassel-Baska (Ed.), *Comprehensive curriculum for gifted learners* (pp. 112–150). Boston: Allyn & Bacon.

Foster, W., & Silverman, L. (1988). Leadership curriculum for the gifted. In J. VanTassel-Baska (Ed.), *Comprehensive curriculum for gifted learners* (pp. 356–380). Boston: Allyn & Bacon.

Freeman, J. (Ed.). (1985). *The psychology of gifted children.* Chichester: Wiley.

George, P., & Gallagher, J. (1978). Children's thoughts about the future: A comparison of gifted and nongifted students. *Journal for the Education of the Gifted, 2,* 33–42.

Hamilton, S., & Fenzel, L. (1987, April). *The effect of volunteer experience on early adolescents' social development.* Paper presented at the Annual Meeting of the American Educational Research Association, Washington, DC. (ERIC Document Reproduction Service No. ED 282 086).

Hauser, J. (1981). Adolescents and religion. *Adolescence, 16,* 309–320.

Hedin, D., & Eisikovits, R. (1982). School and community participation. *Childhood Education, 53,* 87–94.

Hogan, R. (1980). The gifted adolescent. In J. Adelson (Ed.), *Handbook of adolescent psychology* (pp. 536–559). New York: Wiley.

Institute for Staff Development (Eds.). (1971). *Hilda Taba teaching strategies program, Unit 4.* Miami, FL: Author.

Kegan, R. (1980). There the dance is: Religious dimensions of a developmental framework. In J. Fowler & A. Vergote (Eds.), *Toward moral and religious maturity: The first international conference on moral and religious development* (pp. 404–440). Morristown, NJ: Silver Burdett.

Kegan, R. (1982). *The evolving self.* Cambridge, MA: Harvard University Press.

Kohlberg, L. (1972, November/December). A cognitive-developmental approach to moral education. *The Humanist,* pp. 13–16.

Lawrence, J. (1987). Verbal processing of the Defining Issues Test by principled and non-principled moral reasoners. *Journal of Moral Education, 16,* 117–130.

Leroux, J. (1986). Making theory real: Developmental theory and implication for education of gifted adolescents. *Roeper Review, 9,* 72–77.

McKinney, J., Fitzgerald, H., & Strommen, E. (1982). *Developmental psychology: The adolescent and young adult.* Homewood, IL: Dorsey Press.

Maker, C. J. (1982). *Teaching models in the education of the gifted.* Rockville, MD: Aspen.

Miller, N., & Silverman, L. (1987). Levels of personality development. *Roeper Review, 9,* 221–225.

Moore, J. (1988). Adolescent spiritual development: Stages and strategies. *Religious Education, 83,* 83–100.

Nielsen, L. (1987). *Adolescent psychology.* New York: Holt, Rinehart & Winston.

Parker, M. (1985). Identity and the development of religious thinking. In A. Waterman (Ed.), *Identity in adolescence: Processes and contents* (pp. 43–60). San Francisco: Jossey-Bass.

Raths, L., Harmin, M., & Simon, S. (1966). *Values and teaching.* Columbus, OH: Merrill.

Religion in America: The Gallup report. (1984). Princeton, NJ: Princeton Religion Research Center.

Rest, J. (1974). *Manual for Defining Issues Test.* Minneapolis: University of Minnesota Press.

Rest, J., Davison, M., & Robbins, S. (1978). Age trends in judging moral issues: A review of cross-sectional, longitudinal, and sequential studies of the Defining Issues Test. *Child Development, 49,* 263–279.

Strommen, M. (1988). *Five cries of youth.* San Francisco: Harper & Row.

Tan-Willman, B., & Gutteridge, D. (1981). Creative thinking and moral reasoning of academically gifted school adolescents. *Gifted Child Quarterly, 25,* 149–153.

Tannenbaum, A. (1972). A forward and backward glance at the gifted. *The National Elementary Principal, 51,* 14–23.

Torrance, E. P. (1966). *The Torrance Test of Creative Thinking, Form A.* Princeton, NJ: Personnel Press.

Torrance, E. P. (1983, August). *Future images and characteristics of children around the world.* Paper presented at the meeting of the Fifth World Conference on Gifted. Manila, Philippines.

Vare, J. (1979). Moral education for the gifted: A confluent model. *Gifted Child Quarterly, 23,* 13–15.

Ward, V. (1961). *Differential education for the gifted.* Columbus, OH: Merrill.

Wellman, C. (1988). *Morals and ethics* (2nd ed.). Englewood Cliffs, NJ: Prentice-Hall.

Youth volunteers in action (YVA) effects evaluation: Final report. (1986). Washington, DC: ACTION. (ERIC Document Reproduction Service No. ED 271 629).

PART IV

MULTICULTURAL ISSUES

A discussion of gifted adolescents would not be complete without noting the unique problems associated with being a gifted person who is a member of a cultural or racial minority. For two of our groups, black and Hispanic, the stereotypes of limited ability and lack of ambition continue to serve as real barriers to identification, service, and self-esteem. Asians, on the other hand, are becoming known as the "model minority," and many are faced with a growing backlash for their perceived superiority. A fourth group, Pacific Islanders (e.g., Hawaiians and Samoans), are separated from mainland America by both distance and culture. Some of their unique characteristics and needs are introduced and differentiated from those of better known groups that "mainlanders" typically associate with the Pacific Basin.

Prejudice is, of course, applied ignorance. Rehashing prejudice is not our intent. The issues are well known. Specific action plans are needed to break the cycles of misunderstanding and neglect. All but one of those who have contributed chapters to this part are members of the minority group about which they write. The other has chosen to leave his midwestern roots to live and marry within the American-Asian culture of Hawaii. While the approach of each author is somewhat different, the message is similar: Each of us needs to develop an understanding and an appreciation of the subcultures in which many gifted adolescents live and grow. Some will need different identification procedures if we are to find them; others will need unique programs if we are to serve them. All will need our assistance in bridging the gap between the expectations of their families and the educational system. In many instances, in fulfilling the expectations of one, the other is ill-served.

Professionals can best help those about whom they have the most knowledge. Counselors and teachers may wish to use this part to increase personal understanding of the groups described or to replicate the procedures or programs that are mentioned. In either case, we have attempted to provide useful information about both people and programs, so that, through ignorance, we do not inadvertently add to the stresses faced by minority gifted adolescents.

CHAPTER 16

Gifted Black Adolescents: Beyond Racism to Pride

Alexinia Young Baldwin

Adolescence is a period when ideas about the world and their effect on the individual are crystallized. It is a period of unequalled physiological and psychological changes in the natural developmental patterns of human beings. It is during this period that pride in oneself and acceptance by peer groups are crucial to the development of a positive self-concept.

Racism and black pride are two variables that must be seriously considered when planning for the gifted adolescent. Although these variables appear to be primarily related to the planning needs of black American adolescents, all young people, black or nonblack, and particularly gifted adolescents will be affected by the manner in which these variables are handled during this crucial period of their lives.

Racism can play an important role in the adolescent's acceptance by peer groups. It can rear its head through overt as well as covert actions. Most often racism is a result of lack of information and misguided attitudes about people who happen to be different. Another form of isolation, which cannot be accurately termed racism, occurs when members of the gifted adolescent's own race ostracize him or her because they have been identified as gifted and are in specialized educational programs. This form of intraracial racism also occurs because of lack of information and misguided attitudes about racial pride and what giftedness means.

ISSUES RELATED TO RACISM

Racism has taken many overt forms throughout the history of America. These forms have often been cruel and inhuman physiologically;

however, the psychological impact has been even greater. The social events of the 1950s and 1960s diminished the physical forms of racism, but a subtle, covert form of racism took its place. Throughout the 1970s and increasingly in the 1980s, we have experienced a return of some of the overt forms of racism, but the covert forms are the most damaging to the sensitive egos of black adolescents.

The covert forms that directly affect the black gifted adolescent in the educational setting can be found in the research literature (e.g., Jensen, 1987, 1989; Scarr & Weinberg, 1976), in processes for identifying the gifted, in the content of courses designed for the gifted, in the educators themselves, and in the black students' own peer groups.

Research Literature

Jensen (1987) has been the most constant researcher and supporter of the theory of heritability. He has continued through the years to argue the validity of Spearman's "g" factor and has built a case based on scores from intelligence tests to support his theory that blacks are intellectually inferior to whites. It is very clear in Jensen's discussion of the Milwaukee Project (Jensen, 1989) that he has little faith in the theory that the environment plays an important role in depressing or enhancing a person's IQ score.

If persons who work with gifted adolescents accept the validity of assumptions drawn about an entire race of people, the process of identification and the subsequent expectations will be seriously compromised. Research will have succeeded in perpetuating a stereotype that was used centuries ago to establish a social system.

Processes of Identification

Identification of black or other minority gifted students has been the most significant stumbling block to their inclusion in programs for the gifted. Much of the problem has come from the requirement of the federal, state, and city governments that funds for programs be allocated on the basis of certain scores on intelligence and achievement tests. Subjective assessment or nomination of students is often disregarded and considered invalid. On the one hand, this type of assessment might be the only way some students can be included in gifted classes. On the other hand, if the examiner has preconceived notions about black students and their abilities, the subjective measures serve as another covert form of racism.

Content of Courses

Due to centuries of neglect of black history, little information about the contributions and participation of black Americans in the many facets of this nation's development has reached the educational textbooks. The reasons are multifaceted. Textbook companies and publishers respond to society's demands and idiosyncratic prejudices; therefore, historical information is omitted from texts or presented in a way that will be accepted by the buying public. The adolescent who is intellectually capable of absorbing and analyzing events that shaped this country's history is left to seek information about black Americans on his or her own. In the meantime, nonblack students are denied an opportunity to expand their knowledge and erase many built-in stereotypes.

Educators' Role

Educators at all levels play an important role in helping the gifted black adolescent move beyond the effects of racism to black pride. Teacher-training institutions have done an inadequate job of preparing teachers. These teachers' experiences are often limited, and their stereotypical concepts are seldom challenged. Body language and the practice of exclusion are often based on preconceived ideas about a student's ability. Too often, erratic behaviors of black adolescents are treated much more severely than those same behaviors of nonblack adolescents. This can be attributed to a lack of knowledge or simply another type of racism.

Peer Groups' Role

One of the more worrisome phenomena in selecting and placing gifted adolescents (especially males) in programs for the gifted is the negative attitude shown by peers not selected for the programs and the subsequent isolation felt by those selected. Many theories for this phenomenon can be put forward, such as jealousy, distrust of any program that is so predominantly Caucasian, or rejection of what is perceived as taking away any element considered part of blackness.

THE DEVELOPMENT OF PRIDE

Pride is hard to define in terms of its meaning to the black adolescent. The gifted adolescent has experienced pride in many of his or her accomplishments in the particular area of giftedness; however, a less transient feeling of pride must come from a deeper feeling of self-worth. This self-worth begins with the acknowledgment of those with whom the black adolescent interacts that the culture from which he or she comes is rich in history and contributions to society.

If gifted black adolescents are to move beyond the effects of racism to black pride, attention must be given to the attitudes of educators as they respond to the identification process for gifted black adolescents and to the type of content included in courses.

Identification Process

Before proper attitudes toward identification can go forward, the following set of assumptions (Baldwin, 1985) should be accepted:

1. That giftedness can be expressed through a variety of behaviors
2. That giftedness expressed in one dimension is just as important as giftedness expressed in another
3. That giftedness in any area can be a clue to the presence of potential giftedness in another area, or a catalyst for the development of giftedness in another area
4. That a total-ability profile is crucial in the educational planning for gifted children
5. That all populations have gifted children who exhibit behaviors that are indicative of giftedness
6. That carefully planned subjective assessment techniques can be used effectively with objective assessment techniques
7. That behaviors classified as gifted should be above and beyond the average of a broad spectrum of individuals

I have suggested that we define giftedness as above average ability in creative processing ability, and motivation in one or more areas singularly or in combination (Baldwin, 1985). These suggested areas are cognitive, psychosocial, creative products, and psychomotor. Given this definition, it has been suggested that a matrix include these four areas, plus creative processing ability and motivation, as items to be assessed. Appropriately selected objective and subjective tests will give a total profile of the student, showing where the strengths and weaknesses are. After the student's profile has been developed, appropriate extended activities for individual or group experiences should be designed. These activities can occur in different types of organizational structures, for example, self-contained classes, homogenous groupings, independent study, internships outside of school, mentorships, pullout programs, resource rooms, or summer programs.

Course Content

A popular theme in the contemporary educational literature is the development of multicultural curricula. A few decades ago multicultural curricula would have referred to curricula that included information about blacks and possibly native Americans. Today, however, this term embraces a wide range of ethnic groups, and this is as it should be. This chapter has been designed to address the concerns of the black gifted adolescent, but there are two very important issues to consider before making recommendations for course content. These concerns are (1) will there be a negative effect on the sensitive egos of these students as a result of coursework that addresses this ethnic group only, and (2) will the purpose of the course content be better served by including a wide range of ethnic groups in the coursework? This will be a judgment call on the part of the teachers or curriculum planners. This judgment should be based on the environment in which the adolescents live. In a community where the black population is small, a wider range of ethnic groups might make the students feel more comfortable. In a community with a large black population, focus on the black ethnic group might have a more lasting positive effect on the adolescent.

Given the foregoing concerns, I would like to propose the following ideas, which have been drawn in part from Banks' (1979) recommendations for teaching strategies for ethnic studies. These recommendations can be used regardless of which of the two approaches mentioned above is taken by the teacher. As a preliminary step, teachers should engage in a personal reading plan that includes books on ethnicity in the United States and surveys of major ethnic groups. The curriculum development process should begin with a list of key concepts and generalizations. From these concepts, intermediate level generalizations and subsequent lower level generalizations can be related to the ethnic group selected for study.

Suggested Curricula/Teaching Models

Taking Banks' suggestions, I propose that consideration be given to three models that will help develop appropriate activities for the gifted adolescent. These models are sensitivity enhancement, information processing, and concept development (Baldwin, 1989).

Sensitivity-Enhancement Model. The sensitivity-enhancement model is important in the process of developing a nonprejudicial perspective and acceptance of persons that are different in culture or physical appearance. It also provides self-enrichment for the black adolescents themselves. According to Tiedt and Tiedt (1979), student experiences should include cognitive and affective learning such as valuing, describing, relating, discriminating, generalizing, and judging.

Following Banks' suggested structure mentioned above, examples of key concepts for this model would be diversity, prejudice, and worth of the individual. An intermediate level generalization from these concepts could be, This is a richer world because there are different cultures and ethnic groups that enrich our lives. A lower level generalization could be, Stereotypes hinder an understanding of differences. Some ideas for use are as follows:

1. Help students experience what it feels like to be different. Students can use masks and become another ethnic group; they should maintain character for at least 48 hours. A journal and discussion of emotions can be used.
2. Have students produce a resource book on a different cultural group. Include books, film, activities, field trips, and local resource people.
3. Use games that have been developed for the purpose of placing persons in the roles of other ethnic groups (see Sample Resources at end of the chapter).
4. Use other activities such as debates, unfinished stories, and fictional stories such as *Kindred* (Butler, 1988) as a means of developing sensitivity toward different ethnic groups.

Information-Processing Model. The information-processing model provides facts about various events (historical and contemporary). This information should have been included along with general historical information being taught in schools, but for black ethnic groups it is virtually nonexistent. With the three steps of the structured lesson in mind, a key concept could be, Knowledge enhances appreciation of differences. An intermediate level generalization to follow would be, There is much to be learned about various people around us. A lower level generalization could be, Ignorance breeds prejudice. A sample activity would be library research, including letters of inquiry to the Library of Congress and various resource libraries. The NAACP and the Urban League can provide a list of these resources. Other activities include field trips to sites of historical interest, invitations to local historians, becoming historians and sharing information in articles and books, and designing a fictional time capsule in order to explore the activities of certain time periods.

Concept-Development Model. This model involves the use of content from various cultures and ethnic groups to teach a basic concept in math, literature, history, science, and so forth. Using Banks' structure again, we can illustrate the use of this model. The key concept could be, Events that occur in one aspect of society can have concomitant effects in other aspects of society. The intermediate level generalization could be, There are parallels in social and political changes during this century. The lower level generalization could be, The changes in jazz music parallel the changes in national politics in this country.

Using this example as part of a history lesson, the teacher could involve students in analyzing the type of popular jazz music, the attitudes of society, and the elected officials of various periods. Students would have to develop an understanding of jazz and its origins, and of politics and the conservative or liberal attitudes of the governmental administration, and subsequently support or refute the generalization that there are sociopolitical parallels in history. The teacher in this instance will have used material from the culture of the black community to serve as a springboard for teaching a concept.

Similar concepts can be developed through the use of graphic and performing arts, the study of form in poetry, economics, subtleties in the language of various cultures, and so forth. This idea can be extended to learning activities designed to stimulate higher level thought processes. Open-ended questions and research activities could, for example, include information on minority and nonminority women in history.

SUMMARY

The black adolescent who happens to be gifted will be faced with many dilemmas that stem from physiological changes that every adolescent faces; psychosocial influences that result from generations of social stereotypes and prejudices; and the acceptance of his or her own giftedness as a challenge and not a means of separation from his or her own culture. For those who have the responsibility of planning programs for the gifted, there must be a continual review of the attitudes and understanding of those involved. Zeal and good intentions without understanding can be just as damaging to the adolescent as no action at all. The development of a positive self-concept is the underlying theme behind each of the models proposed. This positive concept will come from a generalized acceptance of cultural differences as well as the recognition of exceptional abilities that can be nourished.

As more attention is being focused on programs for the gifted at middle and high school levels, peer pressure on black students becomes a variable with which to contend. The historical precedents of gifted programs have left feelings of bitterness in many black communities. These feelings have been passed on to the peer groups of those students selected to be in programs for the gifted. There is a need for parental and community involvement in programs for the gifted because they can serve as stimulants for improved academic and creative achievement of students at all levels. A beginning step toward the softening of peer pressure would be to involve students who are not gifted as participants in or observers of various activities of a generalized program. These opportunities can include pairing of students on some projects, sharing ideas for special programs, and inviting students not identified as gifted to observe a program or process that has been developed. This strategy proved effective in reducing the tension between students in my class for the gifted and those not in the class.

The movement from racism to black pride cannot be achieved without the support of all elements of society. Black gifted adolescents are particularly vulnerable because the full realization of the potential that exists within them and the recognition of subtle prejudices that prevent the expression and development of these abilities often create more aggressive or defiant students. The movement toward black pride includes the movement toward self-pride and the respect and acceptance of the total society.

SAMPLE RESOURCES

Authentic Afro-Rhythm LP 6060. Kimbo Educational, P.O. Box 246, Deal, NJ 07233.

Banks, J., & Banks, C. (Eds.). (1989). *Multicultural education: Issues and perspectives.* Boston: Allyn & Bacon.

Blacks & Whites. Psychology Today Games, Del Mar, CA 92014.

Canfield, J., & Well, H. (1976). *100 ways to enhance self-concept.* Boston: Prentice-Hall.

Carelli, A. (1983). *Famous and not so famous women enrichment kit.* Unpublished class project. University of Connecticut, Department of Curriculum and Instruction, Storrs.

Haskins, J. (1987). *Black music in America: A history through its people.* New York: Thomas Y. Crowell.

Loewberg, B., & Gogin, R. (1976). *Black women in 19th century American life.* University Park: Pennsylvania State University Press.

Shirts, R. (1971). *Starpower.* Simile, 11–218 12th Street, Del Mar, CA 92014.

Shirts, R. (1977). *Bafa' Bafa'.* Simile, 11–218 12th Street, Del Mar, CA 92014.

The history of black Americans: A study guide and curriculum outline. United Federation of Teachers, Box HBA, 260 Park Avenue South, New York, NY 10010.

REFERENCES

Baldwin, A. Y. (1985). Baldwin Identification Matrix 2. New York: Trillium.

Baldwin, A. Y. (1989, October). *Process for developing multicultural curriculum for gifted children.* Paper presented at the Annual Meeting of the National Association for Gifted Children, Cincinnati, OH.

Banks, J. (1979). *Teaching strategies for ethnic studies* (2nd ed.). Boston: Allyn & Bacon.

Butler, O. (1988). *Kindred.* Boston: Beacon.

Jensen, A. R. (1987). Further evidence for Spearman's hypothesis concerning black–white differences on psychometric tests. *Behavior and Brain Sciences, 10,* 512–519.

Jensen, A. R. (1989). Raising IQ without increasing "g"? *Developmental Review, 9,* 234–258.

Scarr, S., & Weinberg, R. A. (1976). IQ test performance of black children adopted by white families. *American Psychologist, 31,* 726–739.

Tiedt, P., & Tiedt, I. (1979). *Multicultural teaching: A handbook of activities, information, and resources.* Boston: Allyn & Bacon.

CHAPTER 17

Gifted Hispanic Adolescents

Vicente Z. Ortiz
Alexander Gonzalez

For several years it has been recognized that the number of Hispanic adolescents participating in programs for the gifted is critically low relative to the representation of other groups from the general population (Richert, 1987). The reasons attributed to this low participation rate are many and include not only characteristics of the students themselves, such as language and cultural differences, but also other social and political factors. Together they act as barriers to the full participation of these students (Bernal, 1973; Bernal & Reyna, 1975).

However, the most salient issue cited as a cause for the underrepresentation of Hispanics in special accelerated educational programs is the lack of an acceptable set of criteria and procedures that are appropriate for the identification of Hispanic students. Too often, school personnel who have been trained to use a prescribed set of identification methods are reluctant to try new approaches and methodologies. In addition, the schools continue to depend on indices of success such as academic achievement and a narrow definition of "giftedness," which very often act to mask the real potential of many of these students. For example, it may be inappropriate to utilize standardized achievement and reading tests with Spanish-speaking or bilingual children or to attempt to identify gifted Hispanics simply by utilizing IQ scores (Chambers, Barron, & Sprecher, 1980; Evans de Bernard, 1985). The net result is that although some progress has been made in the area, the problem of identifying gifted Hispanic students is still unresolved (Masten, 1985).

This chapter will attempt to address this problem by presenting an alternative strategy for the identification and education of gifted Hispanic adolescents. After a brief review of some of the factors involved, an identification and instruction approach that has been used successfully with gifted Hispanic adolescents will be presented. Since adolescence is a critical stage in the physical, emotional, and intellectual development of all children, it is especially important that the potential of Hispanics be identified as early as possible.

REVIEW OF INFLUENTIAL FACTORS

Demographics

For the past 2 decades, Hispanics in this country have had the largest growth of any group. According to current data, it is estimated that Hispanics in this country number 25 million, and that number is still growing. Not only are Hispanics younger and more fecund, they are also the largest ethnic group in the United States (*Policy Analysis for California Education*, 1989).

The Hispanic population comprises different groups, including peoples of Puerto Rican, Cuban, Mexican, and Central and South American descent. Especially during the more recent past, there has been a tremendous influx of refugees from Central American countries that have experienced social and political upheaval, such as El Salvador and Nicaragua. However, Mexican Americans constitute the single largest group of Hispanics in the United States. They reside primarily in the Southwest, concentrated in California, Texas, Colorado, and New Mexico.

As a group, Hispanics share some common characteristics such as language and a general cultural orientation. But despite these commonalities, there are also differences that serve to distinguish each group. These include a distinct and exclusive history and cultural experience as well as language usage. These differences play an important role in developing an understanding of each group. For purposes of this chapter, most of the reported research has been conducted with Mexican Americans.

Language

Questions about the effects of language on the cognitive and intellectual achievement of Hispanic children continue to be unresolved. Over the years, the debate has centered on whether being bilingual is a handicap in our society; whether cognitive development is hampered as a result of language interference; and the more political issue of whether bilingual programs in the schools should even exist. In the latest major skirmish, bilingualism has been identified as the single most important factor contributing to the low performance of Hispanic children. A series of well-conceived arguments have been developed in response; however, the debate continues (Willig, 1988).

Notwithstanding the various theoretical approaches used in discussing bilingualism, the fact remains that for a majority of Hispanic children, English is still learned as a second language. For them, Spanish continues to be the dominant language for communication at home. However, the reality of the situation is that for many Hispanic children, Spanish is an oral form of communication, with only a limited use of writing and reading. Thus, this form of bilingualism may create further difficulties for these Hispanic children when they are developing second language skills (both oral and written) and, ultimately, it will impede their entire academic performance. By the time these children are adolescents, they may have already become victims of a downward spiral brought about by the early failures of the schools to meet their special needs in this area.

Socioeconomics

Health, education, and welfare agencies report that as a group, the family income of Hispanics falls far below the national average. In addition, the majority of Hispanics hold semiskilled or unskilled jobs and live in lower socioeconomic areas, either urban or rural communities. These circumstances can have a significant impact on the academic performance of Hispanic students and puts them at a higher risk of school failure.

Education

Many schools attended by Hispanic students have mean achievement performance scores well below the national norm. As a result, in these schools very often the main objective is to increase the academic skills of these students. For many Hispanic students with accelerated or gifted potential, this means that the opportunity to be exposed to a higher level, competitive curriculum is nonexistent. As a result of the lack of challenge, they may develop their academic skills only slightly above the average range.

In sum, unstructured or less formal early childhood language experiences, poor socioeconomic conditions, and the lack of exposure to a competitive curriculum at school may be major factors affecting the learning and academic performance of many Hispanic adolescents. These students never reach their full potential as gifted individuals.

IDENTIFICATION

Underrepresentation
of the Disadvantaged Student

One of the first studies to focus on gifted individuals (Terman & Oden, 1947) found that one common characteristic of the subject sample was their socioeconomic background. That is, the majority of the students came from educated and upper middle class families. Only a small percentage of the group studied was from lower socioeconomic or ethnic minority backgrounds. Little has changed since that study. The number of ethnic minority students who have been classified as gifted remains critically low.

The issue of underrepresentation of minorities and lower socioeconomic students in programs for the gifted and talented (GATE) remains an issue of controversy to the present. It has been of particular importance since evidence exists from the earliest research in this area that students with high levels of learning abilities are to be found in all groups (Jenkins, 1948; Sanchez, 1934). However, it has been recognized that factors such as a different language and a poor socioeconomic environment play a vital role in the educational development and academic success of many disadvantaged students (Bernal, 1973; Burns, 1983; Renzulli, 1978). Some research has also indicated that this low representation might be due largely to the approaches being used to identify these students (Gallagher, 1983; Renzulli & Delcourt, 1986).

Student Identification Model

Some positive attempts are being made to provide alternative strategies for identifying gifted students in the Hispanic population. For example, in a recent study with Hispanic students (Ortiz & Volkoff, 1987b), it was found that even after many of the students had been identified as gifted using a standardized IQ test, their academic levels generally were only slightly above the average range. One conclusion of this study was that Hispanic students who attend schools in rural and lower socioeconomic areas are not being exposed to appropriate or competitive academic curricula. This study also concluded that an identification process for GATE programs that depends on high performance on achievement or IQ tests might not be appropriate for identifying Hispanic students who might be gifted.

Since 1985, the Rural and Migrant Gifted Project (RMGP), a special enrichment program developed by the Migrant Education Office of Fresno County, California, has identified many Hispanic students as gifted. Part of this program's success can be attributed to the student identification method, which involves the following procedures.

Informal Procedure. The first step involves a questionnaire/scale form used to help classroom teachers refer those students who exhibit the most potential in the areas of academics, intellectual ability, and creativity. This prescreening process has been very useful in giving teachers an opportunity not only to provide an assessment of reliable observed behavior, but also to consider all the students in a class for evaluation. Another result of this process has been the assurance that more accurate referrals are being conducted.

Formal Procedure. Those students referred through prescreening are recommended for the formal process. This involves the administration of a short version of the Wechsler Intelligence Scale for Children–Revised (WISC-R). This short form has been validated with these students (Ortiz & Gonzalez, 1989) and is administered in both English and Spanish.

Final selection of students for each program in the project is determined by the following criteria:

1. Information provided by the teacher on the prescreening form
2. Performance on the WISC-R screening test (Students performing within the 85th to 94th percentile are considered accelerated, while a score at the 95th percentile or higher is considered gifted.)
3. Achievement test records (Same performance criteria are applied as in the screening test, but in a specific academic area.)
4. Motivation and behavior factors

CURRICULUM AND INSTRUCTION

The second most important aspect of this project is the curriculum selected to teach these students. This curriculum attempts to fit their different learning modes to how and what is being taught. It also emphasizes those needs that have been identified as being the most critical. For instance, in previous research conducted with students participating in this project, it was found that language, particularly reading skills, was the greatest area of need (Ortiz & Volkoff, 1987a). Therefore, the first objective of all curriculum is to expose these students to all forms of language learning experiences. This is accomplished by utilizing various categories and forms of literature to improve reading, as suggested in *Recommended Readings in Literature* (1986). Literature is also emphasized through the use of *Reader's Theater* (Taylor, 1986) and journal writing in each academic area. In addition, students learn various forms of poetry by using formulas such as the couplet, tercet, quatrain, cinquain, diamante, Haiku, and the "I wish."

For the improvement of oral language skills, students are encouraged to participate in class discussions of their reading assignments, and teachers utilize the questioning techniques relating to "Bloom's Taxonomy" (Bloom, 1956). Even when conducting scientific experiments, students are taught to use a scientific method that involves a language activity-based mode. Skills such as observing, defining a problem, questioning, stating a hypothesis, conducting research, collecting data, interpreting results, and stating conclusions are all taught through a group cooperative approach. Finally, for the instruction of mathematics, concepts from the various strand-numbers, measurement, geometry, patterns and functions, statistics and probability, logic, and several other problem-solving abilities are continually taught and followed by reciprocal questioning and class discussion. Other examples of curricular programs adapted for the instruction of students participating in this project include *Family Math* (Stenmark, Thompson, & Cossey, 1986); *Project* AIMS (Weibe, Hyllen, & Youngs, 1986); *Project Wild* (Charles, 1983); *Science on a Shoestring* (Strongin, 1985); and *Young Astronaut* (Young Astronaut Council, 1986).

The curriculum also includes career awareness and educational options. Community leaders and professionals from various fields are invited as guest speakers. Students are also exposed to higher education experiences by attending seminars and summer institutes provided by local colleges and universities. Finally, this program includes a parent component that works with parents on a school involvement training process.

The effectiveness of this project has been measured by the academic gains of the students who have participated. For example, in a study that compared the academic gains made by students who were identified and served with that made by students who were identified but not served, it was found that the students who had participated in the program made gains of about 2 years. In contrast, the students who did not receive services made gains of only one year (Ortiz & Volkoff, 1987a).

CONCLUSION

The Rural and Migrant Gifted Project is a successful model that can be recommended for school districts serving large Hispanic student populations. The screening and identification method can be used to identify at an early stage those Hispanic students with natural ability and/or higher learning potential. In addition, the curriculum used provides these students with needed exposure to higher learning and academic skills that empower them to function at the same competitive levels with their English-speaking peers. Thus, the program helps these students achieve their true levels of giftedness by the time they reach adolescence.

REFERENCES

Bernal, E. M. (1973). Gifted Mexican-American children: An ethno-scientific perspective. *California Journal of Educational Research, 25,* 265–273.

Bernal, E. M., & Reyna, J. (1975). Analysis and identification of giftedness in Mexican-American children: A pilot study. In B. O. Boston (Ed.), *A resource manual on information on educating the gifted and talented.* Reston, VA: Council for Exceptional Children. (ERIC Document Reproduction Service No. ED 117–885).

Bloom, B. S. (1956). *Taxonomy of educational objectives. Handbook I: Cognitive domains.* New York: Longmans, Green.

Burns, E. (1983). Bivariate estimates of giftedness. *Journal of School Psychology, 21,* 261–262.

Charles, C. (1983). *Project Wild.* Boulder, CO: Western Regional Environmental Education Council.

Chambers, J., Barron, F., & Sprecher, J. (1980). Identifying gifted Mexican American students. *Gifted Child Quarterly, 24,* 123–128.

Evans de Bernard, A. (1985). Why Jose can't get into the gifted class: The bilingual child and standardized reading tests. *Roeper Review, 8,* 80–82.

Gallagher, J. J. (1983). Keynote address presented at International Conference on Gifted Students, Sheridan College, Ontario.

Jenkins, M. (1948). Case studies of Negro children of Binet IQ 160 and above. *Journal of Negro Education, 12,* 159–166.

Masten, W. G. (1985). Identification of gifted minority students: Past research, future directions. *Roeper Review, 8,* 83–85.

Ortiz, V., & Gonzalez, A. (1989). A validation study of a WISC-R short form with accelerated and gifted Hispanic students. *Gifted Child Quarterly, 33,* 152–155.

Ortiz, V., & Volkoff, W. (1987a). *Evaluation report of the Rural and Migrant Gifted Project.* Sacramento: California State Department of Education.

Ortiz, V., & Volkoff, W. (1987b). Identification of gifted and accelerated Hispanic students. *Journal for the Education of the Gifted, 11,* 45–55.

Policy Analysis for California Education (Monograph). (1989). Berkeley: University of California, School of Education.

Recommended Readings in Literature. (1986). Sacramento: California State Department of Education.

Renzulli, J. S. (1978). What makes giftedness? Reexamining a definition. *Phi Delta Kappa, 60,* 180–184.

Renzulli, J. S., & Delcourt, M. A. (1986). Legacy and logic research on the identification of gifted persons. *Gifted Child Quarterly, 30,* 20–23.

Richert, E. S. (1987). Rampant problems and promising practices in the identification of disadvantaged gifted students. *Gifted Child Quarterly, 31,* 149–154.

Sanchez, G. I. (1934). The implications of a basal vocabulary to the measurement of the abilities of bilingual children. *Journal of Social Psychology, 5,* 395–402.

Strongin, H. (1985). *Science on a shoestring.* Menlo Park: Addison-Wesley.

Stenmark, J. K., Thompson, V., & Cossey, R. (1986). *Family Math.* Berkeley: University of California Press.

Taylor, C. W. (1986). Be talent developers . . . as well as knowledge dispensers. *Today's Education, 57,* 67–69.

Terman, L., & Oden, M. (1947). *Genetic studies of genius: Vol. 4. The gifted child grows up.* Stanford: Stanford University Press.

Weibe, A., Hyllen, J., & Youngs, D. (1986). *Project AIMS.* Fresno, CA: Pacific College Press.

Willig, A. C. (1988). A case of blaming the victim: The Dunn monograph on bilingual Hispanic children on the U.S. mainland. *Hispanic Journal of Behavioral Sciences, 10,* 219–236.

Young Astronaut Council. (1986). *Young Astronaut.* Washington, DC: Author.

CHAPTER 18

Gifted Adolescents
in the Emerging Minorities:
Asians and Pacific Islanders

Robert Woliver
Gail Muranaka Woliver

When we were approached to write a chapter on the emerging minority—Asians—we smiled, knowing the diversity of Asian groups, especially when Southeast Asian groups such as Vietnamese, Cambodians, and Laotians are included. To compound the matter, we added Pacific Islanders to the title. Asia and the Pacific Islands span more cultures, countries, and territory than any other region; yet, many Americans retain a unitary mental association of the gifted Asian—a serious-minded male chemistry student with thick glasses.

The first step in discovering these gifted youngsters lies in examining demographic information. By 1985, the many faces and cultures of the Asian and Pacific Island peoples constituted the largest group of immigrants to America (46%) ("New Faces," 1989). The census is a starting point to see some of the differences in Asian and Pacific Island American groups. Those that have been here the longest—such as the Japanese—tend to do far better than those who have recently immigrated. There are such cultural and historical differences among Asian and Pacific Island American groups that each group must be examined individually to be understood.

Even within one culture, such as the Vietnamese, there are significant differences between the most recent immigrants and those who arrived in the early 1970s after the fall of Saigon. The earlier Vietnamese, on the whole, were well educated, spoke English, and were from the middle class. They had the skills to propel themselves upward on the U.S. social and economic ladder. Later Vietnamese immigrants often did not possess the education, affluence, and skills of the first wave of immigrants and are having more difficulty adjusting and assimilating ("New Faces," 1989).

In the 1980 census, Asian and Pacific Island Americans numbered more than 3.7 million, more than double the 1970 figure. The percentage of the total U.S. population represented by Asian and Pacific Island Americans in the 1980 census is very small (1.6% of the general population). The largest groups in the 1980 census were Chinese (812,176), Filipinos (781,894), Japanese (716,331), Asian Indians (387,223), Koreans (357,393), and Vietnamese (245,025). Since 1980, almost 900,000 refugees from war-torn Indochina—Vietnam, Kampuchea, and Laos—have immigrated to the United States (U.S. Department of Commerce, 1988).

Among the 259,566 Pacific Island Americans, Hawaiians account for over two-thirds (172,346) and Samoans are the next largest group, with 35,520 (U.S. Department of Commerce, 1988).

Also according to the 1980 census, most (58%) of the Asian and Pacific Island Americans live in the western states. Among the six largest Asian groups, only Asian Indians are more concentrated in the Northeast than the West (U.S. Department of Commerce, 1988).

According to the 1980 census, Asian and Pacific Island Americans have a younger median age, 28.4 years compared with the national median age of 30.0 years. The Japanese, one of the earliest immigrants from Asia, had a median age of 33.5 years, making them the only group over the national median age. The more recent Vietnamese immigrants have a high birth rate and one of the lowest median ages, 21.5 years (U.S. Department of Commerce, 1988).

THE IMPORTANCE OF EDUCATION

The educational statistics of the 1980 census reveal the importance and value attached to learning by Asian and Pacific Island Americans. Of all Americans aged 25 years and over, 66% were at least high school graduates, while 75% of the Asian and Pacific Island Americans were in this category. Among Asian groups, the Japanese had the highest percentage of people (82%) with at least a high school diploma. The Vietnamese had one of the lowest percentages (62%). Among Pacific Island Americans, Hawaiians were the highest (68%); Samoans were among the lowest (61%) (U.S. Department of Commerce, 1988).

A comparison of education at the college level between Asians and the general population was even more pronounced—34% of Asians had completed four years or more of college versus the national average of 16.2%. More than half the Asian Indians and Pakistanis finished at least four years of college compared with the national percentage of 16.2! In contrast, only 13% of Vietnamese, 7.7% of Kampacheans, and 5.6% of Laotians had completed four or more years of college. Pacific Island Americans, at 9.3%, also had a lower completion rate of four years of college than the national average (U.S. Department of Commerce, 1988). These statistics point out the diversity of Asians.

A comparison of gender differences in college attainment among Asians reveals that 41.5% of males had four years of college, versus 28% of females. This emphasis on male education reflects old traditions. Among the Asian groups, only the Filipino women surpassed the men in college education (41% versus 32%) (U.S. Department of Commerce, 1988). It is interesting to note that the most prominent female Asian leader, Corazon Aquino, is Filipino.

The emphasis on education has translated into jobs and economics. In the 1980 census, the median family income for Asian Americans was $23,095 versus the national average of $19,917. However, for Pacific Island Americans, the median family income ($17,984), like college education, lagged behind the national average. Among Asians, Japanese were the highest at $27,354; the lowest were Hmongs at $5,000, Laotians at $5,159, and Vietnamese at $12,840 (U.S. Department of Commerce, 1988).

Education for some Asians, even in precolonial times, served as a major vehicle into government, administration, and bureaucracy. In countries such as China and Vietnam, the emperors relied on a hierarchy of mandarins who obtained positions based on their achievements in examinations on the Confucian classics. Those scholars in turn could afford to educate their sons for the examinations, something the poorer agrarian peasants could not do. Education and scholarship were keys to economic advancement.

In countries where these values were strong, they continue to be upheld by the Asian immigrants. In Amy Tan's *The Joy Luck Club* (1989), one of the characters describes the futile, but thorough, search her Chinese-born mother undertook to discover an American-born daughter's "genius." Private lessons were endured in the unsuccessful quest of uncovering giftedness.

The Japanese have a phrase for parents' sacrificing of themselves for their children—*Kodomo no tame ni*. This is generally reflective of many of the earlier Asian groups—Japanese, Chinese, Korean, and Filipino. These immigrant groups are often seen as both entrepreneurial and as having tremendous faith in education as the tool for upward mobility.

COPING WITH DISSYNCHRONY BETWEEN HOME AND SCHOOL VALUES

Some characteristics of gifted students include extreme sensitivity to people and situations, and a feeling of being different and alienated. Add to this the normal upheaval of physical, emotional, and social changes associated with adolescence in general. Then, to all the above, consider the trauma of looking different and perhaps speaking the English language with an accent. As if that were not enough, now add the simultaneous pressure of parental, traditional values vying with American school-learned values. These constant challenges beleaguer gifted Asians daily. Yet, the success with which each minority group meets this challenge is determined not so much by ethnicity as by socioeconomic level and length of time in this country.

Japanese, Chinese, Korean, Vietnamese, Cambodian, or Filipino—the Asians and Southeast Asians who are children of professionals or who come from wealthier backgrounds, even though their parents may speak no English, seem to do better in school. The second-, third-, and fourth-generation immigrants, freed from taking on several jobs in addition to studying, tend to have the luxury of pursuing their academic interests. On the other hand, there are Asian and Southeast Asian families where economic survival remains the primary priority. As one school administrator puts it, "The parents are so busy working at two to three jobs that there is no supervision and the kids become 'street kids.'" She went on to say, "Soon they're not only alienated from the school but from their families too. After all, we've taught them to enjoy American food in our cafeterias and so even what food to serve at family meals becomes an issue, not that they even have time or space to share a meal together" (M. D. Jones, personal communication, April 18, 1989).

Regardless of socioeconomic status, a number of traditional values are shared by Asians and Hawaiians. These include a high regard for educational achievement; respect for elders, including older brothers and sisters, who are expected to be obeyed without question; avoidance of calling attention to oneself; indirect, rather than direct, communication; and a desire to act as part of a group, rather than as an individual. In communication, Asians are soft-spoken and talk only when they feel they have something significant to say. Often, they will seem to agree because it is the polite thing to do, rather than express their differing opinions. These traits frequently lead to gifted Asian and Hawaiian youngsters not being identified, since teachers tend to call on their more verbal, spontaneous classmates (Boggs, 1985). Therefore, students who are most acculturated are best identified through standardized test scores. After identification, teachers can help by encouraging more verbal activities in class. Small group discussions of four to five students, for example, can be less threatening to these youngsters at first than being expected to voice opinions in front of an entire class.

Clark (1988) and Kitano (1975) identify the following limiting, culturally supported attitudes and abilities that Asian students often bring to the learning situation: critical self-concept; attitude of perfectionism, making "learning by error" experiences quite difficult; strong valuing of conformity, which inhibits creative activity or divergent thinking; little experience with independent thinking; and sex-role differentiation, where the male is seen as more desirable and dominant. On the other hand, facilitating, culturally supported attitudes and abilities are the ability to listen and follow directions; attitude toward discipline as guidance; high achievement; respect for teachers and others; and a tendency to test at or above the norm on all tests of intelligence.

Hawaiians and other Pacific Islanders (Micronesians, Samoans, Marshallese), like Asians, are affiliation-oriented. They direct more effort toward goals that intensify human relationships than toward personal gain or individual achievement. Boggs (1985) found that much effort is directed toward avoiding interpersonal conflict and social disharmony. The general strategy for achieving comfort is to put aside personal gain in order to maximize interpersonal harmony and satisfaction.

Boggs (1969) found that when Hawaiian girls were asked what teachers expected of good students, they responded that compliant obedience, rather than active interest and questioning, was most desired. On the average, when compared with other American teenagers, Hawaiians and Asians are markedly less aggressive toward their parents and are more likely to express hostility by withdrawal from a situation.

Another example of incongruence between home and school values was reported by Boggs (1985), who described the way Hawaiian children learn to obtain assistance from parents by remaining unobtrusive and watching for cues of the adult's receptivity to an approach. When in school, therefore, they try to use unobtrusive, nonverbal means of obtaining assistance, which are often not recognized by the teacher. Students who use such means are not attended to as frequently and are regarded by their teachers as less intelligent.

In the view of both Asians and Hawaiians, questions are seen as a challenge, not as an invitation to dialogue; thus, students are afraid to risk giving the "wrong" answer and feeling humiliated. They prefer to withdraw from such challenges.

Often the ways of interacting developed in school conflict with the values taught at home. Students who begin to behave more individually and independently are chastised by their families for calling attention to themselves and thus begin to suffer increased stress and exhibit problem behavior.

The Teacher's Role

The gifted adolescents from culturally diverse groups who attain success are those who are able to embrace biculturalism: They are adept in intuiting which values to identify with at a particular time. However, much can be done in the way of programming to ensure that such gifted adolescents have the best chance possible to achieve their potential.

As is true for other gifted adolescents, the key to increased motivation and success for the culturally diverse is a flexible and sensitive teacher with the willingness and ability to make the program adjustable for specific students. It has been our experience, for example, that Asian students tend to be visual learners, while Hawaiian children tend to be kinesthetic, rather than aural or visual, learners. Teachers can plan changes in the curriculum to accommodate the special needs of Asians and Hawaiians, especially in the area of individuality and creativity.

Since Asians and Pacific Islanders value group relationships, activities in which students work in teams seem to be successful. At the same time, individuality can be encouraged by having students take turns leading small group discussions. Many teachers attempt to foster leadership skills by giving both a group grade as well as an individual grade for participation. Since precise adherence to directions and fear of making a mistake make it difficult for Asian or Hawaiian youngsters to express creativity or engage in fantasy, patience and repeated assurance that "for *this* exercise, there are no right or wrong answers or correct and incorrect ways of doing this," will help give free rein to the imaginative powers.

There are several ways that teachers can help remove the limits on learning. Many Asian and Hawaiian gifted students tend to do better in mathematics than in verbal skills. According to Julian Stanley (1988), in making predictions of mathematical prowess, students with very high math scores and low verbal scores are more likely candidates than those whose math and verbal scores, though high, are close. Perhaps the most highly gifted students in math are those whose diminished powers in verbal ability force them to excel even more in the world of symbols instead of words. Although this may be true for those few exceptional mathematical geniuses, the majority of Asians and Hawaiians would benefit from more experience in the verbal area, for which habit and family background may not have prepared them. Teachers can encourage them to express themselves through writing and acting out fantasies, short stories about their experiences, and short plays or skits. For those who show an inclination, directing such efforts or filming other students acting would provide leadership opportunities as well as opportunities to work as a group for a common goal.

Michael Chun, President of Kamehameha Schools, a private institution for students of Hawaiian ancestry in Honolulu, credits his success to sensitive, caring teachers. "They are the most important element of any institution," he says. "It was my teachers, not my family, who helped me make my decisions about where to go for college" (M. J. Chun, personal communication, July 21, 1989).

Since parents of Asians and Hawaiians may not be familiar with higher educational facilities and sources of financial aid, teachers and counselors must take a larger role in advising and guiding future efforts.

The Counselor's Role

Being gifted brings about a sense of isolationism—after all, being in the top 2% of the population intellectually means having few people around who can communicate at one's level. Being an adolescent brings its own brand of difficulty—and being Asian or Hawaiian and looking different from the dominant majority tends to exacerbate an already lonely situation. At a time when most adolescents enjoy being with and like others, the gifted Asian or Pacific Islander adolescent must forge a path that may lead away from loved ones.

The counselor's role is to show that biculturalism is both possible and desirable. Counselors can work with these students to support their efforts to develop traits that will help further their education and achievement, yet not alienate them from their family environments. Setting up small groups that meet regularly to discuss such issues and also working individually with the students would help them develop coping strategies. Because of changes in some college admissions programs, which require not only high grade point averages but also active participation in extracurricular activities, some Asian students are attacking this problem with the same zeal that they formerly attacked their studies. Counselors may need to help such students maintain a sense of balance and overcome their feelings of never quite measuring up to what is seen as needed.

Parenting seminars to help bring the parents closer to what the school is trying to do may help both sides resolve to work together for the benefit of the student.

The Parent's Role

Gifted Asian and Hawaiian students, who have a tendency to be ultra sensitive to their environment and to people's feelings, agonize over conflicting feelings of loyalty to both peers and family. It is natural for adolescents to want to assimilate and accommodate since they spend so much time with their peers; yet, many minority parents may see this as an effort on the part of youngsters to pull away from their roots and their heritage. The school, through counselors, can help alleviate such parental anxiety about the loss of their culture.

Asian parents, in particular, can be perfectionists. One teacher reports how hard a student was working at a sport and how a parent berated him angrily on the field for mistakes he made that "shamed the family." Counselors can work with parents on some of these issues and help them develop roles that will make them feel more a part of what is going on in school.

Since Asian and Hawaiian students tend to have had little opportunity to get involved in life outside the family, it is important that the parents learn about opportunities for their children during the summer. To foster individuality and independence, this would ideally take place away from their home, in other parts of the country; for example, the Duke University Talent Identification Program in North Carolina or the Carleton College Writing Program in Minnesota, which awards minority scholarships. Florence and Al Apo, parents of three gifted children, described summer programs their children benefited from: a bike trip through Alaska, a school-sponsored trip to Japan, a science workshop at the Naval Academy, the Northwestern journalism and engineering program, the American Legion Freedoms Foundation program, and the Washington and Lee University four-week program for high school juniors in business and anatomy (F. and A. Apo, personal communication, May 23, 1989). Such programs can give a gifted student a wider window to the world, providing an important break away from the insular, sometimes overprotected world of family and friends. The school can help parents learn about other such programs and opportunities for financial aid.

THE BARRIERS

In all these groups, there are gifted individuals. Studies have shown that the Japanese have a higher percentage of youngsters scoring over 130 on IQ tests than Caucasians. Asians are frequently described as the "model minority." They are depicted as quick to learn and follow directions. Traditionally, teacher, *sensei*, has been placed in a position of respect and authority. Asians are viewed as serious students with high achievement motivation.

Racism has always been the biggest barrier to Asians in America. Although Germany was a far greater threat to America during World War

II, as evidenced by U.S. strategy to defeat Germany first, Americans feared and despised the Japanese more than the Germans. War bonds whose advertising promoted fear of the Japanese always outsold anti-German promotions. Racism and jealousy over the economic successes of Japanese-Americans were the root of the policy of placing them in internment camps during World War II. This was done under the guise that Japanese-Americans would be disloyal; yet, not a single case of espionage was ever recorded. In Hawaii, very few Japanese were interned; and Hawaii raised the famous 442 Regiment comprising Japanese-Americans, which became one of the most decorated combat forces in American history. Outside the European combat zone, this group remained segregated.

While less overt, racism now takes other forms. Recently, a large California university was revealed to have weighted the entrance criteria to discriminate against Asians because the school felt it had too many Asians. Rumors of quotas for Asians among prestigious eastern schools are often heard. The message to Asian youngsters seems to go something like this: "We want you to succeed, but not to excel past the white majority."

This same cry is echoed in the world of business and commerce. Americans want quotas because we feel we cannot compete with Japan and other emerging nations of Asia as they industrialize. This is a reversal from the traditional policies of America. It was the American fleet of Black Ships under Perry that forced the Japanese out of isolationism and commanded Japan to compete. What Perry and the West did not expect was that the Japanese would compete so well.

In spite of the many areas in which Asians have excelled, racism plays a major role in the self-esteem of Asian-American adolescents. We can rejoice that Michael Chang, in winning the French Open at 17, broke both the age barrier and the stereotype that Asians are scientists, not sports heroes. On the other hand, Asians are the group for which blue contact lenses and "Western style eyes" have the most appeal. Both the Asian and majority culture must realize that diversity enriches our country and our world. Rather than blindly following the majority, Asian youths need to balance acceptance of majority values with reaffirmation of their own cultural and racial heritage.

REFERENCES

Boggs, J. (1969). Hawaiian adolescents and their families. In R. Gallimore & A. Howard (Eds.), *Studies in a Hawaiian community* (pp. 12–18). Honolulu: Bernice P. Bishop Museum.

Boggs, S. (1985). *Speaking, relating, and learning: A study of Hawaiian children at home and at school*. Norwood, NJ: Ablex.

Clark, B. (1988). *Growing up gifted* (3rd ed.). Columbus, OH: Merrill.

Kitano, H. (1975). Cultural diversity and the exceptional child. In J. Miley, I. Sato, W. Luche, P. Weaver, J. Curry, & R. Ponce (Eds.), *Promising practices: Teaching the disadvantaged gifted* (pp. 40–59). Ventura, CA: Ventura County Superintendent of Schools.

New faces of America's people, The. (1989, January 16). *Insight*, pp. 8–17.

Stanley, J. (1988, August). *Research bases for four program models for the gifted*. Paper presented at the American Psychological Association, Atlanta, GA.

Tan, A. (1989). *The Joy Luck Club*. New York: Putnam.

U.S. Department of Commerce, Bureau of Census. (1988). *We the Asian and Pacific Islander Americans*. Washington, DC: U.S. Government Printing Office.

THE GIFTED ADOLESCENT
IN PERSPECTIVE

Judy Genshaft

As they leave childhood, adolescents are asked to put behind them the simple play, diversions, and amusements they have known and enjoyed and, within 10 years, they are expected to be transformed into caring, sensitive, well-adjusted adults. Every aspect of an adolescent's life undergoes change—relationships within the family; relationships with peers and adults in the school and the community; and the adolescent's personal beliefs, goals, and objectives. For the first time, career becomes more than just a word, as adolescents must consider how they want to spend their adulthood. The transition from adolescent to adult can be traumatic for any adolescent. Gifted adolescents face the additional pressure of "realizing their potential."

Parents, counselors, teachers, and other adults are crucial to this process. However, understanding what adolescents are experiencing and helping them to cope during this transition are difficult, because adolescence is one of the least studied and understood stages of the human life cycle. Adding the phenomenon of giftedness to this stage of growth and development further muddies our understanding of the dynamics involved.

The family plays a critical role in the process of adolescents growing into adults, especially if a gifted adolescent is part of the unit. Family personalities and interactions affect the psychosocial adjustment, maturity, and development of the special talents of the gifted teenager. Parents face the challenge of achieving a balance between the time and financial responsibilities devoted toward these ends and overinvolvement. Gifted adolescents seem to thrive in families where mutual trust and cooperation are the norm.

Teenagers in these families seem to be able to transfer the attitudes of trust and cooperation easily to adults and peers in school. At times, parents may find themselves in a conflict with schools, especially when adequate challenges and supplementary experiences are not available to gifted students. Parents then must take an active role in working with schools to correct this deficiency. It cannot be assumed that critical thinking, creativity, and autonomy are inherent skills. Instead, these skills must be taught, encouraged, and maximized in the curriculum of secondary schools. Talent is nurtured by practice and concentration, and it is important that schools provide the environment within which that potential can grow.

The challenge of understanding and developing leadership skills also must be given a higher priority in homes, schools, and communities. Separate courses and internships with school, community, business, and political leaders need to be incorporated into the curriculum for gifted students. Leadership programs also need to be created for parents and educators.

Assessing the progress of gifted students is an area that needs further refinement. How do we determine underachievement in gifted students? Are there patterns to this underachievement, and how can these patterns be broken? Educational considerations unique to gifted adolescents who have a disability must be addressed as well. This subpopulation of the gifted community has special program and counseling needs, depending on the disability. Psychological support, technological aids, and other support services are important additions for these gifted adolescents. Alternative programs and summer opportunities, offered at colleges, universities, and schools and in community settings, do exist for gifted adolescents. No matter which program is being considered, parents and adolescents must ask some basic questions before enrolling, including, How does the program meet my special needs? What are the qualifications of the staff members? How is the program evaluated?

Peer and sibling relationships undergo many changes during the transition from adolescence to adulthood. Problems in family dynamics can arise if a family has more than one gifted adolescent, has other children who are less gifted, or has both underachieving and achieving gifted children. Power struggles can result in the best of families, but the balance of power and the maintenance of the adolescents' individuality can be negotiated. Special techniques can be used that will permit adolescents to listen to the experience and wisdom of their parents and yet retain their own unique expressions of thought.

All adolescents undergo psychosocial adjustment during this transition to adulthood. Learning coping skills is necessary for everyone, gifted or not. One maladjustment that seems to occur in gifted adolescents more frequently than the general population is perfectionism. Perfectionism may manifest itself in eating disorders, anxiety and stress disorders, and/ or substance abuse. Curiously, little or no research has been conducted to determine the prevalence of these problems in gifted adolescents. Yet, there is reason to believe that because of the nature of these disorders and the traits of gifted adolescents, this group of adolescents may be at higher risk than the general adolescent population. Breaking the cycle of perfectionism is important to the attainment of "balance" in life.

Adolescence is a time of soul searching and trying to find meaning and purpose in life. Gifted adolescents search for spirituality through organized religion and community service. More attention needs to be given to providing appropriate programs and models that could assist gifted adolescents in their search for spirituality. The moral development of gifted adolescents allows them to search for the right behavior, value, or the good in their relationships with others. The role of teachers, counselors, and parents is very important in this search. Adults should provide balance to this growth process by giving unconditional acceptance to the adolescent while providing appropriate challenges to the belief systems the adolescent is investigating.

Choosing a career is a complex and difficult process for anyone, but gifted adolescents may experience even more anxiety than average teenagers because of the expectation that they should "realize their full potential." Gifted adolescents are no different from other adolescents in that they have a variety of learning styles and personality types. Knowledge of these learning styles and personality types can be helpful in counseling career decisions. Various test instruments are available to help counselors work with, for example, the artist son of a military officer.

The phenomenon of stereotyping, which can restrict one's choices regardless of ability and aptitude, must be dealt with. Positive career exploration requires that gifted adolescents be introduced to options through role models, mentors, career programs, and other training experiences without the typical biases or stereotypical beliefs that often accompany traditional views of careers. Counselors, parents, and other adults must be careful to examine their own views and become aware of their biases so as not to let them interfere with the advising of gifted adolescents.

Black, Hispanic, and Asian gifted adolescents face additional issues. Blacks must face racism and black pride. The attitudes and understanding of those involved with gifted black students must be continuously reviewed to ensure that those adolescents develop a positive self-concept and understanding, pride, and acceptance of cultural differences. Parental and community involvement in programs for gifted black adolescents is critical to stimulating academic and creative achievement. The movement from racism to black pride will permit gifted black adolescents to fully realize their potential.

Problems in identifying minority gifted adolescents are the major cause of underrepresentation of these groups. The Rural and Migrant Gifted Project has been successful in identifying gifted Hispanic youngsters at an early age and providing educational opportunities that foster higher learning and advanced academic skills. This program has enabled gifted Hispanic adolescents to be competitive with their majority counterparts.

Racism is also a major problem for gifted Asian-American adolescents. The prevalent attitude that Asian and other minority adolescents must contend with has been stated in this way: "Americans want you to succeed, but not to excel past the white majority." Racism can have a devastating effect on self-esteem. In addition, Asian adolescents face problems with school and university quotas that close the door to future advancement. The dissynchrony between the values learned at home and those learned at school can cause internal conflict for these gifted students, too. Teachers, counselors, and parents must work together for the benefit of these gifted adolescents.

From the wide-ranging reviews and suggestions in this book, the possibilities for future research with and for gifted adolescents seem to be endless. It should come as no surprise that in almost every chapter of the book more information, research, and resources are requested. In many ways, we know more about what is not known than about what is clearly understood from the literature. We hope the information in this book will provide background information and stimulate further experimentation, study, and research of the personal and educational issues of gifted adolescents. This book represents not the end of a journey, but the very beginning.

ABOUT THE EDITORS
AND THE CONTRIBUTORS

INDEX

About the Editors
and the Contributors

Marlene Bireley received her B.S. in elementary education from Bowling Green State University in 1957. Her M.A. in special education and Ph.D. in the psychology of exceptional children were received from the Ohio State University in 1961 and 1966, respectively. She has taught elementary school, learning disabled, and developmentally handicapped children; served as a school psychologist; and taught various topics in special education and school psychology at the Ohio State University. In 1969 she joined the faculty of Wright State University as coordinator of (and the first faculty member in) special education. In that capacity, she developed programs in special education, gifted education, and school psychology. She continued to teach, write, and consult in these three areas of interest until her early retirement in 1988. Since that time, she has devoted her time to writing, consulting, and adjunct teaching at the university.

Judy Genshaft received her B.A. in psychology and social work from University of Wisconsin–Madison. Her M.A. in school psychology and Ph.D. in counseling psychology were earned at Kent State University. Currently Dr. Genshaft serves as Professor and Chairperson of the Department of Educational Services and Research at the Ohio State University. In addition, she has been a visiting professor at the University of British Columbia, Vancouver, Canada. Prior to her academic positions, Dr. Genshaft worked as a school psychologist in the public schools, and as a therapist in a community mental health center. She has written numerous journal articles and chapters focusing on such issues as mathematical anxiety in female adolescents, improving study skills, professional ethics and practice, and assessment of intellectual abilities. Dr. Genshaft has received several awards and honors for her leadership for women and for her contributions to the National Association of School Psychologists. She is a member of the board of trustees of Support for Talented Students.

Miriam Adderholdt-Elliott received her undergraduate degree from Lenoir-Rhyne College, Hickory, North Carolina, in intermediate education. She received her master's degree in special education for the gifted from the University of Tennessee and Ph.D. from University of Georgia in educational psychology with a concentration in gifted education. Currently, she is a Clinical Assistant Professor at University of North Carolina–Charlotte. Prior to this position, she has been an Assistant Professor at Lenoir-Rhyne College, has worked as a classroom teacher in programs for the gifted, and has been employed in a variety of summer enrichment programs for the gifted. Dr. Adderholdt-Elliott is the author of two books, *Perfectionism: What's Bad About Being Too Good* and *Perfect to a Fault*, and has published numerous journal articles.

Susan R. Amidon earned an undergraduate degree in biology from Wittenberg University and a master's degree in gifted education from Wright State University. She received both a master's degree in anatomy and her Ph.D. in gifted education from the Ohio State University. Currently she is supervisor of Gifted and Talented Programs for the Columbus Public Schools, Columbus, Ohio. Prior to this position, she served as a senior research associate in the Center for Special Needs Populations. She has been an adjunct faculty member at several colleges and universities in Ohio, and presented at international, national, regional, and local conferences in the areas of science education, adventure education, secondary gifted education, and insight.

Alexinia Young Baldwin received her B.S. degree from Tuskegee Institute, M.A. degree from the University of Michigan, and Ph.D. from the University of Connecticut. She is presently Professor and Head of the Department of Curriculum and Instruction at the University of Connecticut, Storrs. Her professional experiences have included serving as an elementary school teacher, including teaching classes for the gifted; as a professor of curriculum and education of the gifted at the State University of New York at Albany; as the director of an international teacher education program; and as a lecturer, consultant, researcher, and writer of several articles on the identification and program development process for gifted students, with particular emphasis on students from underrepresented groups. Dr. Baldwin is an active member of several professional organizations and has served as president of the Association of the Gifted (TAG), associate editor of *The Journal of Exceptional Children*, and U.S. delegate to the World Council for the Gifted.

Suzanne Meriweather-Bean received her Ph.D. in special education with emphasis in gifted education from the University of Southern Mississippi. She is currently employed as Assistant Professor of Education at Mississippi University for Women. Dr. Meriweather-Bean has taught gifted students at preschool, elementary, and secondary levels and has coordinated summer and weekend programs for gifted students. Her research interests include the development of leadership potential, family influences on giftedness, creativity, curriculum for the gifted, and the culturally diverse gifted. Dr. Meriweather-Bean has published several articles in the field of gifted education and is co-author of an upcoming book on developing leadership potential.

Jim Broyles earned his B.S. degree in education and M.A. in school psychology from the Ohio State University. He is currently completing his dissertation for the Ph.D. degree in school psychology at the Ohio State University and serves as a graduate research associate in the Department of Educational Services and Research. Previously Mr. Broyles worked as a school psychologist in a public school setting. His research interests include cognitive assessment and counseling with children and families.

George R. Fichter received his M.A. degree in speech pathology and audiology from Kent State University. He currently serves as Governmental Relations Liaison to the State Associations for Gifted Children, and as Secretary of Support for Talented Students; he also provides consulting services in gifted education in Ohio and several other states. From 1968 to 1988, Mr. Fichter was educational consultant for the State Department of Education in Ohio. He served as supervisor of speech and hearing services from 1968 to 1974, and of gifted education from 1975 to 1988; he was the director of the Martin W. Essex School for the Gifted from 1976 to 1988. He is currently evaluator of a seminal project, Teaching and Learning About Japan, for the State Department of Education in Indiana and Earlham College. Mr. Fichter's research interests lie in the area of justification of the provision of special education for gifted children, including the relationship of success in careers and special school experiences. He has written several articles and book chapters in the area of gifted and talented children.

Diane E. Frey earned her Ph.D. in counseling from the University of Illinois and is currently Professor of Counseling at Wright State University. In addition to her graduate level teaching and writing, Dr. Frey maintains a private practice as a licensed clinical psychologist. Dr. Frey is co-author of *Enhancing Self-Esteem* and *Practical Techniques of Enhancing Self-Esteem*. She is the author of *100 Inspirational Quotations for Enhancing Self-Esteem* and *Intimate Relationships, Marriage and Family*. Dr. Frey has been a keynote speaker and/or major presenter at numerous conferences concerning the gifted, counseling, and self-esteem.

David M. Garner earned his B.A. and M.A. degrees in psychology from Cleveland State University and Ph.D. degree from York University, also in psychology. He is currently a Professor of Psychiatry at Michigan State University and the Director of Research for the Eating Disorders

Program. He was a scholar of the Medical Research Council of Canada from 1980 to 1985 and the recipient of a Research Associate Award from the Ontario Mental Health Foundation from 1985 to 1988. Dr. Garner served as Director of Research in the Department of Psychology at the Toronto General Hospital from 1982 to 1987, and then took a position as Professor of Psychology at the University of Toronto until 1988. Dr. Garner has published over 100 scientific articles on eating disorders and has co-authored or co-edited five books including: *Anorexia Nervosa: A Multidimensional Perspective, Handbook of Psychotherapy for Anorexia Nervosa and Bulimia*, and *Diagnostic Issues in Anorexia Nervosa and Bulimia Nervosa*. Dr. Garner and his colleagues have developed the widely used Eating Disorder Inventory and Eating Attitudes Test. Dr. Garner has given over 150 invited lectures over the past ten years on every phase of research and treatment of eating disorders.

Alexander Gonzalez received his training at Pomona College, Harvard Law School, and the University of California, Santa Cruz, where he completed the doctorate in psychology. In addition, he was also a postdoctoral fellow at Stanford University under the sponsorship of the National Research Council. Currently, he is serving as the Assistant to the President of California State University, Fresno, after having completed a three-year term as chairperson of the Department of Psychology. His experience and interests are broad and include involvement in programs at the community, educational, business, and government level. His research interests include the impact of assessment of Hispanics, cooperation and competition, intergroup relations, and the psychology of time. He is co-author with Elliot Aronson of "Desegregation, Jigsaw, and the Mexican-American Experience," in *Eliminating Racism: Profiles in Controversy*. His most current work is the development of the Stanford Time Perspective Inventory, with Philip Zimbardo of Stanford University.

Constance L. Hollinger earned her Ph.D. in educational psychology from Case Western Reserve University. She currently is Associate Professor and Coordinator of School Psychology at Cleveland State University. Prior to this position, she was dean of students at Lake Erie College for Women. Her research interests include longitudinal studies on the career development of gifted and talented women, with particular focus on the internal barriers to the realization of potential and self-perception. She also conducts research in the area of assessment of intellectual ability. Dr. Hollinger has written numerous journal articles and is the co-author of *Project Choice: A Diagnostic-Prescriptive Model of Career Education for Gifted Young Women*.

Frances A. Karnes earned her Ph.D. in education from the University of Illinois. Currently she is the Director of the Center for Gifted

Studies and a Professor in the Department of Special Education at the University of Southern Mississippi. Dr. Karnes is best known for her work in the education of the gifted and talented. Her current interests are in the leadership training of youth and the legal aspects of gifted education. She is the co-author of the *Leadership Skills Inventory* and the accompanying manuals. In addition, she has published over 100 articles in scholarly journals and is the co-author of *A Handbook of Instructional Resources and References for Teaching the Gifted, Issues and Trends in Basic Adult Education: Focus on Reading, Assessment in Gifted Education*, and *Programs, Leaders, Consultants, and Other Resources in Gifted and Talented Education.*

Vicente Z. Ortiz earned his B.A. degree in psychology from the University of California, Santa Cruz, M.S. from the California State University–Sacramento, and Ph.D. from Columbia Pacific University. He is currently the GATE and bilingual school psychologist with Madera Unified School District in California. Dr. Ortiz has conducted research for the California State Migrant Education Department on appropriate identification processes with gifted Hispanic students. He is author and co-author of a number of journal articles on this topic. Dr. Ortiz also developed the Rural and Migrant Gifted Project with the Fresno County Office of Education. He has also been a university lecturer in psychology and assessment at the undergraduate and graduate levels. Gifted education, assessment, and the underrepresented student continue to be Dr. Ortiz's research priorities.

Jane Piirto received her Ph.D. from Bowling Green State University. She is presently Associate Professor and Director of Gifted Education at Ashland University in Ashland, Ohio. Formerly, she was principal of Hunter College Elementary School, a school for gifted children in New York City; a gifted coordinator in Michigan and Ohio; a college humanities instructor; and a high school teacher and counselor. She has research interests in creative adolescents, particularly those with special writing abilities. Her book *Creativity and Giftedness* will be published in 1991. An award-winning novelist (*The Three-Week Trance Diet*) and published poet (*mamamama* and *Postcards from the Upper Peninsula*), she has also written articles for scholarly journals. She gives literary readings and workshops in gifted education around the country and abroad. She was awarded a Fulbright-Hays Fellowship in 1990 to study in Argentina.

E. Susanne Richert earned her Ph.D. from Brown University and is presently Director, National Clearinghouse for Gifted Education Resources at the Educational Information and Research Center, Sewell, New Jersey. She is the author of more than 15 articles and chapters, including an article on special populations of gifted students and patterns of underachievement among the gifted, *The National Report on Identification* for the U.S. Department of Education, and two teaching guides for the United States Supreme Court. She is co-authoring a forthcoming book for gifted girls and boys and has written the New Jersey Department of Education's manual for *Identification of Gifted Children* and the Kentucky Department of Education's manual for *Curriculum Standards for Gifted Education*. Dr. Richert is on the editorial boards of four journals for gifted education: *Gifted Child Quarterly, The Roeper Review, Journal for the Education of the Gifted,* and *Gifted Children Monthly*. She has been consultant to over a dozen state and national departments of education, and to local districts in more than 30 states, as well as to the U.S. Supreme Court. Her specialties in gifted education include identification, particularly of disadvantaged populations; program design and evaluation; curriculum; underachievement; and emotional needs.

Sylvia B. Rimm received her B.A. in sociology from Rutgers University. Her M.S. and Ph.D. in educational psychology were received from the University of Wisconsin–Madison. Currently she is a psychologist specializing in working with gifted and creative children who are not performing up to their ability in school. She directs the Family Achievement Clinic with four offices in Wisconsin. She has taught graduate courses in the areas of gifted and talented, creativity, and underachievement, and is the author and researcher of several internationally validated creativity instruments, including GIFT, GIFFI, and PRIDE, and three inventories for the identification of underachievement patterns (AIM, AIM-TO and GAIM). She is the co-author of *Education of the Gifted and Talented,* and author of *Underachievement Syndrome: Causes and Cures; Guidebook—Underachievement Syndrome: Causes and Cures;* and *How to Parent So Children Will Learn*. She speaks and publishes nationally on family and school approaches to working with gifted, creative, and underachieving children.

Raymond H. Swassing earned his M.Ed. and Ed.D. from the University of Kansas in the areas of special education and special education administration. He currently serves as Coordinator of Gifted Programs in the Department of Educational Services and Research at the Ohio State University. He has served as Assistant Director of Ohio's Martin W. Essex School for the Gifted for 14 years and as Coordinator of OSU's Summer Institutes for the Gifted for 5 years. He edited the text *Teaching Gifted Children and Adolescents,* co-authored *Teaching Through Modality Strengths* with Dr. Walter B. Barbe, and with Dr. Barbe developed the Swassing-Barbe Modality Index.

Karen B. Tye received her B.A. degree with honors from Transylvania University, M.A. from United Theological Seminary, and Ed.D. from Presbyterian School of Christian Education in Richmond, Virginia. Currently she is the Frank and Belva Gleiss Associate Professor of Christian Education at American Baptist Seminary of the West, Berkeley, California. Her research interests include teaching and teacher education in the church context and educating for spiritual formation. She has published articles in *Baptist Leader* and *Religious Education.*

Gail Muranaka Woliver received her M.Ed. from the University of Hawaii. She has taught in Connecticut at Yale University and in the East Haven and Wethersfield school systems. She currently teaches at Kamehameha Schools, a private boarding school for students of Hawaiian ancestry in Honolulu, Hawaii. For 1990–91, she received a Christa McAuliffe Fellowship awarded by the U.S. Department of Education for innovative projects and excellence in teaching. A consultant in education, she also enjoys acting and freelance writing.

Robert Woliver earned his doctorate in psychology at the University of Hawaii and is a clinical psychologist in private practice and a lecturer for the University of Hawaii–Windward Community College. He serves as a mental health consultant for the Hawaii Job Corps with its population of Asian, Hawaiian, and Pacific Island adolescents. He was the founding president of the Hawaii School of Professional Psychology and the founding dean of the Forest Institute of Professional Psychology–Hawaii campus.

Index

Abt, L., 111
Academic advising, 205–206
Acceleration, in school, 10
Acceptance, need for, 38
Achievement
  family environment and, 29–30
  giftedness *vs.*, 139–140
  of Hispanic adolescents, 242
  perfectionism and, 68–69
  self-exploration and, 208
  sibling relations and, 28–29
  stress and, 80–81
  time and financial commitment of
    parents required, 22–24
  See also Underachievement
Adaptive thinking, 110
Adderholdt-Elliott, M., 56, 65–75, 65, 68,
    72
Addiction, 33
Addison, L., 123, 126
Adjective Check List, 10
Adler, M., 222
Adolescence, 8–14
  career issues, 13–14
  combatting stereotypes during, 204–210
  educational issues in, 12
  emotional issues in, 9–12
  ethical issues in, 12–13
  extended, 27, 36
  identifying giftedness in, 8
  lifestyle issues, 13–14
  social issues in, 9–12
  spiritual issues in, 13
African-American adolescents. *See* Black
    adolescents
Albert, R. S., 23, 25, 29, 30
Albo, D., 139
Alexander, P. A., 98
All-or-nothing thinking, 65, 69
Altman, R., 80, 82

Alvino, J., 2, 11, 14, 71, 115, 129, 141, 155,
    159
Amabile, T. M., 113
American Association for Gifted Children,
    35
American Guidance Services, 43
Amidon, S. R., 91–103
Analogical reasoning, 98
Anderson, M., 97
Anderson, R. S., 45
Andreasen, N. C., 77
Androgyny, 42, 205, 207
Andron, S., 221
Anorexia nervosa, 50–61
Anxiety, symptoms of, 78–79. *See also*
    Stress management
Apo, A., 255
Apo, F., 255
Arguing, 30–31
Arieti, S., 111
Arnold, J. D., 44
Arts students, 3, 104, 105–106, 177–179
Asian-American adolescents, *x*, 229,
    248–257, 261
  demographics of, 248–249
  home vs. school values and, 250–255
  importance of education to, 249–250
  racism and, 255–256
Assertiveness training, 45
Astin, H. S., 208
Atkinson, J., 168
Attention Deficit Disorder with
    Hyperactivity (ADD-H), 163–164
Attention-Deficit Hyperactive Disorder
    (ADHD), 163–164
Autonomous gifted, 5
Autonomy, 36, 172–173

Babigan, H. M., 51
Bagley, M., 111

Bakan, D., 203
Baker, L., 57
Baldwin, A. Y., 231–239, 234, 235
Baldwin, B., 69, 70
Baldwin, L. J., 171
Bales, R. F., 203
Banks, J., 235, 237, 239
Barnette, E., 35
Baron, J., 3
Barr, L., 123, 129
Barr, N., 123, 129
Barrell, J., 95, 98
Barrett, G. V., 123
Barrett, M. J., 60
Barron, F., 106, 108, 240
Barrow, J., 69, 71
Bass, B. M., 123, 124, 129
Beck, L., 182
Behavioral disorders, 164–165
Behling, O. C., 123
Belenky, M., 116
Bell, L. A., 210
Bem, S. L., 207
Bemis, K. M., 54, 55, 58–60
Benbow, C., 10, 106
Bennett, W. J., 129
Benson, H., 84
Bergman, S., 44
Bernal, E. M., 240, 243
Betts, G., 2, 5, 6, 35, 153*n*
Beumont, P. J. V., 51
Beyer, B., 96
Bibliotherapy, perfectionism and, 72
Biculturalism, 235–237, 244–245, 253–255.
    See also Bilingualism
Bidell, T., 108
Bielen, P., 44
Bilingualism, 240, 241–242, 244–245
Bireley, M. K., x, 1–17, 43, 163–175, 172,
    189–200, 193, 195, 196, 215–227
Birnbaum, J., 169
Birth order, 28–29, 66
*Birth Order Book, The: Why You Are the
    Way You Are* (Leman), 66
Black, J. D., 125
Black adolescents, x, 229, 231–239, 261
    development of pride in, 233–237
    racism and, 231–233
Blackburn, A., 82
Blackman, J., 165, 167

Blake, R. R., 123
Blake, W., 139, 144
Blanchard, K. H., 123–124
Bleck, E., 167
Bleedorn, B., 72
Bloom, B. S., 22, 23, 25, 30, 106, 111,
    114–115, 176, 245
Blume, B., 7
Boggs, J., 252
Boggs, S., 251, 252
Borgers, S., 72
Borman, C., 182, 210
Boston, B., 170, 181
Boyd, T. A., 164
Boyle, J., 184
Bradshaw, G. L., 95
Braiker, H. B., 207
Brainstorming, 114
Brandt, G., 139
Brandt, R. S., 92
Bransky, P., 65
Bray, H., 210
Briggs, K. C., 192, 194
Brody, L., 10, 37, 163, 210
Broedel, J., 152
Bronowski, J., 95
Brook, D., 40
Brook, J., 40
Brooks, L., 209
Brophy, B., 70
Brounstein, P., 36
Brown, L., 53
Broyles, J., 76–87
Bruch, C. B., 93
Bruch, H., 51, 54, 55, 57
Buescher, T. M., 23, 30, 36, 39, 40, 218, 221
Bulimia nervosa, 50–61
Burka, J., 69
Burks, S., 1, 9–10
Burns, D., 55, 65, 69, 72
Burns, E., 243
Butler, O., 236

Callahan, C. M., 11, 126, 212
Campbell, D., 129
Campbell, J., 193
Canfield, J., 44
Career Awareness Model for Girls, 210
Career Data Books (Flanagan et al.),
    207

Careers, 13–14, 201–214, 261
  of disabled gifted, 172–173
  evaluating intervention efforts
      regarding, 211
  learning style and, 13–14, 197–198
  mentorship programs and, 181
  programs to explore for, 208
  self-exploration and, 207–208
  stereotypes in, 201–211
Carey, R., 44
Carlock, J., 38, 42, 44
Carlson, J. E., 96
Carnegie Corporation of New York, 177
Cartledge, G., 44
Casserly, P., 206, 209
Cattell, M. D., 126, 127
Cattell, R. B., 126, 127
Cerebral palsy, 167
Challenge, stress and, 82
Challenging gifted, 5
Chambers, J., 240
Chance, P., 99
Chang, M., 256
Change, 77–78, 224
Chauvin, J. C., 125, 128, 130–131
Chi, M., 95
Chiodo, J., 57
Chodorow, N., 56
Chun, M. J., 254
Clabby, J., 44
Clark, B., 11, 70–72, 92, 218, 252
Clark, G. A., 23, 106
Clark, W., 218
Clarke, J. I., 44
Clinch, B., 116
Clinkenbeard, P., 112
Coddington, R., 77
Cognitive appraisal, stress and, 77
Cognitive information processing, 93
Cognitive relabelling, 44–45
Cognitive therapy, perceptions of reality
    and, 79–81
Colangelo, N., 35, 139, 151, 152
Coleman, J., 38
Collaborative instruction, 97
College programs, 179–180
Colson, S., 182, 210
Commitment, 151
  of parents, 22–24, 27
  stress and, 82–83

Community service, 128–129, 220
Competition, 21, 24–25
  eating disorders and, 50–51
  sibling relations and, 28–29
  withdrawal from, 149
Concept-development model, 237
Conflict, 224
Conformity, 145, 146, 147–149, 154
Conger, J., 12, 13, 218
Conn, J., 216
Connors, M. E., 58
Conradie, S., 126
Control, stress and, 82
Convergent thinking, 112–113
Cook, E. P., 203
Copeland, E. P., 77, 78
Coping skills, 42–43
  failure and, 155–157
  need for, 37
  stress and, 82–83
Corn, A., 172
Cornell Critical Thinking Test, 99–100
Coscina, D. V., 53
Cossey, R., 247
Costa, A. L., 96, 97, 99, 100
Counselors, 42–43, 259
  academic advising by, 205–206
  disagreement and learning style, 198–199
  psychosocial interventions and, 43–45
  role of, in biculturalism, 254
  role of, in moral and spiritual
      development, 221–225
Cousins, N., 72
Cox, C., 1
Cox, J., 170, 181
Cox, P. W., 168
Craig, G., 12
Creatively gifted
  defined, 105
  development of, 108–110
  types of, 110
Creative thinking, 92
Creative visualization, perfectionism and,
    71–72
Creative Visualization (Wiehl), 72
Creativity, 104–121
  concept of, 6–7
  defined, 104
  and development of the creative person,
      108–110

Creativity (*continued*)
  encouraging, 155–157
  Gardner's multiple intelligences and, 3,
    7–8
  gender differences in, 115–117
  intellective characteristics and, 104–105
  intelligence vs., 140–142
  IQ and, 6–7
  nonintellective characteristics and,
    105–108
  overexcitability and, 2, 4, 7, 109–110
  perfectionism and, 73
  situational factors and, 111–115
  in theories of giftedness, 6–7
Creativity training, 111–115
Crisp, A. H., 50, 51, 60
Critical thinking, 92
Csikszentmihalyi, M., 105, 106
Cults, 221
Cunningham, K., 109
Curriculum
  development of multicultural, 235–237,
    244–245
  for Hispanic students, 244–245
  leadership training in, 133–134

Dabrowski, K., 2, 4, 7, 109, 143
Dally, P. J., 51, 55
Daniel, N., 170, 181
Davidson, J. E., 3, 4, 6, 93, 94
Davis, G. A., 218, 220, 221
Davis, G. L., 218, 219
Davis, R., 54, 58
Davison, M., 218
Dean, R., 221
Debaters, 30–31, 42, 198–199
de Bono, E., 111
Decision-making, developing skills in,
  43–44
Defining Issues Test (DIT), 217, 218
DeHaan, R. F., 122
Delcourt, M. A., 243
Delisle, J. R., 40, 46, 70, 71, 78–80, 82,
  153*n*
Dellas, M., 106
Demographics
  of Asian-American and Pacific Island
    adolescents, 248–249
  of Hispanic adolescents, 241
Depression, 67–69, 165

Descartes, R., 35
Desch, L., 166
*Developing Minds: A Resource Book for
  Teaching Thinking* (Costa), 99
Development
  characteristics of maximum human, 142
  of creative people, 108–110, 116
  of leadership potential, 130–134
Developmental dysplasia, 33, 37, 67, 76
Developmental thinking, 110
Diaries, 85
Dichotomous thinking, perfectionism and,
  65, 69
Dick, S., 26, 30
Diener, C., 168
D'Ilio, V., 8, 128–131
*Dimensions of Thinking: A Framework for
  Curriculum and Instruction* (Marzano
  et al.), 92
Dirkes, M., 78
Disabled gifted, 2, 5, 163–175
  education of, 169–173
  identification of disabilities of, 163–167
  motivation in, 168–169
Disagreement, 30–31, 42, 198–199
Dissonance, 39
Divergent thinking, 112–113, 149–150
Divoky, D., 164
Divorce, 31
Doman, G., 67
Dorf, J. H., 125
Double-labelled gifted, 5. *See* disabled
  gifted
Dowdall, C., 139, 151, 152
Downing, C. J., 98
Drew, C., 166, 170
Dropouts, 5, 30
Drug use, 42
Dually labeled. *See* Disabled gifted
Dunn, K., 190
Dunn, R., 189, 190
Dweck, C., 168
Dysfunctional families, perfectionism and,
  67

Eagle, M., 54
Eating Attitudes Test (EAT), 56
Eating disorders, x, 33, 50–64
  competition and, 50–51
  intellectual functions and, 51–52

predisposing factors for, 52–57
social class and, 51
treatment of, 57–61
Eby, J. W., 126, 127
Eby Gifted Behavior Index, 126, 127
Eccles, J. S., 203
Edelstein, C. K., 58
Edgette, J. S., 58
Edlind, E. P., 129, 209
Education
acceleration by grade in, 10
of disabled gifted, 169–173
of gifted students, 12
of Hispanic adolescents, 242
importance of, to Asian-American and
Pacific Island adolescents, 249–250
Educational Programs That Work
(National Diffusion Network), 99
Education for All Handicapped Children
Act (PL 94-142), 165
Egan, M. W., 166, 170
Ehle, John, 177
Eisikovits, R., 220
Elaborative thinking, 110
Elias, M., 44
Elkind, D., 40, 67
Ellingson, M. K., 183
Ellis, A., 79
Emerick, L. J., 25
Emotional issues
defined, 11
disorders, 164–165
giftedness and, 9–12
See also Psychosocial needs
Endorphins, 111
Ennis, R. H., 92
EQUALS, 210
Ericcson, K. A., 94
Erickson, D., 82
Erikson, E., 9, 108
Ethics, 12–13, 216. *See also* Moral
development
Evaluation, of thinking skills, 99–100
Evans de Bernard, A., 240
Events and Life Change Units for Use
with Four Age Groups, 77–78
Expectations
of others, 39–40, 153–155
strategies for handling, 145, 147–151
Extended adolescence, 27, 36

External locus of control, 83
Extracurricular activities, 26, 128–129

Failure
coping with, 155–157
fear of, 69–70, 155
Fairburn, C. G., 58
Fallon, P., 56
Family, 259
achievement and, 29–30
of creative people, 108
dysfunctional, 67
eating disorders and, 56–61
as source of stress, 77
values of Asian-American and Pacific
Island, 250–255
See also Parents; Sibling relations
Family Math (Stenmark et al.), 245
Farmer, H. S., 208
Fear of failure, 69–70, 155
Feldhusen, J. F., 8, 112, 132, 183, 222
Feldman, D., 10, 117
Fenzel, L., 220
Feuerstein, R., 171
Fichter, G. R., 176–185, 178
Fiedler, F. E., 123
Field, T., 44
Fine, M. J., 31
Fiorello H. LaGuardia High School of
Music and Art and Performing Arts
(New York City), 104–106, 114
Fischer, P., 36
Fitzgerald, H., 218
Flanagan, J. C., 207
Flavell, J. H., 93
Fleming, E. S., 42, 207, 210
Florey, J. E., 125
Folkman, S., 76, 77
Foster, W. H., 122, 123, 125, 223
4Mat system of teaching, 194
Fox, C. F., 51
Fox, L. H., 37, 106, 163, 210
Fox Dember, 31
Frankl, V., 143
Freeman, J., 218
Freud, S., 13, 108, 209
Frey, D. E., *ix*, 35–49, 38, 40, 42, 44
Friedman, M., 68, 81
Friedman, P. G., 126
Friedman, R. J., 126

Friedrich, W. N., 56
Frieze, I. H., 202
Fromm, E., 143
Fugit, E., 44

Gaier, E., 106
Galbraith, J., 11, 45, 72, 153n
Gallagher, J. J., 132, 151, 218, 243
Galligan, J., 209
Galton, F., 115
Gardner, H., 2, 3, 6–8, 112, 141, 142
Gardner, J., 123
Garfinkel, P. E., 51, 52, 55, 58
Gargiulo, D. A., 171
Garner, D. M., x, 50–64, 51–55, 57–60, 65
Garner, M. V., 54
Gelatt, H. B., 44
Gelcer, E., 26, 30
Gender differences, 2
    in college attainment of Asians, 250, 252
    in creativity, 115–117
    leadership and, 128, 129
    in learning style, 196
    in moral reasoning, 217
    in psychosocial needs, 41–42
    sex-role stereotypes and, 14, 37, 129,
        201–211
    in social skills, 10–11
    in underachievement, 145, 147–151, 159
Generative instruction, 97
Genshaft, J., 1–17, 76–87, 259–262
George, P., 218
Getzels, J. W., 6, 105, 106
Ghiselin, B., 111
Gibb, L. H., 210
Gifted Kids Survival Guide (Galbraith), 72
Giftedness
    academic achievement vs., 139–140
    defined, 2, 105, 234–235
    defining maximum gifted potential,
        140–144
    eating disorders and, 51–52
    identification of, 8, 232, 234–235, 240,
        243–244, 251, 261–262
    perfectionism and, 70–71
    sibling relations and, 27–29
    stereotypes concerning, 1–2, 201–211
    vulnerabilities of, 9, 11–12
Giftedness, theories of, 1–8
    creativity and, 6–7

Gardner's multiple intelligences, 2, 3,
        7–8
    leadership and, 8
    Marland's six types, 2–3
    psychic overexitabilities and, 2, 4, 7,
        109–110
    Renzulli's three-part definition and
        talent pool models, 2, 4–5
    Sternberg's triarchic theory of
        intelligence, 2, 3–4, 93
    subtypes of giftedness and, 5
    talent and, 7–8
    Terman stereotypes, 1–2
Gilligan, C., 56, 116
Girls/women. See Women/girls
Glaser, E. M., 91
Glaser, R., 95, 97
Glasser, W., 72, 73
Gleick, J., 95
Goertzel, M. G., 25, 109, 115
Goertzel, T. G., 115
Goertzel, V., 25, 109, 115
Goff, K., 112, 113
Goldberg, M. L., 140, 151, 152
Goldberger, N., 116
Goldbloom, D., 54
Gomez, J., 51
Gonzalez, A., 240–247, 244
Goodenough, D. R., 168
Gordon, W., 97
Gottfredson, L. S., 203
Gourley, T. J., 111
Govinda, L. A., 143
Gowan, J. C., 92, 116, 140
Gowers, S., 51
Graphic organizers, 98
Great Ideas, The: A Syntopicon of Great
        Books of the Western World (Adler),
        222
Gregorc, A., 191, 192
Gregorc Style Delineator, 191–192
Greiger, R., 79
Gridley, B. E., 83
Grouping, underachievers and, 152,
        158–159
Guiding the Gifted Child (Webb et al.), 43
Guilford, J. P., 106, 108, 111–113
Guttentag, M., 210
Gutteridge, D., 215, 217

Hackney, P. W., 171
Haden, T., 37
Haeger, W. W., 183
Haensly, P. A., 129, 209
Haily, A., 51
Halkitis, P., 105
Hall, D. J., 51
Halpern, D. F., 91, 92, 94
Hamilton, S., 220
Hammer, T., 116
Hankins, N., 218
Hanson, J. R., 193, 194, 196
Hanson, R., 97
Harding, B., 51
Hardman, M., 166, 170
Harmin, M., 222
Harmon, P., 94-95
Harris, L. J., 116
Hartman, R. K., 126
Hauser, J., 221
Hausman, C., 111
Havighurst, R., 8-9, 40
Hayes-Roth, F., 95
Hearing impairments, 166
Heath, P., 44
Hedin, D., 220
Hefner, R., 205
Heiman, M., 44
Heisel, J., 77
Helmstetter, S., 44, 45
Herman, C. P., 53
Herman, J., 169
Herrman, D., 95
Herrmann, N., 192, 197
Herrmann Brain Dominance Instrument, 192
Hersey, P., 123-124
Hess, K., 111
Higham, S., 40, 116, 206
High School Personality Questionaire, 126, 127-128
Hillman, D., 108
Hispanic adolescents, *x*, 229, 240-247, 261
  factors influencing, 241-242
  identification of gifted, 240, 243-244
Hobbs, N., 176, 177
Hoehn, L., 43, 193, 195, 196
Hoffman, L. W., 203
Hoffman, M., 13
Hogan, R., 218

Holahan, W., 36, 209
Holland, J., 139
Hollander, E. P., 122
Holleman, J. L., 51
Hollinger, C. L., 42, 201-214, 207, 208, 210
Hollingworth, L. S., 2, 10, 76, 124, 140
Holmes, T. H., 77
Homosexuality, *x*, 40, 116
Hooper, S. R., 164
Horowitz, F., 35
Hothousing, perfectionism and, 67
Houtz, J., 168
Howard, B. E., 96
Howell, H., 191
Howell, R. M., 169
Howley, A., 125
Howley, C. B., 125
Hoyt, D. P., 139
Hughes, C. S., 92
Humor: Lessons in Laughter for Learning and Living (Bleedorn and McKelvey), 72
Huon, G. F., 53, 57
Hyllen, J., 245
Hynes, K., 132

Identification
  of disabled gifted, 163-167
  of giftedness, 8, 232, 234-235, 240, 243-244, 251, 261-262
  of leadership potential, 124-130
  of minority giftedness, 232, 234-235, 240, 243-244, 251, 261-262
Identity, 38, 40
Identity crisis, 9
Imagi/Craft, 112
Impatience, 40
Independence, 36, 172-173
Individuality, need for, 37
Inductive/directive instruction, 96
Information-processing model, 236-237
Insight, 93-94
Instructional strategies
  in combatting stereotypes, 206
  learning style research in, 194-198
  multicultural, 235-237, 244-245
  for thinking skills development, 96-99
Instrumental Enrichment Program (IE), 171-172

Intellective characteristics, defined,
　104–105
Intellectually gifted, defined, 105
Intelligence
　creativity *vs.*, 140–142
　eating disorders and, 51–52
　See also IQ
Interests, sharing of, with parent, 25
Internal locus of control, 150–151
　developing, 157–158
　in disabled gifted, 168
　perfectionism and, 72–73
　stress and, 82–83
IQ, 240
　creativity and, 6–7, 105
　eating disorders and, 51–52
　environment and, 232
　in identification of giftedness, 240, 243
　of intellectually gifted, 105
　leadership and, 10, 124
　of mathematically creative youth, 107
　psychosocial issues and, 10
　of scientifically creative youth, 107
　of Terman's gifted population, 2
　See also Intelligence
Irvine, M. M., 58

Jacklin, C. N., 201
Jackson, P., 6, 106
Jacobs, T. O., 123
Janis, I. L., 211
Janos, P., 38
Jellen, H. G., 132
Jenkins, M., 243
Jenkins-Friedman, R., 65
Jensen, A. R., 232
Jensen, D., 1, 9–10
Jersild, A., 40
Johns, E. F., 126–128
Johns Hopkins University, 10, 179
Johnson, C., 53, 58
Johnson, J. H., 77
John-Steiner, V., 107
Johnstone, L. C., 51
Jonas, B. S., 172
Jones, B. F., 92
Jones, M. D., 251
Journal of Pediatrics, 77
Journals, 85
Joy Luck Club, The (Tan), 250

Julian, J. W., 122
Jung, C. G., 128, 143, 193

Kalucy, R. S., 50, 51, 55
Kamehameha Schools (Hawaii), 254
Kaplan, L., 43
Karchmer, M., 172
Karnes, F. A., 8, 80–82, 122–138, 125,
　128–131, 178
Kaufman, A. S., 164
Keating, D. P., 92, 179
Keefe, J. W., 190
Kegan, R., 223, 224
Kelly, M., 78
Kendell, R. E., 51
Kennedy, D., 132
Kerr, B. A., 10, 145, 207, 210
Kiefaber, M., 66
Kindred (Butler), 236
King, D., 94–95
Kirby, D. F., 176
Kitano, H., 252
Kitano, M. K., 176
Knaus, W., 69
Knowledge engineering, 183
Kobasa, 82
Koestler, A., 111
Kog, E., 56–57
Kohlberg, L., 12, 108, 143, 205, 216–218,
　222
Kohut, H., 143–145, 147, 149, 153, 157
Kolb, D. A., 191, 192, 194, 197
Kolloff, P. B., 183
Kopp, H. G., 165
Krathwohl, D. R., 143
Krawetz, M., 44
Kreinberg, N., 210
Kretschmer, R. E., 169
Krug, 31
Kuczen, B., 77, 79–84
Kulieke, M., 23, 30

LaGuardia High School (New York City),
　104–106, 114
Lakein, A., 73
Landers, M. F., 172
Langley, P., 95
Language, Hispanic adolescents and, 240,
　241–242, 244–245
Lao Tzu, 143

Larkin, J., 95, 97
Latimer, P. R., 57
Laughter, perfectionism and, 72
Lawrence, G., 129
Lawrence, J., 217
Lazarus, R. S., 76, 77, 79
Leadership, 3, 122–138
  concept of, 8
  definitions of, 122–123
  development of, 130–134
  identifying potential for, 124–130
  IQ and, 10, 124
  moral education and, 223
  theories of, 123–124
Leadership: A Speical Kind of Giftedness
  (Sisk and Rosselli), 132–133
Leadership: Making Things Happen (Sisk
  and Shallcross), 132
*Leadership Education: Developing Skills
  for Youth* (Richardson & Feldhusen),
  132
Leadership Network Newsletter, 134
Leadership Potential Score (LPS), 127–128
Leadership Skills: A Training Program, 132
Leadership Skills Development Program,
  130–132
Leadership Skills Inventory (Karnes &
  Chauvin), 130
*Leadership Skills Inventory Activities
  Manual* (Karnes & Chauvin), 130–131
Leadership Training Model, 133
Learned helplessness, 168–169, 172–173
Learning disabilities, 7, 163–164
Learning Preference Inventory (LPI), 193,
  194
Learning Style Inventory (Dunn et al.),
  190
Learning Style Inventory (Kolb), 191
Learning Style Profile, 190–191
Learning styles, 43, 187, 189–200, 261
  assessment of, 189–193
  career choice and, 13–14, 197–198
  disagreement and, 198–199
  using research on, 194–198
Learning Styles Inventory (Renzulli &
  Smith), 191
Lecroy, C., 44
Lehr, S., 169
Leman, K., 65, 66
Lenat, D. B., 95

LeResche, L., 36
Lerner, J., 164, 165
Lerner, R. M., 202
Leroux, J. A., 29, 41, 81, 82, 218
Lessner, W. J., 108
Lester, C. P., 45
Levine, E., 35
Levine, M. P., 59
Lewandowski, 7
Lewin, K., 123
Licht, B., 168
Lifestyle choices, 13–14
  of disabled gifted, 172–173
Lifework planning, 198, 210
Lindsay, B., 125
Lippitt, R., 123
Lockhead, J., 97
Locus of control
  external, 83
  internal, 72–73, 82–83, 150–151, 157–158,
    168
Loeb, K., 116
Loew, B., 24–26, 29
Lomanaco, S., 169
Low incidence disabilities, 165–167
Lubeck, S., 108
Lupkowski, A. E., 129
Lyons, N., 116
Lyth, W., 172

MacDonald, C. T., 210
MacKinnon, D., 106, 108
Maddi, 82
Magic Friends and Places (Alvino), 71
Magoon, R. A., 132
Mahoney, M. J., 59
Maier, S., 168
Mainstreaming, 169
Maker, C. J., 12, 93, 169, 173, 222
*Managing the Social and Emotional Needs
  of the Gifted* (Schmitz & Galbraith),
  45
Mangrum, C. T., 172
Mann, L., 211
Marland, S., Jr., 2–3
Martin, D., 172
Maryanopolis, J., 7
Marzano, R. J., 92
Maslow, A., 143, 144, 159
Masten, W. G., 240

Masuda, M., 77
Mathematics, 10, 105, 106–108, 179–180,
    245, 253
  "girl-friendly" classes in, 206
  summer programs in, 10, 179–180
McAleer, N., 111
McCarthy, B., 194
McCaulley, M. H., 14, 43, 126, 128, 129,
    194–197, 199
McCuen, J. T., 145, 151, 152
McCutcheon, R., 153n
McDaniel, S., 44
McDonnel, R., 2, 141
McGregor, D., 123
McIntyre, J. M., 191, 197
McKelvey, S., 72
McKinney, J., 218
McLaughlin, D. H., 207
McMahon, J. B., 51
McNamara, J. F., 129
Meckstroth, E. A., 43, 152, 153n
Media influences, perfectionism and, 66
Mediative instruction, 96–97
Meeker, M., 111
Meisgeier, C., 126, 128, 193
Mentoring, 36–37, 180–183, 209, 210
Meriweather, S., 8, 129, 131
Meriweather-Bean, Suzanne, 122–138
Miklus, S., 111
Milburn, J. F., 44
Miller, A., 108, 143, 145, 147, 149, 157
Miller, G. P., 44
Miller, N., 218, 224
Miller, T., 169
Mills, C., 43
Milwaukee Project, 232
Mindstroms (Papert), 73
Minority groups, 2
  gifted programs and, 144
  underachievers in, 152
  See also Asian-American adolescents;
    Black adolescents; Hispanic
    adolescents; Pacific Island
    adolescents
Minuchin, S., 57, 60
Mitchell, B., 105
Mitchell, J. E., 58
Mitchell, P. B., 58
Money magazine, 145
Monk, J. S., 190

Moodswings, perfectionism and, 68, 69
Mookerjee, A., 143
Moore, A. D., 183
Moore, C., 69, 71
Moore, C. A., 168
Moore, J., 218
Moral development, x, 12–13, 215–227,
    216–218, 261
  role of teachers, counselors, and parents
    in, 221–225
  search for meaning and, 219–221
Morgan, H. G., 51
Morris, S., 53
Moseley, V. A., 183
Motivation, in disabled gifted, 168–169
Mouton, J. S., 123
Muktananda, S., 143
Mumford, E., 123
Murphey, F., 7
Murphy, A. J., 123
Murphy, D., 65
Murphy, E., 126, 128, 193
Murphy, J., 165
Murphy-Meisgeier Type Indicator for
    Children (MMTIC), 126, 128, 193
Murray, H., 69
Myers, I. B., 14, 43, 106, 107, 126, 128, 129,
    189, 192, 194–197, 199
Myers, P. B., 106, 107, 129
Myers, R. E., 111
Myers-Briggs Type Indicator (MBTI), 106,
    126, 128, 129, 192–193, 194, 196, 197,
    199

Nagel, D., 167
Narcissism, 147, 157–158
Nash, W. R., 182, 210
National Association of School
    Psychologists, xiii
National Science Board Commission on
    Pre-College Education, 91
Navarre, J. P., 111, 116, 206
Neihart, M., 2, 5, 6
New Directions in Creativity, 112
New Jersey Test of Reasoning Skills,
    99–100
Newlon, B., 165
Newman, 31
Niehart, M., 35
Nielsen, L., 12, 13, 218, 220

Noble, K. D., 204, 208
Nochlin, L., 116
Nonintellective characteristics
  of arts students, 104, 105–106
  defined, 105
  of mathematics students, 105, 106–108
  of science students, 105, 106–108
Nonverbal behavior, 41, 45

Oden, M. H., 1, 140, 243
Oehler-Stinnet, J., 80–82
O'Brien, M., 35
O'Neil, J. M., 210
Oleshansky, B., 205
Olivero, J. L., 126
Olmsted, M. P., 53, 54
Olsen, M., 152
Olszewski, P., 23, 30
On Being Gifted (American Association
  for Gifted Children), 43
Only Child, The: Being One, Loving One,
  Understanding One, Raising One
  (Sifford), 66
Organizational Psychology (Kolb et al.),
  191
Organized religion, 219–220
Ortiz, V. Z., 240–247, 243–245
Osborn, A. F., 111
Overachievement, eating disorders and,
  51–52
Overexcitability, 2, 4, 7, 109–110
Ownership, of giftedness, 39

Pacht, A., 69
Pacific Island adolescents, x, 229, 248–257
  demographics of, 248–249
  home *vs.* school values and, 250–255
  importance of education to, 249–250
  racism and, 255–256
Palmer, R. L., 50
Papert, S., 73
Paralyzed perfectionsim, 70
Parents, 18–31, 259
  competition and, 21, 24–25
  disagreement and, 198–199
  expectations of, 39–40
  extended adolescence and, 27, 36
  financial commitments of, 22–24, 27
  moral development and, 13
  perfectionism and, 66, 71, 73

power in relationships and, 29–31
relationship of, with school, 26–27
as role models, 24–25, 159
role of, in biculturalism, 254–255
role of, in moral and spiritual
  development, 221–225
sharing interests and, 25
sibling relations and, 27–29, 260
styles of, 13
time commitments of, 22–24
underachievers and, 156
as volunteers in school, 27
Parker, J. P., 133
Parker, M., 220
Parks, P., 36
Parnes, S. J., 97, 111
Parsons, T., 203
Passow, A. H., 100, 122, 140, 151
Pearce, N., 178
Peer relations, 38, 115, 260
  perfectionism and, 66–67
  racism and, 233
  sex-role stereotypes and, 204
Pendarvis, E. D., 125
Perception, stress and, 79–81
Perfectionism, 33, 65–75, 255, 260–261
  breaking away from, 71–73
  eating disorders and, 55–56, 59–60
  giftedness and, 70–71
  major traits of, 69–70
  mind games and, 67–69
  reasons for, 66–67
  reduction of, 44
  stress and, 80–81
Perfectionism: What's Bad About Being
  Too Good? (Adderholdt-Elliot), 72
Performing arts, 3, 104–106
Perkins, D. N., 92, 112, 113
Perkins, H. V., 152
Perrone, P., 82–83
Persistence, 4–5, 25
Person, H. S., 123
Personality type, 261
  of art students, 106
  assessment of, 189–193
  response to external expectations and,
    147–151
  of science and mathematics students,
    107–108
  stress and, 81–82

Petersen, A., 12, 13
Pfleger, L., 35
Physical impairments, 167
Physical symptoms, stress and, 77, 83
Piaget, J., 108
Piechowski, M., 2, 4, 6, 7, 109
Piirto, J., 104–121, 109, 110
Planning
  lifework, 198, 210
  teaching skills in, 157
Plowman, P. D., 125
Polivy, J., 53
Powell, P., 37
Power, 29–31, 260
  debaters and, 30–31
  dysfunctional alliances of, 31
  positive trust and, 29–30
Prejudice, 229
Presseisen, B. Z., 92, 95, 99
Prevention, 43
Price, G., 190
Pride, 233–237, 261
Prisoners of Childhood (Miller), 145
Problem finding, 95
Problem solving, 84–85, 94–95
Procaccini, J., 66
Procrastination, perfectionism and, 69
Productive Thinking Program, 112
Proff, F., 152
Project AIMS (Weibe et al.), 245
Project CHOICE, 210
Project REACH, 210
Project Wild (Western Regional
  Environmental Education Council),
  245
Protocol analysis, 97–98
Prout, M. F., 58
Psychological education, 206–207
Psychological type, leadership and, 129
Psychomotor ability, 3
Psychosocial needs, 35–49, 152, 153
  adjustment and, 36
  of adolescents, 9–12
  coping strategies for, 42–43
  defined, 9
  gender differences and, 41–42
  general, 36–38
  of gifted adolescents, 38–41
  interventions for, 43–45
  learning style and, 196–197

Purdue Creative Thinking Program,
  112

Quigley, S. P., 169

Racism, x-xi, 231–233, 255–256, 262
Raitz, R., 77
Rand, D., 210
Rankin, S. C., 92
Raph, J. B., 140, 151
Rappaport, M., 77
Raths, L., 222
Raven, 98
Reality therapy
  cognitive therapy and, 79–81
  perfectionism and, 72
Ream, J., 77
Reasoner, R. W., 44
Rebecca, M., 205
Rebellion, 29, 145, 146, 148, 149–150, 154
Recognition, need for, 37–38
Recommended Readings in Literature, 245
Redden, M. R., 169
Reflective thinking, 98
Reineke, J., 172
Reis, M., 11
Reis, S. M., 2, 4, 93, 204, 212
Relaxation techniques, 71–72, 84
Religion, x, 13. *See also* Spiritual
  development
Religion in America, 219–220
Renzulli, J. S., 2, 4–5, 93, 94, 99, 126, 140,
  141, 169, 191, 243
Repucci, N., 168
Resnick, L. B., 95, 97
Resolution of Conflict Strategy (Taba), 222
Rest, J., 217, 218
Reyna, J., 240
Ricca, J., 191
Richardson, W. B., 8, 132
Richert, E. S., 2, 5, 6, 139–162, 140, 141,
  143, 144, 152, 155, 156, 159, 240
Richter, N. C., 84
Riggs, G., 70
Rimm, S. B., 2, 5, 6, 18–32, 24–26, 29–31,
  152, 218, 220, 221
Risk-taking, 39, 41, 112, 155–157
  perfectionism and, 69–70
  in self-actualization, 151
Robbins, S., 218

Robinson, B., 67
Robinson, N., 38
Rockert, W., 53, 54
Rodin, J., 53
Roe, A., 107
Roedell, W., 9, 37, 38
Roeper, A. M., 143
Roets, L. S., 126, 127, 132
Roets Rating Scale for Leadership, 126, 127
Rogers, J., 7
Role models
  career choice and, 209
  need for, 36-37
  parents, as, 24-25, 159
  providing, 158-159
Roopnarine, J., 44
Root, M. M. P., 56, 60
Rosen, L. W., 60
Rosenman, R., 68, 81
Rosman, B., 57
Rosner, S., 111
Rosselli, H. C., 132-133
Rothenberg, A., 111
Rowell, J., 66
Rowland, C. V., 51
Rubin, I. M., 191, 197
Rudman, G. J., 44
Rule for School Foundation Units for Gifted Children (Ohio Department of Education), 182
Runco, M., 106
Runions, T., 183
Rural and Migrant Gifted Project (RMGP), 243-244, 245-246, 261-262
Russell, G. F. M., 51
Rutter, M., 77

Saba, G., 60
Sabatino, D., 169
Safter, H. T., 113
Sanchez, G. I., 243
Sanford, T., 177
Sargent, M., 152
Sartre, J. P., 143
Scales for Rating Behavioral Characteristics of Superior Students (SRBCSS), 126-127
Scarr, S., 232
Schakel, L., 124-125

Schlaerth, P., 172
Schmidt, C., 169
Schmitz, C., 45
Schoenfeld, A., 95
Scholastic Aptitude Test-Mathematics (SAT-M), 179
Schools, parent relationships with, 24, 26-27
Schriescheim, C. A., 123
Schurenberg, E., 145
Schwartz, L. L., 204
Schwartz, R. C., 60
Science, 105, 106-108, 206
Science on a Shoestring (Strongin), 245
Seeley, K., 39
Segal, M., 44
Seiden, R., 152
Self-actualization, 4, 144-146, 148, 150-151, 154, 159
Self-awareness, stress and, 83-86
Self-concept
  of black adolescents, 231-238
  external expectations and, 147-151, 153-155
  strengthening, 153-155
Self-confidence, stress and, 81
Self-esteem, 38, 42
  eating disorders and, 54
  enhancement of, 44
  external expectations and, 147-151, 153-155
  perfectionism and, 68, 69
  in stress management, 85
Self-evaluation, 157-158
Self-exploration, 207-208
Self-knowledge, need for, 38
Seligman, M., 168
Selye, H., 76
Sensitivity-enhancement model, 236
Set-breaking, 114
Sex-role stereotypes, 11, 129, 201-211
  careers and, 14
  individuality and, 37
Sexuality, *ix-x*, 40-41, 116
Shallcross, D. J., 132
Shamanoff, G. A., 210
Shank, S. B., 44
Shaw, M. C., 145, 151, 152
Sheppard, W. C., 44
Sibling relations, 27-29, 260

Sifford, D., 66
Silberstein, L. R., 53
Silver, H. F., 97, 193, 194, 196
Silverman, I. K., 35
Silverman, L., 2, 109, 125, 218, 223, 224
Simon, H. A., 94, 95
Simon, S., 222
Simonton, D. K., 107, 109, 110, 115–117
Sisk, D. A., 8, 126, 132–133
Skill development
  career choices and, 208
  mentorship programs and, 181
Slade, P. D., 52, 54, 55
Slomianko, J., 44
Smeriglio, V., 36
Smith, F. H., 126
Smith, L. H., 2, 4, 191
Smith, M., 45
Sociability
  gender and, 10–11
  IQ and, 10
Social issues
  defined, 11
  giftedness and, 9–12
  See also Psychosocial needs
Socialization, 44, 85
Socioeconomic status
  of Asian Americans, 250, 251
  eating disorders and, 51
  of gifted students, 243
  of Hispanic adolescents, 242
  of Terman's gifted population, 2
Socratic methods, 96–97
Spearman, 98, 232
Spiritual development, x, 13, 218–219, 261
  role of teachers, counselors, and parents
    in, 221–225
  search for meaning and, 219–221
Sprecher, J., 240
Stage theory, x
Stanish, B., 44
Stanley, J., 106, 253
Stanley, J. C., 179
Steiner-Adair, C., 56, 60
Stenmark, J. K., 245
Stephens, T., 44
Stereotypes, 261
  combatting effects of, 204–210
  of eating disorders, 57
  effect of, on gifted adolescents, 202–204

gender, 11. *See also* Sex-role stereotypes
  of giftedness, 1–2, 201–202
  individuality *vs.*, 37
  minority groups and, x–xi
  nature of, 202
Sternberg, R. J., 2–4, 6, 93, 94, 98, 112,
    141, 142
Stewart, E., 183, 191
Stewart, W. J., 44
Stogdill, R. M., 124, 129
Storr, A., 117
Stress management, 33, 44, 76–87
  coping skills and, 82–83
  interventions in, 83–86
  origins of theories on, 76–77
  physical illness and, 77, 83
  signals of, 78–79
  sources of stress and, 77–78
  vulnerability to stress and, 79–83
Strichart, S. S., 172
Striegel-Moore, R. H., 53
Strobino, D., 36
Strommen, E., 218
Strommen, M., 219
Strong, R., 97
Strongin, H., 245
Strop, J., 42–43
Study of Mathematically Precocious Youth
    (Johns Hopkins University), 10,
    179–180
Subotnik, R., 106
Success, coping with, 155–157
Successful gifted, 5
Suhor, C., 92
Suicide
  perfectionism and, 71
  prevention of, 44
  warning signs for, 78–79
Summer programs, 177–179, 255
  college and university programs, 10,
    179–180
  governor's schools, 177–179
Super, D. E., 207
Super woman syndrome, 56, 60, 208
Support groups, career choice and, 209
Swassing, R. H., 176–185, 178

Taba, H., 222
Talent
  concept of, 7–8

time and financial commitment of
parents, 22–24
Tan, A., 250
Tannenbaum, A. J., x, 6, 11, 105, 107, 113,
115, 140, 141, 215
Tan-Willman, B., 215, 217
Tarule, J., 116
Taylor, C. W., 139, 245
Teachers, 259
disagreement and, 198–199
perfectionism and, 66–67, 73
psychosocial interventions and, 43–45
racism and, 233
as role models, 159
role of, in biculturalism, 253–254
role of, in moral and spiritual
development, 221–225
use of learning research by, 194–198
*Teaching Models in the Education of the
Gifted* (Maker), 222
Technology, for disabled persons, 170–171
Teidt, I., 236
Teidt, P., 236
Telescopic thinking, 68
Television, perfectionism and, 66
Terman, L. M., x, 1, 2, 9–10, 71, 124, 140,
163, 243
Terry, P., 93
Tetenbaum, H., 168
Textbooks, racism and, 233
Theander, S., 51
Thinking in the Classroom (Chance), 99
Thinking skills, 91–103
application of theory in teaching, 95–99
characteristics of gifted and, 92–95
creative, 92
critical, 92
program evaluation for, 99–100
triarchic theory of intelligence and, 3–4
Thinness, as cultural value, 53, 59
Thompson, V., 247
Thought stopping, 44–45
Tiedeman, D. V., 207
Tiedt, I. M., 96
Tittle, C. K., 208
Tobin, D., 37, 163, 210
Todd, E. W., 183
Tolan, S. S., 43, 152, 153n
Tolliver, J. M., 123
Tonelson, S., 169

Torrance, E. P., 7, 72, 106, 111–113, 141,
143, 217, 218
Torrance Tests of Creative Thinking, 7,
112, 113, 217
Touyz, S. W., 51
Trant, T. J., 128
Trauma, childhood, 108–110
Troxell, J., 77
Trust, 29–30
Trybus, R., 172
Tucker, S., 35
Tuttle, D. W., 165
Tye, K. B., x, 215–227
Type A personality, 68, 81–82, 203
Type B personality, 81–82

Ullian, D. Z., 205
Underachievement, 6, 26, 139–162, 260
defining, 142–144
defining maximum gifted potential and,
140–144
gender differences in, 145, 147–151, 159
overcoming, 151–159
patterns of, among the gifted, 144–151
rebelliousness in, 29
sibling relations and, 28–29
See also Achievement
Underground gifted, 5
University programs, 10, 179–180
Ussery, R., 115

Vandereycken, W., 56–57, 59, 60
Vanderlinden, J., 56–57
Van Dyke, M., 126
Vare, J., 215
Varenhorst, B., 44
Velsor, E. V., 129
Vernooy, J. F., 172
Visual arts, 3, 104–106, 142
Visualization, 71–72
Visual impairments, 166–167
Volkoff, W., 243–245
Volunteer work, 27, 128–129, 220
Vomiting, 53–54, 57
Vroom, V., 124

Walberg, H., 106–108, 115
Wallace, T., 115
Wallas, G., 111
Ward, V., 177, 222

Wasek, P., 77
Wassermann, S., 91
Watanabe, K., 96
Waterman, D. A., 95
Watson-Glaser Critical Thinking Appraisal,
    99–100
Webb, J. T., 43, 152, 153n
Wechsler Intelligence Scale for
    Children-Revised (WISC-R), 164, 244
Weibe, A., 245
Weible, T. D., 44
Weight loss, 53–54
Weinberg, R. A., 232
Weisberg, R., 112
Wellman, C., 216
When I Say "No" I Feel Guilty (Smith),
    45
Whimby, A., 97
White, A. J., 126
Whitmore, J. R., 71, 84, 152, 163, 169, 171,
    173
Wiehl, A., 72
Wikoff, R., 191
Willig, A. C., 242
Willings, D., 110
Willis, M. B., 207
Wilson, D., 44
Wisnyai, S. A., 94
Withdrawal, 145, 146, 148, 149, 154
Witkin, H. A., 168, 169

Wolf, J. S., 178
Woliver, G. M., 248–257
Woliver, R., 248–257
Wolkind, S. N., 77
Women/girls, 2
    career choices of, 11, 14
    dating relationships of, 41
    mentor relationships for, 209, 210
    responses to expectations and, 145,
        147–151
    role conflicts of, 37
    sex-role stereotypes concerning, 201–211
    super woman syndrome, 56, 60, 208
Women Mentor Project, 210
Wooley, O. W., 57, 60
Wooley, S. C., 57, 60
Workaholism, 68–69, 70, 147
World War II, 255–256

Yager, J., 58
Yetton, P. W., 124
Young Astronaut (Young Astronaut
    Council), 245
Young-Bruehl, E., 209
Youngs, D., 245
Youth Volunteers in Action, 220
Yuen, L., 69

Zimmerman, E. D., 23, 106
Zytkow, J. M., 95